WITHDRAWN FROM
TSC LIBRARY

ML   Gaisberg, Frederick W.
1055   The music goes round
.G15
M8
1977

DATE DUE

DEC. 12, 1988			
APR 2000			

A FINE WILL BE CHARGED
FOR EACH OVERDUE BOOK

Opera Biographies

This is a volume in the
Arno Press collection

Opera Biographies

Advisory Editor
ANDREW FARKAS

Associate Editor
W.R. MORAN

See last pages of this volume
for complete list of titles

THE MUSIC GOES ROUND

F[rederick] W[illiam] Gaisberg

ARNO PRESS
A New York Times Company
New York / 1977

Editorial Supervision: ANDREA HICKS

Reprint Edition 1977 by Arno Press Inc.

Reprinted from a copy in
 The University of Illinois Library

OPERA BIOGRAPHIES
ISBN for complete set: 0-405-09666-6
See last pages of this volume for titles.

Manufactured in the United States of America

Library of Congress Cataloging in Publication Data

Gaisberg, Frederick William.
  The music goes round.

  (Opera biographies)
  Reprint of the 1942 ed. published by Macmillan, New
York.
  1. Musicians--Biography. 2. Phonograph--History.
ML1055.G15 1977   789.9'1'0924 [B]   76-29936
ISBN 0-405-09678-X

THE MUSIC GOES ROUND

Fox Photos, Ltd., London

F. W. Gaisberg

THE
MUSIC
GOES
ROUND

By F. W. GAISBERG

NEW YORK

THE MACMILLAN COMPANY

1942

Copyright, 1942, by
F. W. GAISBERG

All rights reserved—no part of this book may be reproduced in any form without permission in writing from the publisher, except by a reviewer who wishes to quote brief passages in connection with a review written for inclusion in magazine or newspaper.

First Printing

PRINTED IN THE UNITED STATES OF AMERICA
BY H. WOLFF, NEW YORK

TO MY SISTER CARRIE

Author's Note

My thanks are due to Mr. Perceval Graves, for his assistance throughout, in the compilation of these memoirs.

Acknowledgment is also made to Glyn, Mills & Co., literary executors for the Elgar estate, for permission to reproduce the Elgar letters in Chapter XIV, and to George Bernard Shaw for permission to use his postcard in this same chapter; and to the Gramophone Co., Ltd., for access to their library, and the use of many photographs found in this volume.

I also wish to express gratitude for great help cheerfully given me by Gwenn Mithias.

F. W. G.

Contents

CHAPTER		
I	Cylinder versus Disc (1890-1902)	3
II	We Go to Europe (1898)	23
III	From Zinc to Wax (1901)	37
IV	The Gramophone Goes East (1902)	53
V	The War Years (1914-1918)	69
VI	The Procession Passes (1906-)	83
VII	Here Comes the Prima Donna (1908-)	103
VIII	Chiefly Wagner (1919-)	123
IX	Conductors and Their Sorrows (1912-)	141
X	Opera Recording—Home and Abroad (1903-)	165
XI	Masters of the Keyboard (1911-1939)	181
XII	Kreisler—and Others (1913-)	203
XIII	Feodor Chaliapin (1912-)	225
XIV	Elgarian (1908-)	241
XV	And So, Good Day!	259
	Index	269

Illustrations

F. W. Gaisberg	Frontispiece
	Facing Page
Emile Berliner, inventor of the gramophone	4
Goura Jan, famous classical Indian singer	56
Janki Bai	58
Lunching at Frascati, Italy. Marconi the tenor, and the author	96
Bruno Walter	128
Lauritz Melchior with his wife, "Kleinchen"	132
Group outside the recording studios at Hayes, Middlesex— L. G. Sharpe, Artur Nikisch, and the author's brother Will	144
Paderewski making his first gramophone records	182
Arthur Rubinstein with Jascha Heifetz	190
Kreisler recording in Berlin	204
Kubelik, Seidler-Winkler, and Max Hampe	210
Casals recording Dvořák's violoncello concerto in Prague	212
Chaliapin in his famous grey topper	232
Sir Edward Elgar with Yehudi Menuhin and the author	246
Alfred Clark with the author	260

Illustrations

Cylinder

Versus Disc

in public parks, gardens and fountains. No factories are permitted other than those engaged on government work, like the bureau for engraving and printing paper-money.

Taking advantage of its many libraries and museums, scientists and research-workers come from all over the world to work out their problems. Its important centres for research are the Library of Congress, the Smithsonian Institution, the Bureau of Patents, with its vast Museum of Working Models, and the National Museum.

To this congenial town came an emigrant boy, Emile Berliner, from Hanover at the age of twenty. He made his living as a draper's clerk, but devoted his spare time to solving electrical problems connected with telephones and phonographs which fascinated every young boy of the period. At twenty-six years of age, though barely versed in the language, he was already writing out in English the patent-specifications of his telephone transmitter, the sale of which to the Bell Telephone Company was to lay the foundation of his fortune and give him the means for carrying out experiments on the phonograph. For his telephone patents Berliner received $75,000 in cash and $5,000 per year as a retaining-fee from the Bell Telephone Company. Later these patents were the subject of one of the classic lawsuits of the day.

From Berliner's own lips I heard the story of his telephone experiments. He slept and worked in a third-floor bedroom of a modest boarding-house, run by a widow with three children. To the ground-floor he ran a circuit with a transmitter. The widow and her children would speak into this and Berliner would receive their messages on the third floor. Working of an evening with odd bits of string, wire and batteries he converted a soap-box into a transmitter. As the crucial exhibit in the great lawsuit, *The U.S.A. versus Emile Berliner*, it became the most famous soap-box in the world. It embraced the basic principle of all successful telephone and radio microphones, past and present.

To Washington also came Alexander Graham Bell and Charles Sumner Tainter, having just won the coveted Volta Prize for the invention of the telephone. With their prize-money they established the Volta Laboratory from which issued the master-patent for "cutting a sound line in a solid body" (in other words, "wax")—a discovery which was to make practical the recording of sound to which

CHAPTER I

Cylinder versus Disc

To ANYONE looking back on the Washington of fifty years ago, it seems a fitting place for the birth of so picturesque and romantic an industry as the gramophone. In the nineties it was still an overgrown, self-satisfied town of 180,000 inhabitants (the 80,000 being negroes). Every spring, the Potomac River would flood the lower part of the city, known as the "Swamppoodle" district, for a week at a time. Boats would ferry Congressmen up and down Pennsylvania Avenue from the White House to the Capitol.

It was a common sight to see droves of cattle and sheep driven through the stately Massachusetts Avenue (the "Avenue of the Ambassadors") on their way to the market. For years a vast tenderloin district, patronised by high and low, was tolerated within a stone's throw of the White House. It thrived until the Theodore Roosevelt administration when the city was cleaned up and Congress passed a bill decreeing the return to the original L'Enfant plans for building up and beautifying Washington. However, with all Roosevelt's high hopes, the low standard of living of the negroes and their segregation remain as much a problem today as they were then and to this problem is added another, almost equally insoluble—car-parking for the city's 100,000 motor-cars.

Washington is a city given over entirely to the Federal Government, and its endless avenues of smug, comfortable homes reflect the security and repose of the many Civil Servants employed in Government offices. It is laid out like a miniature Paris, abounding

[3

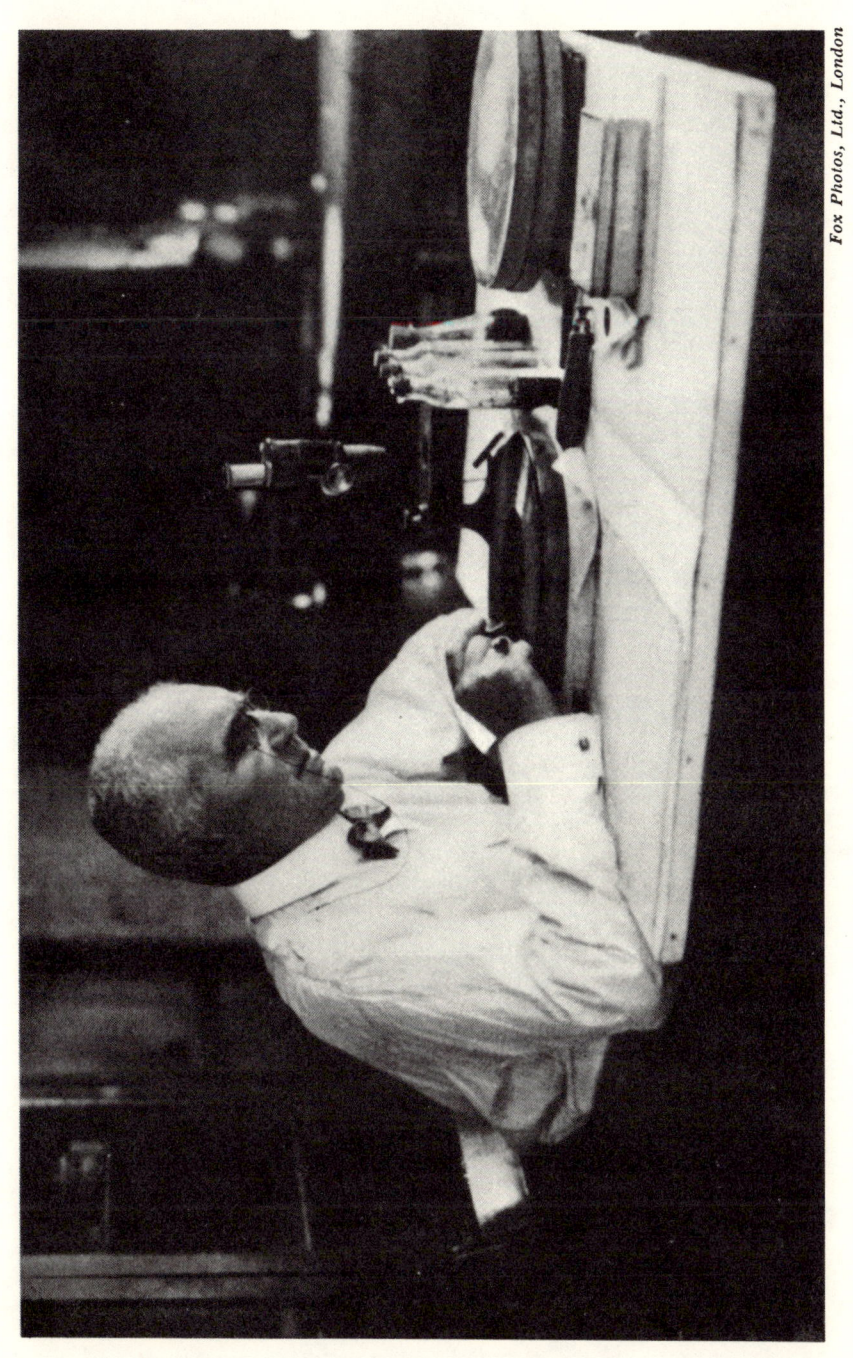

Emile Berliner, inventor of the gramophone. This picture shows him as a man in his sixties.

Fox Photos, Ltd., London

CYLINDER VERSUS DISC

even Edison himself had eventually to subscribe. In their Volta Laboratory Bell and Tainter evolved the graphophone. Until the advent of the graphophone, with its governed speed and wax cylinder, all talking-machines were really toys.

The Columbia Phonograph Company (licensees of the Edison Phonograph), founded by E. D. Easton and Paul Cromlin, stenographers to the Supreme Court, was also established in Washington. Quite naturally they saw the machine as an ideal substitute for shorthand. Their purpose was to exploit it as a dictating-machine for office use. In this respect, however, it proved a failure. I remember some hundreds of the instruments being rented to Congress and all being returned as impracticable. The Columbia Company seemed headed for liquidation at this failure, but it was saved by a new field of activity which was created, almost without their knowledge, by showmen at fairs and resorts demanding records of songs and instrumental music. Phonographs, each equipped with ten sets of ear-tubes through which the sound passed, had been rented to these exhibitors. It was ludicrous in the extreme to see ten people grouped about a phonograph, each with a tube leading from his ears, grinning and laughing at what he heard. It was a fine advertisement for the onlookers waiting their turn. Five cents was collected from each listener so the showman could afford to pay two and three dollars for a cylinder to exhibit.

As an embryo pianist I was able during school vacation to earn good pocket-money by playing the piano accompaniments for the singers and comedians employed by these different laboratories.

In 1893 I met Dan Donovan, a big, fat Irishman who announced the train departures at the Potomac railway station: "Richmond, Atlanta, Savannah and all points South." He had a mighty bass voice and I was particularly proud to accompany him at our local "smokers" in songs like "Rocked in the Cradle of the Deep" and "Anchored." He was the means of bringing me into touch with Charles Sumner Tainter, the mechanical genius of the Volta Laboratory. Tainter had just obtained a concession for coin operated talking machines at the Chicago World's Fair and was engaged in recording music on the cylinders for use with these machines. His cylinders took the form of a roll of paper eight inches long and about one and a half inches in diameter, coated with ozokorite, on

[5

which a sapphire point cut the sound. In his studio he had installed a battery of twenty recording heads that worked as a unit. From each head hung a trumpet directed towards the piano behind which stood the singer. One performance produced twenty records, but from the singer and accompanist plenty of volume was required.

To earn my $10 a week I had to find the artists, load up each of the twenty units with the paper cylinders, set the recording horns and play the accompaniments. Our entire repertoire consisted of "Daisy Bell" and "After the Ball Was Over," and sometimes we would perform the latter as many as seventy times a day.

Tainter was an Englishman and a confirmed tea-drinker. Indeed, he taught me how to brew and enjoy it. The perfume of that special China blend of his haunts me still. Between the cups he would mount the diaphragm and adjust the angle of the cutting stylus. In his clear Yorkshire voice he would test them with "Caesar, Caesar, can you hear what I say—this, which, s-ss-sss." The stress was always laid on the sibilants, these being the most difficult sounds to record. In playing back the test, at the slightest indication of the "s" sound, he would smile with joy and treat himself to another cup.

Charles Sumner Tainter was a scientist as well as a mechanical genius. I can see him now working at a watchmaker's lathe with a glass to his eye; he had a touch as delicate as a woman's. I never knew anyone who lived so abstemiously.

His slot-controlled automatic phonograph was a truly remarkable achievement for that period but proved too delicate to stand the rough handling at the Chicago Fair Grounds. It was withdrawn and shipped to Washington where, acting on Tainter's instructions, I installed some dozens in the local saloons, restaurants and beer-gardens. They were not infallible and sometimes would accept a coin without giving out a tune. In carrying out my job of collecting the coins in the morning and reloading the machines with cylinders, I would at times be badly handled by an irate bartender who accused me of taking money under false pretences.

With the failure of the World's Fair venture, I was free to work for the Columbia Phonograph Company * which had begun to make musical records on a large scale. For this company I acted as accom-

* The Columbia Phonograph Company, founded in 1889, Licensees for the Edison Phonograph for the District of Columbia and for Maryland.

CYLINDER VERSUS DISC

panist to such famous cylinder artists as Daniel Quinn, Johnny Meyers, George Gaskin, Len Spencer and Billy Golden.

And here let me present John York Attlee, with his pompous announcements that introduced each performance in tones which made the listener visualise a giant. But in reality he was a mere shrimp of a man, about five feet in his socks, that little Government clerk with a deep, powerful voice. Of this and his fine flowing moustache he was mighty proud. After his office hours as a wage-slave of the U. S. Government, from nine till four, he would return to his modest home where I would join him. In the parlor stood an old upright piano and a row of three phonographs, loaned him by the Columbia Phonograph Company. Together we would turn out, in threes, countless records of performances of "Whistling Coon," "Mocking Bird" and "The Laughing Song." I can still hear that reverberating announcement: "THE MOCKING BIRD" BY JOHN YORK ATTLEE, ARTISTIC WHISTLER, ACCOMPANIED BY PROFESSOR GAISBERG.

I was then only sixteen. *Some* professor! Years after, Australians and New Zealanders meeting me would register amazement at my boyish appearance. I suppose I should have grown a beard to live up to my title. Attlee's unaccompanied repertoire included Mark Antony's speech in *Julius Caesar*, commencing "Friends, Romans, Countrymen," the Lord's Prayer, and "The Ravings of John McCullough, The Mad Actor." What a nuisance we must have been on those long summer nights to our suffering neighbors seeking rest and fresh air on their front porches! From our open window, evening after evening that beastly little man, with myself as sole accessory, would keep up this infernal racket till all hours.

The late nineties can be rated as the "high spot" of the phonograph cylinder as an entertainer, brought about, strangely enough, through the vogue of the slot machine. Automatic Phonograph Parlors, as they were called, sprang up like mushrooms on the busy streets of most towns in the United States.* They did a flourishing business for just two years and then the craze vanished. A singer with a loud voice could record to five machines simultaneously. If the Company had an order for 100 cylinders of "Maggie Murphy's Home" the artist would have to sing the "title" twenty times over.

* The renaissance of the disc was brought about in America in 1938-39 by the automatic gramophones in roadhouses and cafés.

Favorite records of those days were the U. S. Marine Band playing Sousa's Marches, the Boston Cadet Band, Eisler's Band, the minstrel-comedian Billy Golden whistling "The Mocking Bird" and in his negro shout "Turkey in de Straw," and the tragic negro George W. Johnson in "The Whistling Coon" and "The Laughing Song." George achieved fame and riches with just these two titles. His whistle was low-pitched and fruity, like a contralto voice. His laugh was deep-bellied, lazy like a carefree darky. His life ended in tragedy.

Women's voices and stringed instruments such as violins did not record well, but the piano was possible if the instrument was old and had a tinny, shallow tone.

Perhaps because of his unsavory reputation, my particular pet and hero of this time was the handsome Len Spencer. His father, the originator of the florid Spencerian handwriting, was the chief bugbear of thousands of schoolboys, myself included. The son had many and varied gifts. As a popular baritone, I accompanied him at concerts and for record-making. I first saw him seated at a small table on Pennsylvania Avenue, surrounded by admiring darkies, writing out visiting-cards at six for a dime. His beautiful, ornate Spencerian writing, ending up with two doves, looked like engraving. Later I was always to remember his handsome face disfigured by a scar, the result of a razor-slash in an up-river gambling brawl. He was said to have been an adroit poker player. His records of "Anchored," "Sailing," "The Palms" and "Nancy Lee" were important items of our meagre record repertoire.

The star attraction of the phonograph parlors was the series of "Michael Casey" records written and spoken by Russell Hunting. Russell Hunting at the age of 21 had been a member of the Edwin Booth Company, when the great actor was playing in "The Taming of the Shrew" at the Fifth Avenue Theatre. For nine years he was a member of the Boston Theatre Stock Company and was for three years its stage manager. After this he acted as stage manager in Meyer Lutz's *extravaganza* "Faust Up to Date," playing the rôle of Mephistopheles. During his spare time he earned thousands of dollars recording his inimitable Irish scenes from life, such as "Casey as a Judge," "Casey Takes the Census," "Casey at the Telephone." They consisted of rapid-fire cross-talk between two Irish characters, with Hunting taking both parts. His fine voice had an infinite capacity

CYLINDER VERSUS DISC

for mimicry. He had a sense of humor and a lively imagination with a genuine gift for accurate portrayal of scenes from real life. Thomas A. Edison became very fond of Hunting, and Berliner found his company a tremendous tonic. Later he emigrated to Europe where he became a business associate of Louis Sterling in London and then was recording-manager for the Pathé Brothers Studios in Paris and New York. I give this lengthy "aside" on Russell Hunting because, in the nineties, his "Casey" records gave pleasure to thousands the world over and they were undoubtedly the zenith of phonograph achievement by an entertainer.

It was Billy Golden who one day in Washington asked me if I would go with him to see a funny German who had started experimenting with a flat disc talking machine record and wanted to make some trials. I was only too eager to see him at work. We found Emile Berliner in his small laboratory on New York Avenue and received a warm welcome from the inventor. Billy was right, Berliner certainly did make me smile. Dressed in a monkish frock he paced up and down the small studio buzzing on a diaphragm. "Hello, hello!" he recited in guttural, broken English, "Tvinkle, tvinkle, little star, how I vonder vot you are." * Berliner delighted in creating effects, and the youthful enthusiasm I showed must have gratified him.

I was introduced to the inventor and invited to witness the making of the *first gramophone record*. Berliner placed a muzzle over Golden's mouth and connected this up by a rubber hose to a diaphragm. I was at the piano, the sounding-board of which was also boxed up and connected to the diaphragm by a hose resembling an elephant's trunk. Berliner said "are you ready?" and upon our answering "Yes," he began to crank like a barrel-organ, and said "Go." The song finished, Berliner stopped cranking. He took from the machine a bright zinc disc and plunged it into an acid bath for a few minutes. Then, taking it out of the acid, he washed and cleaned the disc.

Placing it on a reproducing machine, also operated by hand like a coffee-grinder, he played back the resulting record from the etched groove. To our astonished ears came the play-back of Billy Golden's

---
* Sibilants remained strangers to the gramophone record until the introduction of the electrical recording process in 1925.

[9

voice. Berliner proudly explained to us just how his method was superior to the phonograph. He said that in his process the recording stylus was vibrated laterally on a flat surface, thus always encountering an even resistance, and this accounted for the more natural tone.

Acquainted as I was with the tinny, unnatural reproduction of the old cylinder-playing phonographs, I was spell-bound by the beautiful round tone of the flat gramophone disc. Before I departed that day, I exacted a promise from Berliner that he would let me work for him when his machine was ready for development. A few months later, I received a postcard asking me to come and see him. In great anticipation I called at his house.

I was then 21 and had already acquired in the new talking machine industry a varied practical experience which, besides the musical side of it, included laboratory training in the Volta Laboratory with the Columbia Company. I had also spent a year with the American Graphophone Company at Bridgeport, Connecticut, in their Research Department, then in the charge of Charles MacDonald. I detailed these qualifications to Berliner who told me I was just the person he was looking for. He informed me that in recent months his laboratory experiments had culminated in the production of a recording and reproducing apparatus and also a recording process sufficiently advanced to place on the market. He also confided to me that three of his relatives and friends had formed a small syndicate to exploit his gramophone. With the limited funds available he wanted to make a small programme of songs and music for demonstration purposes in order to raise capital for promoting a company.

My value to Berliner rested in the fact that I could collect quickly a variety of effective talent to make these demonstration records. Professional phonograph vocalists of established reputation like George J. Gaskin, the Irish tenor, Johnny Meyers, the baritone, and Dan Quinn, the comedian, were expensive but they had loud, clear voices and provided us with effective records of "Down Went McGinty to the Bottom of the Sea," "Anchored," "Sweet Marie," "Comrades" and so forth. We averaged up by employing lower-paid local talent secured from the beergardens and street corners of Washington.

One of these, George Graham, was a character of Washington

life, a type of happy-go-lucky vagabond met with in the saloons, mostly near the free lunch counter, dodging the eyes of the bartender and cadging for drinks. He steered the easiest course through life, sometimes as a member of an Indian Medicine Troupe doing one-night stands in the spring and summer and in the winter selling quack medicines on the street corners. His tall, lanky figure, draped in a threadbare Prince Albert coat and adorned with a flowing tie, his wide-brimmed Stetson hat and his ready stream of wit combined to extract the dimes and nickels from his simple audience in exchange for a bottle of colored water. I discovered him one day on the corner of Seventh and Pennsylvania Avenue selling a liver cure to a crowd of spellbound negroes. He was assisted by John O'Terrell, who strummed the banjo and sang songs to draw the crowd.

I brought this pair to Emile Berliner. Always a student of humanity, he was delighted and found them amusing types. Perhaps their carefree existence, when contrasted with his own busy and fettered life, afflicted him with a sense of nostalgia. George recorded his lecture on "Drink." In this he hammered home his point as follows: "Drink is an evil habit; all my life I've devoted to putting drink down, and I'm *still* putting it down." Then also his talk, "My Celebrated Liver Cure," became a classic. In this he cited the case of a man aged 95 who died immediately after taking one bottle of the cure. Before they could bury him they had to take out his liver and kill it with a club.

I have a guilty conscience when I reflect that my introduction led kindhearted Berliner to many a "touch" from this precious pair. But I will give him the credit of never refusing a "touch" or failing to smile. I have lived long enough to know that Berliner was never so happy as when he was giving.

It was John O'Terrell who actually made the first wax-record disc. His number was "I'm Gonna Telegraph Ma Baby." I remember it because in 1900 it was the turning point of sound-recording.

Berliner himself contributed a record of the Lord's Prayer, spoken with his fruity German accent. Listeners were amused when hearing this record and always exclaimed "How distinct! I can understand every word." It was the only talking-record we exhibited, and Berliner confessed that as ninety-nine out of every hundred people knew the Lord's Prayer by heart everyone could understand it with ease.

THE MUSIC GOES ROUND

I took Donovan, the train-announcer, to record for Berliner and also a boy I discovered on the train selling sweets and magazines between Baltimore and Washington. Above the noise of the locomotive you could hear his powerful voice calling "Magazines, peanuts, bananas, apples, *Harper's, Youth's Companion, Saturday Evening Post.*" Both of these big voices performed in turn before our sluggish recording diaphragm. They needed quantity rather than quality in those days.

Berliner had been using ebonite or vulcanised rubber for pressing records. Ebonite took a lot of pressure and would not retain the impression permanently. Pondering over this he remembered that the Bell Telephone Company had abandoned vulcanised rubber and adopted a plastic material for their telephone receivers. The Durinoid Company of Newark, N. J., were button manufacturers who undertook to furnish pressings on a similar substance from matrices supplied by Berliner. The new substance was a mixture of powdered shellac and byritis, bound with cotton flock and colored with lampblack. It was rolled under hot colanders into "biscuits." When heated, these "biscuits" were easily molded under pressure and when cooled they retained the impression.

I was present when Berliner received the first package of gramophone records from the Durinoid Company. With trembling hands he placed the new disc on the reproducer and sounds of undreamed quality issued from the record. It was evident that the new plastic material still in use today and consuming nearly one quarter of India's entire shellac production, when under pressure had poured into every crevice of the sound-track, revealing tones hitherto mute to us. Berliner shouted with excitement and all of us, including the venerable Werner Suess, danced with joy around the machine.

Werner Suess, our eighty-five-year-old mechanical genius, deserves a few words of loving memory. Suess was a little roly-poly German who out of his clever brain designed machines in turn for those great scientists Helmholtz and Bunsen in Germany, Tyndall and Huxley in England, and Henry and Berliner in the U. S. A., and was able thereby to demonstrate their theories and lectures. In the Frankfurt Opera House in the fifties, standing on a chair in the wings, he held two sticks of carbon in contact. These were fed by

CYLINDER VERSUS DISC

the current of 200 Bunsen cells. It was thus he produced the first electrical sunrise ever seen in any theatre.

His spontaneous smile was as sunny as the whole nature of the man. To have known him was to have loved him. He has been a life-long inspiration to me.

For us the sun, hitherto hidden by clouds, now came out in all its glory. Once more fortune smiled on Berliner. With our new record-material, a simple gramophone machine which one turned by hand like a coffee-grinder, and a score of newly-recorded titles we thought we really had something to offer prospective investors.

A stream of punters and speculators, rich and poor, visited Berliner's small laboratory. They were all interested and amused but sceptical. They would not part with their money and Berliner's funds and courage were getting lower and lower. Even his friends began to doubt and avoid him. He often confided to me that something would have to be done or he would be forced to close down. I had been weeks without my modest salary, but as I was earning money with my piano playing in the evenings this was no great hardship for me. Still, my heart warmed towards Berliner and I was sorry to see him discouraged. I searched my young brain as to what could be done to raise the wind.

Among my friends was the apparently flourishing Karns family living on Capitol Hill. B. F. Karns was a retired Methodist minister, at that time engaged in lobbying a bill through Congress to secure a right-of-way for his Eastern Shore Railroad scheme. This imposing gentleman, by frequent references to Rockefeller, J. Pierpont Morgan, Harriman and the rest, impressed my youthful imagination and I was hopeful that he would be the very man to rescue Berliner. That Karns was a persuasive talker and magnetic personality was proved by the fact that within twenty-four hours after I had brought them together the nearly bankrupt Berliner advanced him $500. Then we waited for the miracle to happen. At each appointment for a demonstration to Rockefeller or Morgan the most devilish forces seemed to intervene to obstruct their appearance. Rockefeller's wife had measles or Morgan's wife was going to have a baby. At the end of six months we were no further along, except that I personally had loaned Karns $200 and Berliner $1,000, and Karns' family was reduced to living on liver at ten cents a pound. But Karns never lost

[13

heart; he told Berliner that if he would only furnish him with a Talking Doll he could get him a million dollars.

Eventually Berliner got Karns and myself on the train headed for Boston, equipped with a first-class gramophone exhibit and letters to the directors of the Bell Telephone Company. At the close of a directors' meeting we were shown into the board-room. The directors, oozing opulence and exhaling fragrant Havana cigars, signalled to us to proceed to demonstrate our gramophone. When I played Berliner's record of the Lord's Prayer they wept with joy; they thought his recitation of "Twinkle, Twinkle Little Star" especially touching, but in the gramophone as a musical instrument they could positively take no interest. Perhaps in turning the crank I was too nervous to give a steady pitch. "Well," they chuckled, "has poor Berliner come down to this? How sad! Now if he would only give us a Talking Doll perhaps we could raise some money for him."

Back in New York City we demonstrated to Mr. Schwarz, the greatest toy dealer in America, and to many others, all of whom asked for a Talking Doll. Then in March 1895 a great blizzard struck New York. We were snowed up in a dollar-a-day hotel for one whole week without funds and with all communications cut off. For food we patronised the free-lunch counters when the bartender's face was turned away. Altogether we spent a week of great discomfort.

In Philadelphia things brightened up. Although our records, to say nothing of our patience, had by this time nearly worn out, some citizens were found who agreed to hazard a gamble. Twenty-five thousand dollars was the amount subscribed, mostly by gentlemen connected with the Pennsylvania Railroad Company. With this the Gramophone Company was founded and the manufacture of gramophones and records started in a small way.

Sales were very slow and we soon discovered that unless the gramophone could be fitted with a clock-driven motor it would only remain a toy for the curious; it could never become a serious commercial proposition. How to do this was the problem uppermost in our minds. The modern man might smile at the bare idea of so simple a requirement presenting such absurd complications. After all, clock-making is one of the oldest of the crafts. But in our case, the clock-motor had to perform the work of rotating a turntable at an

CYLINDER VERSUS DISC

even speed for two consecutive minutes against the resistance of a heavy soundbox. One day, while reading the *Philadelphia Ledger*, my eye caught the following advertisement:

WHY WEAR YOURSELF OUT TREADING A SEWING-MACHINE?
FIT ONE OF OUR CLOCKWORK MOTORS.

Thinking perhaps the advertiser could help us solve our problem I sped hot-foot to the address given. In a back street I found a dingy workshop and a venerable old gentleman with a flowing beard who announced that he was the inventor. When I saw that his motor was a vast, unwieldy contraption like a beer-barrel my heart sank. For an incredibly long time the old man wound it up with a crank, like a man hauling a bucket of water from a deep well. Then for an absurdly short time the sewing-machine buzzed away. I asked the inventor how many clockwork sewing-machines he had sold and he answered: "As yet, none at all." He assured me, however, that he could easily design a clock-motor for my gramophone as it was a much simpler problem. I left him my gramophone and commissioned him to go ahead. A week later he appeared before our directors with the results.

The motor he produced was impracticable, but the workshop that built his model was in Camden, N. J., and was owned by a young mechanic, destined to dominate the talking-machine industry for the next thirty years and to forge it into a world institution. The mechanic was Eldridge R. Johnson. His quick, inventive brain saw what the old man was trying to do. On his own account he built and submitted to our directors a clockwork gramophone motor which was simple, practical, and cheap. It was the answer to our prayer and brought Johnson an order for two hundred motors with a cash advance to finance their manufacture. He was tall, lanky, stooping and taciturn, deliberate in his movements and always assuming a low voice with a Down-East Yankee drawl. I can see him now as he was when I went to that little shop across the river, to report that the governors of the motors did not and would not function unless a flat type of spring was adopted, similar to that employed by Edison in his clock-motor phonograph. The change was made with complete success and, in fact, it is the principle used to this very day and cannot be improved upon.

[15

The tide turned and the hand-driven gramophone was buried. From now on, the demand for the new gramophones and records was always greater than the supply. The little shop in Camden grew like a mushroom until it covered many acres of the waterfront facing Philadelphia. Its trademark, "Victrola," which superseded the generic term "gramophone," became known the world over.

When I revisited Camden, N. J., in 1928, my friend B. G. Royal, one-time Treasurer of the Victor Talking Machine Company, mentioned that Johnson had sold out to a group of bankers for $30,000,000 the previous year. Of this, he intimated, Johnson had received somewhere around $23,000,000—and *that* after having cashed in a like sum in dividends over the past twenty-five years. The bankers, in their turn, sold out at a substantial profit to that Colossus, the Radio Corporation of America, during the frenzied flood of mergers that preceded the financial crisis of 1929. Yet Johnson was not the only millionaire produced by the gramophone. I once heard mention of thirty others as a rough estimate.

I have heard that Johnson, in spite of his great wealth, was not happy in retirement and actually at one time tried or contemplated buying back the control.

These developments occupied the year 1897, when in Philadelphia I installed and operated the first commercial studio for recording sound on discs. All recordings were made on 7-inch zinc discs by the etching process. Later, that same year, by introducing C. G. Child, a friend and colleague of my phonograph days, to Emile Berliner, I secured a recording expert for his New York Studio. Later Child was to fill the post of Chief Recorder and Artists' Director for the Victor Company and retained this position until its sale to the Radio Corporation. He played the chief part in building up their great Red Seal Catalogue. His foresight and acumen secured under long contracts such great artists as Alma Gluck, Emma Eames, Geraldine Farrar, Caruso, Scotti, John McCormack, Kreisler, Galli-Curci, and others. His efforts mostly covered the pre-electric recording period. In fact, he led the Victor Company in their competition with their powerful Columbia rivals for the world-celebrities of the pre- and post-World War periods.

Progress in sound-recording was still hampered by the ban of

Tainter and Bell's patent for "cutting sound on wax." This was to continue until 1901, when Johnson's foresight brought about a plan among the contending parties to pool their patents and stop fighting. This will be touched upon in a later chapter.

Its novelty alone accounted for the gramophone's great popularity, since the repertoire recorded at this time covered only popular and comic songs, valses, and marches in their simplest settings. The records were single-sided, 5″ and 7″ in diameter, with a playing time of 1½ to 2 minutes. A fee of two to three dollars per song was paid to singers, and sales-royalties to artists and music publishers were undreamed of. We pirated right and left without remorse.

On a visit to Atlantic City one day I discovered the handsome tenor Ferruccio Giannini in a provincial Italian opera company. The next day he came to my studio and made records of "La Donna e Mobile" and "Questa o Quella." These were most successful and were the first opera excerpts we ever brought out. They filled us with pride and for many months represented our only concessions to highbrow taste. Thirty-five years later in Berlin I made a contract with Dusolina Giannini, the celebrated dramatic soprano, and taxed her with being Ferruccio's daughter. She admitted that this was true and was surprised to learn that her father was a pioneer record-maker. I was glad to know that Ferruccio was still living and owned an atelier for making plaster casts of well-known statues. He had given up singing many years before.

Another fortune resulted from the American tour of the *Artist's Model* company. I had a Syrian friend, a cigarette manufacturer, who for months had boasted of a fellow-countryman from Smyrna called Maurice Farkoa who was the greatest singer of chansonettes in the world. Now Farkoa was to visit Philadelphia with the company and my friend undertook to bring him to our studio. True to his word, one bright afternoon the greatest exquisite of his day, Farkoa, arrived with his friend and accompanist, Frank Lambert, composer of that lovely and still popular ballad "She Is Far From the Land." My friend did not exaggerate. As an artist Farkoa more than justified his extravagant praise. A most successful record of the famous laughing-song, "Le Fou-Rire," was made. It was the first time he had heard his own voice reproduced and Farkoa was amazed and delighted. In fact, this record served as one of our great stunt-records for climaxing a recital.

The main record sales were from such popular titles as "Down Went McGinty to the Bottom of the Sea," "Daddy Wouldn't Buy Me a Bow Wow," "Maggie Murphy's Home," "After the Ball," "Daisy Bell," "Sunshine of Paradise Alley," "Comrades," "Drill, Ye Tarriers, Drill!" and ditties that wrung the heartstrings, such as "The Fatal Wedding," "Only a Picture of Her Boy," "Her Father Turned Her Picture to the Wall," "It Was Only a Faded Picture." Irish songs, Sousa marches and simple valses were also in great demand. The thirst for music among the people must have been prodigious to endure the crude and noisy records produced at that time. I remember my own affection for those rough tunes. I seemed never to tire of repeating the record of "Ben Bolt" from *Trilby* or "Oh, Promise Me" from *Robin Hood* or "Steamboat Medley" ("Steamboat comin' round de bend, Don't you hear dem darkies singin'?") sung by a negro male quartet.

One day when things were slack Berliner and I improvised a record called "Auction Sale of a Piano." He did the auctioneering and called out to me: "Professor, show dem vat a peautiful tone dis instrument has." When no bids were forthcoming, with anguish in his voice he would complain: "Why, ladies and gentlemen, on *dis* piano Wagner composed *Die Götterdämmerung*. Still no bids? I see you know nothing about music. Johnny, hand me down dat perambulator!"

For many years Berliner was the only one of the many people I knew connected with the gramophone who was genuinely musical and possessed a cultured taste. This love of music was no doubt the inspiration that nourished his faith in the future mission of that instrument.

Disc recording might have developed more rapidly had there not been such a prejudice on the part of phonograph fans against the Berliner system. One who realised the possibilities of the disc was young Alfred Clark, then working for Thomas A. Edison. In the summer of 1896 he made a special trip from Newark to interview Berliner in his Pennsylvania Avenue studio and investigate his gramophone claims. Obviously Clark's impression was favorable since, a few months later, he accepted a position from him and was marked

CYLINDER VERSUS DISC

out to play a leading rôle in the European development of the gramophone.

Another young visitor was Joe Jones. Jones spent one summer vacation working in Berliner's laboratory and, from watching our experiments, was able to file a patent claim for "engraving a groove of even depth." The uncanny perception that led this seventeen year old boy to pick out the key-wording of his claim stamped him as a mechanical genius of the first order. Looking well ahead the Columbia Company bought up this patent for, it is said, the modest sum of $25,000, when searching for a spring-board to dive into the disc business. The patent would have been cheap at a hundred times that amount, as it was to give Columbia a stranglehold over the record-disc industry and eventually a share with the Victor Company in the monopoly of the discs in the U.S.A.

The stumbling-block to the rapid development of the old phonograph was the difficulty of duplicating record cylinders. This delay actually enabled the gramophone disc to overtake it with its simple method of stamping endless copies from the master, despite the superior recording-qualities of the cylinder. Hunting has told me in a most amusing way how he awoke to the realization that duplication of cylinders had arrived.

Leeds and Catlin were leading distributors in New York City of phonograph cylinders and they had quietly perfected a machine on the pantograph system for duplicating original cylinder-records. Unknown to the artists engaged to record they were fairly coining money with duplicated cylinders. They engaged Hunting to make ten rounds of his famous sketch, "Casey at the Telephone," at $5 a round. While carrying out this contract he was just finishing the fifth round when a boy crossed the end of the studio with a tray of twenty-four cylinders. Hunting stopped him and examined the label and was amazed to read "Casey at the Telephone." There were *twenty-four* of them although he had only completed four rounds of four records to each round, making a total of *sixteen*. It dawned on him that he was being duped. Leeds and Catlin were duplicating his originals by some secret process. Hunting indignantly charged them with unfair dealing and threatened to expose them if they did not make good all past pilferings. This they promptly did.

Inventors of genius made heroic efforts to match up the phono-

[19

graph cylinder to the gramophone disc, but they could never get round the two basic advantages of the latter: simple stamping of endless copies from one master, and the sound-track in the disc to guide the reproducing tone-arm. Scientists of the Bell and Tainter school had promptly rejected the Berliner process of disc recording as being fundamentally wrong. Their criticism was that the surface-speed of the outside of the disc was greater than that of the inside. This was wrong in 1890 and it is so today, fifty years later, but it was practical and simple; further, the gramophone record could be manufactured cheaply enough to bring it within the means of the poorest families.

We Go

to Europe

CHAPTER II

We Go to Europe

In order to cash in on his European rights before rival inventors could steal his markets, Emile Berliner decided to send an agent to London. He selected William Barry Owen, the son of an old New Bedford whaling captain and a typical high-pressure American business man and go-getter; he was, in, fact, a forerunner of the modern publicity and advertising school.

For one year Owen exhibited his gramophone in his rooms at the Hotel Cecil to a stream of prospects without a single bite. His weekends he spent up the Thames at a most comfortable old-fashioned pub. The owners were a youngish couple with the genius that has made English inns famous, she a good cook and housekeeper, he a convivial host and authority on the best horses, wines, and food. To crown all, her pretty niece was the type of barmaid that gladdens the heart and is a consolation and hope to the mere male. (All this is to tell how the merest chance brought fortune to one quick to grasp it.) The hostess had been a nurse and some of her grateful patients still looked in on her occasionally. While talking to one of these, a young gentleman of position with many friends, she drew attention to Owen's gramophone. The introduction was to net her a handsome reward and start the disc a-turning.

The final scheme Owen presented to Berliner looked very modest compared with his original dream of selling his European rights for £200,000 spot cash. A small trading syndicate with a modest £15,000 credit was started; gramophones were to be imported from America, and record pressings from a factory in Hanover, Germany, to be built by Berliner.

On July 1st, 1898, I embarked on the old Cunarder *Umbria* (minimum first-class passage $90) bound for Liverpool. My baggage consisted of a complete recording outfit plus a twenty-five dollar bicycle, with penumatic tires, and a notebook stuffed with receipts, addresses, and advice in Berliner's own handwriting. Berliner's chief concern was to safeguard his interests from intriguing associates. As his personal agent, I was also entrusted with the secrets of his then unpatentable recording process, and thus had a serious responsibility towards my benefactor—a trust which I can boast to have successfully carried out.

I remember arriving in London at the tail end of a strawberry glut of which I took the fullest advantage. That first evening, which was a Sunday, Owen gave a supper to myself, Joe Sanders (a nephew of Emile Berliner, who had been sent by him to Hanover to erect the pressing plant) and B. G. Royal. Royal was E. R. Johnson's great personal friend and was then in London as his observer. We were all small town boys, and Owen was in the seventh heaven of delight at our astonishment at the luxury of the Trocadero Grill and the "wickedness" all round us on that sabbath night. I actually found my first artist here in the person of Leopold Jacobs. He and his band made many a successful record.

The autumn of '98 saw me making the first records in London and preparing a list for the first English Gramophone Christmas. We were sold out of machines and records easily a week before Christmas. For the next ten years the gramophone played a big part in Christmas festivities: publicity and recording programmes pyramided up to this climax and dealers counted on the December sales to change their year's trading losses into a handsome profit.

Berliner could have selected no finer agent than Owen to exploit his invention. He was an opportunist of quick decision and a bold gambler, heads or tails, odds or even. He would always call a *stand pat* in a poker game and his eyes would bulge as he laid a full house on the table. On his many Atlantic crossings he would bid high when there was a following wind and in foul weather on the low field in the ship's pool. You would always find him sitting at the stiffest game of poker in the smoking-room. On one crossing, however, when we were travelling together he never played after the first night when he was trimmed by professional card-sharpers. They afterwards took him on deck and muscled him to the rail, threatening to throw him overboard if he squealed. The threat did not deter Owen from warning the captain that he had three dangerous crooks aboard. They were locked up for the rest of the voyage—I really believe to Owen's regret, as it left him without worthy opponents at poker.

I remember a holiday at Vineyard Haven when he missed the boat to Europe in order to watch a ball game between the Martha's Vineyard nine and his home team. At a horse race, in his excitement his eyes would nearly pop out of his head as the horses approached the judges' stand. I liked to watch the way he would stuff the five-pound notes into his pocket as he cashed in his winnings. He brought to London an infectious enthusiasm and energetic leadership which I believe was quite new to the conservative English City man of that day.

During the Owen régime in England he was able to introduce many up-to-date American advertising stunts, and the Gramophone Company became famous for its modern methods. Owen was one of the first to take a whole front-page in the *Daily Mail*, then in its infancy. He also purchased from the artist Francis Barraud the well-known dog and gramophone picture entitled "His Master's Voice." This picture Barraud had first submitted to the Edison Bell, and on their rejection he painted out the phonograph. Then, when Owen accepted the picture, he substituted a gramophone. In many other ways Owen showed his business genius, especially in quickly organising all the world markets for records before others could step in. Only in one aspect did his vision fail and that was in regard to the future of the gramophone as a permanent home entertainer.

After two years of profitable trading, he recommended that the Company should add other strings to their fiddle—which they did. In December 1900 they adopted a typewriter and an electric clock and began to manufacture the typewriter. It was a most complicated machine, presenting insuperable manufacturing problems for a small factory. Their name was changed to "The Gramophone and Typewriter Company" but later turned back to the Gramophone Company as soon as the typewriter had proved a failure. In this venture a good deal of money was lost before the directors decided to abandon other lines and concentrate solely on the gramophone.

After remaining for five years as Managing Director in England, Owen sold out and returned to the United States with a tidy little nest-egg. Unfortunately he lost it all within a few years.

Pursuing the policy of quick expansion, Owen sent me on a short recording circuit of Europe embracing Leipzig, Vienna, Budapest, Milan, and Madrid. I had a most congenial companion on this trip in my young colleague W. Sinkler Darby, also from Washington. In each city I recorded a few hundred titles as a start for trading operations. This expedition gave me vast experience in recording under various conditions and produced a rich harvest of musical records, both exciting and delightful to my provincial mind. The successful result prompted the decision to send me to that Eldorado of traders, Russia. Here the types of people I came into contact with were vastly different from those I had previously met.

Our agent was Max Rubinsky, the well-educated son of a Russian-American Rabbi. Max was handsome and ruthless in business and love, his two absorbing pursuits. He pretended to speak Russian well but he stuttered so badly that he was never able to convince me of this claim. The combination of American and Russian business methods, introduced by him, showed a versatility that amazed even the hardened Polish and Russian-Jewish dealers of the old Russian Empire. It is possible that Max was not so corrupt and that it could all be traced to his stuttering. He would begin by making it known that his wife's name-day was April—or his own birthday or wedding anniversary was March—and that, of course, credit to a certain dealer would be reduced unless he d—d—d—. The dealer in question, without waiting for him to finish, would rush out to a jeweller's and return with a diamond brooch or a gold watch with a card saying "Many Happy Returns of the Day." The tap of credit would be given one or two more turns according to the purity of the diamond or the weight of the gold watch.

The dealers also were a comic crowd. One, Rappaport by name, would draw me apart and whisper in my ear: "Don't trust Lebel, he'd cheat his own father." Then Lebel would take me in a corner and advise me: "Look out for Rappaport, he seduced a girl-pupil and was transported to Siberia; he's only free because of the amnesty on the Romanoff Centenary."

Our agent had devised a clever scheme to feather his own nest. Remaining always in the background, he organised a printing company that did all our catalogues or brochures, a credit-company through which dealers were forced to discount their bills, a big Moscow retail shop which had first call on all our new records or machines—and the system of gentle hints concerning his or his wife's birthdays, wedding-anniversaries, and other festivals like Easter and Christmas, which produced a galaxy of presents ranging from fur coats to grandfather clocks.

One day on coming home from a recording trip he greeted me on the doorstep of his apartment, saying: "C—c—come here, Fred. I want to show you s—s—something." With that he threw open the door of his salon, in which an array of gifts was displayed, comprising silver samovars, cutglass vases, gold cigarette cases, baskets of hothouse fruit and elaborate photograph frames. "Look, Fred," he said, "at the response to my birthday. Don't they l—l—love me?"

His dealers, as will be seen, carried heavy burdens; most of them were Hebrews and therefore barred from living in the better cities. They resented the overbearing swank of their American co-religionist. These people, particularly Lebel and Rappaport, tried to win me over from my Company and make me join them in forming a rival gramophone syndicate; naturally, I did not succumb.

Some years later I heard that they had made some progress in promoting a rival concern with the promise of financial backing from a wealthy young Russian officer. An agreement was to be signed in Paris with record-engineers and manufacturers. Loaded with *vodka* and *zakuska* the tricky trio took the Nord Express for that city; at Vilna Rappaport and Lebel were awakened from their drunken sleep by the conductor who told them their friend had jumped off the train. Quickly both got off and searched for him right up as far as St. Petersburg, only to find their faint-hearted capitalist had changed his mind and the deal was off.

In spite of the graft which was rampant, Russia paid us handsome dividends year after year. When eventually Max resigned to pursue bigger game, he knew every channel for landing profitable contracts so that when the World War broke out he was in a position to make a clean-up. Clever Max died playing poker on an Atlantic liner.

Our uncovering of this rich new gramophone field was by no means unchallenged, and we had continual fights with competitors, some scrupulous but most of them the reverse. Russia was one of the countries where international patent and copyright laws did not hold good.

In the spring of 1912, for example, I was recording in St. Petersburg in our studio on the Fontanka when Joe Cummings, a colleague from a competing concern, dropped in to see me. I was, of course, surprised at this visit. He was a little Englishman and, in answer to my query, went on to tell me that he had signed a year's contract with the Finkelstein Company. After having worked for them for six months, he was still without any salary and was very anxious to get back to England to his sick wife to whom he was unable to send money. It was for this reason that he had come to ask my assistance.

I had known that there was a Finkelstein Company operating in St. Petersburg. They were pirates in the gramophone trade. In other words, they were forging our Chaliapin, Sobinoff, Caruso, and other Red Label celebrity records and selling them at reduced prices. Naturally there was a hue-and-cry raised by the artists, who were being cheated out of their royalties, and for some time we had been trying to take legal action against this firm. They were, however, too wily and our only hope was to get evidence somehow that they were pressing records from our own records. Joe Cummings' appearance offered me the solution to this problem, and I told him I just wanted a little favor from him, and then he could have the money for his wife. He asked what it was, and I replied: "Give me a signal when Chaliapin records are actually in the press and being stamped in the Finkelstein factory."

It was arranged that the signal should be the dropping of a handkerchief. The time and place were agreed upon and we notified the police. The plot moved successfully, the police raided the factory and obtained all the evidence we wanted. Their action enabled us not only to confiscate all the forged matrices but also to destroy their entire stock of accumulated records of our celebrity artists and to close down their plant.

One of our first inspirations was the idea of recording the voice

WE GO TO EUROPE

of the Tsar. With this end in view, Rappaport arranged for an actual demonstration of gramophone recording in the palace of the Grand Duke Michael. We drove in a sleigh with our apparatus to the great palace where we were directed to the servants' entrance. We passed the guards, who examined us suspiciously, and were shown by a major-domo, with his snub Russian nose in the air, to a corner in a vast salon, furnished with chandeliers, tapestries and soft Persian carpets. With bated breath we set up our modest outfit near a Steinway grand piano. Just after nine o'clock the company trooped out from the dining room and ranged themselves round our machine.

There was His Excellency, General Bobrikoff, Governor of Finland, and Alexander Taneiev, the Chancellor to Lerche, Secretary to the Tsarina. Taneiev's two lovely young daughters and his two sons were also present with their mother. As they came up one by one and introduced themselves to me I was amazed and almost ashamed at having had to come the whole way to Russia to hear such flawless English. Each of them was ready with an impromptu message for the recording trumpet. To crown all, Taneiev himself, a great musician, played one of his own compositions on a wonderful Steinway. My colleague and I added a humorous touch by recording a negro ditty. It was the zinc-etching process that we employed, and twenty minutes after we played back these records to the delighted company. This was their first introduction to the miraculous talking-machine. My diary concludes: "They served us with tea and fruit and treated us fine; they expressed themselves as highly delighted." We never achieved the recording of the Tsar's voice nor, to my knowledge, did any other company do so.

That year, 1900, we completed recording at St. Petersburg of a rich programme performed by Russian choruses, and gypsy singers, among whom was the beloved Panina, as well as by such artists as the romance-singer Tamara, the popular comedian and concertina-player Peter Nevsky, whose records sold in thousands, and the great operatic baritone Kamionsky. Panina was a Tolstoyan type of gypsy with a deep-throated alto voice. At her recitals she would remain seated, accompanied only by a Tyrolean zither. Tamara was an equally great *chanteuse* but easygoing and not too fond of work: she frequently broke off a tour in a particular town if she found agreeable company and was well entertained; it took a bottle or

[29

two of champagne to put her in her best mood for a Russian gypsy song and then she could melt a heart of stone. On receiving her first cheque for 6,000 rubles, representing six months royalty earnings, she said "Not bad for an afternoon's work." Later her earnings were much larger.

We opened negotiations to record Chaliapin, but at that time he was still dizzy with success and would not respond to our humble offers. The same can be said of that marvellous lyric tenor, Sobinoff, who was even more spoilt and unattainable than Chaliapin. A few years later both of these men signed long term contracts with us which continued for the rest of their lives. These negotiations were unnecessarily protracted because of the lifelong jealousy between these two artists, each being afraid the other was getting the larger fee from us. I remember that on the night when Chaliapin signed his contract he invited us to a party at Yar's restaurant and engaged the largest *chambre séparée*. With his cronies from the chorus he sang Russian and gypsy songs the whole night through. It was a tireless night: no women were present and Chaliapin was happy as a schoolboy.

I wonder what has become of Yar, and of that handsome American negro Thompson, Yar's proprietor, who knew every nobleman and plutocrat in Moscow. He was always perfectly dressed and would personally welcome his patrons with a calculating eye in the vestibule. He was a general favorite everywhere, especially amongst the ladies, who made a pet of him. Paris, Berlin, Vienna, Budapest—none of them could compare in my opinion with St. Petersburg and Moscow if one wanted carefree night life.

As I write these lines I can see excited dealers lining up when the word went out that a fresh consignment of Chaliapin or Sobinoff records had arrived from the factory. The price was $5 each, single-sided, first come first served, and they sold like hot cakes. Is it any wonder that I called Russia our Eldorado?

It was Rappaport, whom I should have called a double-dealer when I first referred to him, who preached to us that to be a success in business one had to be *frech* (Yiddish or German slang for "fresh"). And so he at once opened a de luxe gramophone store on the Nevsky Prospect, with red-plush chairs and palms complete. He also advised affixing a Red Label to the Figner and Sobinoff records and selling them for $5 each. Needless to say, only the aristocracy and the wealthy merchants could afford to own a gramophone. It was really this rogue who, to secure goods of distinction for his emporium, always forced us to attempt the impossible in music and artists. Still, he lifted us out of our small town mentality.

On this trip we also began a siege to secure that sweetest and dearest of all Russian romance singers, Vialtseva, an artist I can only liken to one other person who, to my mind, flutters over the borderline of angels and human beings, Gracie Fields. She was one of the busiest of artists and only after extended negotiations was she signed up to sing ten songs for £2,000. When we asked her to repeat a record that was returned from the factory as defective she demanded further payment: indeed she literally worked herself to death piling up a large fortune. Her greatest hit and moneymaker for us was a record of the world-popular sleigh song, "Gai-da, Troika." Her sad and untimely demise in 1914 at the age of 40 at St. Petersburg was marked by an overwhelming demonstration of the people's love. Thousands of mourners who had known her humanity and generosity thronged the streets to pay their last tribute to her.

Newspapers reproduced telegrams announcing the hurried arrival at her bedside of a famous Berlin specialist to perform the then new transfusion of blood operation. We who loved her waited with bated breath on the result of this daring experiment. But there was no recovery.

Our next stop was to be Moscow, to obtain records of church choirs, Cossack soldier songs, military band marches and Little Russian choruses of the Don River. The railroad journey was marked by an incident that will always live in my memory. Occupying the opposite berth in my sleeping compartment was a distinguished gentleman. The conductor called to collect tickets. I produced mine but the gentleman fumbled in his pockets, unable to find his. The conductor said he would call later. Again the passenger excitedly searched his pockets but without success. This time the conductor was impatient and said he would return in an hour and if the ticket was not produced he would have to stop the train and expel the traveller. As the railway between St. Petersburg and Moscow is a straight line drawn on the map by Tsar Alexander, III, it passes through no town or village of any size. This time, my fellow-traveller, protesting frantically that he had a ticket but could not find it, was deposited on the open fields as the train stopped. In Moscow, a few days later, Lebel showed me a newspaper account about a body discovered near the railroad track. On enquiries being made this was found to be M———, a Government official travelling on a pass which was discovered in the ticket-pocket of his waistcoat, just where a ticket should be carried.

I was fortunate to arrive in Moscow in time to see the procession when the Tsar passed rapidly through the streets on the only state visit to that town in many years.

Our programme included a stop in Warsaw, then very much under the heel of Russia. I remember a city very beautiful in parts, yet with a high proportion of slums and ghettos. A first-class National Opera created a number of fine singers like Gruschelnitska (dramatic soprano), Didur (bass), Messal and Kavetskaya (lyric and operetta sopranos). Gruschelnitska was to become a favorite at La Scala and Didur leading basso at the New York Metropolitan Opera for over twenty-five years. Messal was beautiful and equally fine in opera and operetta. We made their first records. In common with all Polish artists they were suspicious of us and made us pay in advance before they sang: the artists in Russia were more trusting.

Here also were the best theatres and synagogues. The celebrated Cantor Kwartin made the first records of the age-old Temple chants, unaccompanied, which were to find their way to Hebrews in all parts of the world. Strange to say, today the appreciation of these devotional numbers no longer obtains with the younger generation. When their elders complain of this neglect, they regard them as hopeless fanatics.

As previously mentioned, on this expedition we were still employing the zinc-etching process and on this account a disagreeable incident occurred. One cold night a big earthen vat containing the etching-acid burst. The bright red fluid dripped through the ceiling on to a sleeping guest; when his body began to smart he aroused the hotel. At two in the morning there were furious hammerings at our door, and we were confronted by an angry crowd who wanted our blood. We were summarily kicked out of the hotel and before our baggage was surrendered we had to pay a thousand rubles in damages.

WE GO TO EUROPE

I returned to Moscow to record three Russian artists of Red Label rank, although at that time, April 1901, this exalted category of records had not yet been instituted. The artists were Davidoff, Sobinoff, and Tartakoff. Davidoff was a light tenor, a master of *bel canto*. With very little vocal material but perfect mastery, he made pleasing records of Russian lovesongs. He continued to be a great favorite in opera and through his records extended his popularity throughout Russia right up to the Revolution. I last saw him in Paris earning a precarious living in an obscure cabaret—the fate of so many fine Russian artists shattered and scattered by the Revolution.

Sobinoff was then the greatest lyric tenor in Russia. His fine voice and handsome appearance in such rôles as Lohengrin, Lenski, Hermann, Werther and Des Grieux made him the idol of the operatic world. To honors and gifts showered on him were added the royalties from the sales of his gramophone records, which made him a rich man. In the heyday of his career, between 1900 and 1912, his every performance was sold out by noon on the day it was advertised. In this respect his only rival was Chaliapin. Sobinoff sang at the Scala for two or three seasons, but only once in London—during the Beecham season of 1913—when he had passed his prime. He was to experience great poverty during the Revolution and until his death his only income was small sums earned outside of Russia on the sales of his old records, made in 1910.

The third artist was Tartakoff, a fine baritone and actor of the Titta Ruffo school. Those baritones were always wonderful fellows, intelligent and dependable; to me they always personified human sanity. Was it Hans von Bülow who said "A tenor is a disease"?

During the long Easter holiday I took a side trip to Nizhni Novgorod and down the Volga by steamer to Kazan, to make a few hundred Tartar records. Interesting, if for no other reason, was the fish dinner on the open deck of the steamer, during which the ragged, half-naked stevedores sang while loading sacks of meal and cement. Shall I ever forget the rhythmical swing as the green water-melons were passed from deck to barge? On every hand one heard music. Cossacks mounted on their sturdy, shaggy ponies rode through the streets singing soldier songs; their leader in a high-pitched tenor sang four lines and the chorus of a hundred masculine voices shouted the refrain. It was grand. The haulers moved in rhythm to their

[33

song; the loafers on the docks or the passengers on the decks below, with a small concertina, mouth-organ or balalaika, joined in groups. Through all these sounds threaded the clang of Russian church bells, with their distinctive changes of five tones. Life seemed easy and lazy, or was it simply the holiday spirit after a long, hard winter?

But of Tartar music we discovered little; musically these people have remained stationary. Being Mahometan, their women are strictly secluded and cover the face whenever they go abroad. The better-class Tartars adapt European music to their native idiom. So to the working-man's cafés and to the low-class brothels we went, since they were the only avenues for the Tartar songs we wished to record. Altogether it was an unsavory business that we concluded as quickly as possible before our return to Moscow.

I had put in six months, beginning in a zero winter of deep snow, fur coats, and troikas, and finishing in a blazing summer of buzzing bees and flies, with scarcely a lull intervening. I had seen opera performances on a scale unbelievably lavish. Only the wealthiest family in the world, the Romanoffs, could support them. I had heard and negotiated with a bevy of the greatest and perhaps most spoiled artists of that epoch. Added to this were my first impressions of Russian music, ballet, and decorative art, then at the height of their freshness and vigor. Then and there I decided to return, and return frequently, to Russia. Another and totally strange world of music and people was opened up to me. I was like a drug addict now, ever longing hungrily for newer and stranger fields of travel. Already I began to lay plans for a trip to the Far East.

From Zinc

to Wax

CHAPTER III

From Zinc to Wax

LOOKING back, it is hard to realise my state of nerves at the responsibility of recording Patti, Melba, Caruso, Paderewski, and other stars in those pioneer days when every new artist presented fresh problems. The recording art never had time to develop at leisure, but was urged on by rapidly expanding trade and the profits that were to be earned. Mine not to argue why, mine but to do or get kicked out! Enough to say that rarely could I sleep the night before an important session. I would busy myself till late at night, making preparations and attending to the last details, examining the surfaces of wax discs for flaws or re-surfacing waxes, trying out diaphragms and remounting them, setting up the positions of the orchestral players and even stringing up the clumsy Stroh violins then in use. I would even make certain that the special orchestrations were duly in order, and that the transpositions, if needed, were on hand.

Think, as I did, of a recorder's responsibility. A diva's record might be lost to posterity if I failed. In those days of star worship, the artists' patience with us was short and to ask "Her Grace" to repeat an aria because of any fault other than her own would probably send her off into a tantrum that would capsize the session. Moreover, I would get all the blame.

I remember poor Max Hampe, our Berlin recorder, and a complaint lodged against him by our German manager, who begrudged Max his success and independence of character. "Hempel doesn't like Hampe because when he wants her to get closer, he shoves her forward and when he wants her to get farther off, he pushes her away, all without gentleness." You must bear in mind that when recording high and loud notes the artist was instructed beforehand to recede from the diaphragm, and for low notes to approach it. Hampe's method was to make sure the artist did not forget this instruction in the heat of her performance. In this particular case, Hempel's dignity in front of the orchestra was ruffled, as rough hands pushed her backwards and forwards. He could only see that the lady was being paid £100 a song and that it was up to him to produce results. He also knew that the manager's job of greeting the diva with a bouquet of flowers and a smile, once the red carpet had been laid down, was simple compared to his. Successful records meant glory for the manager, but failures the sack for the recorder.

Nor, in those days, could one waste time on repeats as one can so easily do today. Why, you ask? Because time was a vital factor. Six to ten records had to be made at a session, simply because, in a whole season, the diva could spare only two hours. It was a case of take it or leave it. One must remember that gramophone fees were only chicken feed to the artists of that day. At the opera house the diva would be performing three times a week under contract, with a day's rest before and after each performance. Two rehearsals had to be fitted in and some allowance made for the usual colds, indispositions, and other ailments. How could a prima donna find time to make records? And she must be in her top form, because it was always impressed on her that she was singing for posterity.

Recently I read a long account of the recording of Patti's voice which made no mention whatever of the technician. One would have thought records recorded themselves. The recorder in this case happened to be myself, and later on I will tell the whole story from beginning to end.

The beginning was the evening of March 14, 1900, when I went to a performance of *Florodora* at the old Lyric Theatre and sat directly behind the conductor, Landon Ronald. It was my second year in London as chief recorder and artist scout for The Gramophone Company. My visit to the Lyric was as a scout and when, for two hours, I watched the dynamic youngster conduct, I said to myself "That's the man our Company needs." I lost no time in approaching him and here was manna from heaven! Ronald recited his qualifications—associate conductor at Covent Garden, accompanist to Melba, Patti, Plançon, Renaud, and so on. For our young company it was like finding the Koh-i-Noor diamond. I immediately informed my Manager, William Barry Owen, of my find. It is important to reflect what a primitive little affair the gramophone was in 1900. 10" records were not yet introduced nor was wax recording. Our recorded repertoire consisted only of ballads, comic songs, and band records. Whenever we approached the great artists, they just laughed at us and replied that the gramophone was only a toy. But our faith and ambition were too great to be put off like this. In Landon Ronald we saw the agent who could bring us into contact with those unapproachables, so he was given a contract and a roving commission to bring them in—a job that terminated only with his death two years ago. His service lasted nearly forty years and came near to rivalling my own record of forty-two.

As the recording art developed and with the introduction of the three and four minute (10" and 12") playing records, we became bolder and more enterprising. We lived on excitement. Before this we were satisfied to cope with such national and popular celebrities as Dan Leno, Eugene Stratton, R. G. Knowles, and Bert Sheppard, whose material lent itself to the primitive gramophone. Bert Sheppard was an old minstrel I had met on the S. S. *Umbria* when crossing the Atlantic, and Knowles and Stratton were his poker companions at Savoy Court where he lived. I never risked being included in their game of poker, because I was warned that between them I was bound to be trimmed. However, as their rendezvous was Rule's in Maiden Lane, next door to the premises we had taken as a recording studio, Sheppard brought his companions to us to be amused and this served to give us contact with the greatest artists of the then flourishing music-hall world. Their names proved lodestones that brought to our catalogue other stars—Ada Reeve, Vesta Victoria, Gus Ellen, Albert Chevalier, Herbert Darnley, George Mozart, Marie Lloyd, Vesta Tilly, Connie Ediss. Tears come to my eyes even to recall those sterling characters—there was not a mean or ungenerous one amongst them. They had climbed the hard ladder of life, but all had arrived at the top quite unspoiled. How easy it was to deal with them in comparison with our dealers and factors!

In Maiden Lane we kept open house and our good friend Mr.

Hyde, himself a publican, acted as runner. I had my recording machine ready to receive at any time the interesting visitors Mr. Hyde would bring in from Rule's. I remember Dan Leno arriving without an accompanist, so that I had to start the recording machine and then quickly run to the piano and accompany "Mrs. Kelly." He was also the champion Lancashire Clog Dancer, so we hoisted him up on a table to record his foot-taps. After that we always kept Airlie Dix, composer of "The Trumpeter," standing by to act as accompanist. Even this did not always work, as he would often disappear to a nearby tavern. This gifted pianist could not keep off the bottle, but those were hard drinking days and Scotch was only 3/6d. a bottle, full proof.

Other visitors were Jimmie Fawn and his son-in-law Scott Russell, to sing "Jack's the Boy," Louis Bradfield "The Military Man," Henry Lytton his "Laughing Song," and Maurice Farkoa, accompanied by Frank Lambert, to sing "I Like You in Velvet" and "Le Fou-Rire" again, the most natural and contagious laughing song ever invented. Connie Ediss was a child of Drury Lane, but always the lady. She kept our studio in an uproar and could never be serious. I heard that in her last days at the Middlesex Hospital, bedridden though she was, she kept the patients in the ward and the nurses in continual laughter.

My second Atlantic crossing brought me into contact with the *Belle of New York* Company, coming to London to launch that wonderful operetta. All England fell under its spell. This led to Frank Lawton recording his famous whistling solo. Even beautiful Edna May herself, the dazzling daughter of a Schenectady letter carrier, sang her "Purity Brigade" song. Were we thrilled when she entered our grimy studio!

Yes, grimy was the word for it. The smoking room of the old Coburn Hotel was our improvised studio. There stood the recording machine on a high stand; from this projected a long thin trumpet into which the artist sang. Close by, on a high movable platform, was an upright piano. If there was an orchestral accompaniment, then half-a-dozen wind instrumentalists, also on high stands, would be crowded in close to the singer. Perhaps one Stroh violin, its trumpet bearing close on the singer's ear, would be the sole representative of the string section, and he would be left inaudible if he did not exag-

FROM ZINC TO WAX

gerate heavily the *pizzicato, glissando* and *vibrato* characteristics of his instrument.

The recording process was to employ a thin flat zinc disc with a highly polished smooth surface. This would be coated with a protective film of fat and placed on a turntable. A stylus attached to a diaphragm would trace a spiral groove through the fat when the turntable revolved. The diaphragm terminated in a horn, down which the artist sang, causing the stylus to vibrate from side to side. Lateral vibrations, Emile Berliner called them in his patent specification, to avoid clashing with the Edison phonograph patent, which specified an up-and-down, or hill-and-dale, vibration. The artist having performed, the zinc disc was immersed for ten minutes in an acid bath. The result was a thin shallow groove of even depth etched into the zinc. This formed a sound-track that carried the reproducing sound-box when the record was played back. In the middle of the studio, in full view of the artists, I carried out this process and when I played back the record it never failed in those days to amaze the artists. In particular, they could not grasp how just one line could contain both voice and accompaniment. I had to explain that it was the composite result of all impacts on the diaphragm.

Our diaphragm was not very sensitive and we still required robust, even voices to make good records. Fat, jolly Bert Sheppard, with his powerful tenor voice and clear diction, gave us our most successful results. We used him under many names and as an old minstrel man he was very versatile. His repertoire comprised negro airs, Irish and English ballads, comic and patter songs, parodies and yodels. The spontaneous and boisterous laugh he could conjure up was most infectious and was heard by thousands through his records. Bert Sheppard's "Whistling Coon" and "The Laughing Song" were world-famous. In India alone over half a million records of the latter were sold. In the bazaars of India I have seen dozens of natives seated on their haunches round a gramophone, rocking with laughter, whilst playing Sheppard's laughing record; in fact, this is the only time I have ever heard Indians laugh heartily. The record is still available there and I believe that to this day it sells in China, Africa, and Japan as well. These songs I brought over from America, having transcribed them from memory and taught them to Bert. I had acquired them from George W. Johnson, the tragic negro mentioned

[41

earlier, who was hanged for throwing his wife out of a window when in a drunken frenzy.

Another powerful singer was Ian Colquhoun, called the "Iron-Voiced Baritone," who dressed in kilts and sang patriotic songs in the old Alhambra Theatre. In the days leading up to the Boer War, his mighty voice brought down the house with "MacGregor's Gathering" and "The Absent-Minded Beggar." Both of these songs were successfully recorded and sold in great quantities.

But the star turn during the Boer War period was a descriptive record entitled "The Departure of the Troopship," with crowds at the quayside, bands playing the troops up the gangplank, bugles sounding "All ashore," farewell cries of "Don't forget to write," troops singing "Home Sweet Home," which gradually receded in the distance, and the far away mournful hoot of the steamer whistle. The record became enormously popular and eventually historic. It brought tears to the eyes of thousands, among them those of Melba, who declared in my presence that this record influenced her to make gramophone records more than anything else. I was directly and solely responsible for acquiring "The Departure of the Troopship" for my company, and, together with my good colleague Russell Hunting, its author, staged the recording.

My duties were becoming increasingly heavy as my company started to develop their foreign markets, and early in 1900 they offered my brother Will a position as associate recorder. Will was short and rotund, with an amiable smile that reflected his good and generous nature. He regarded artists as children (and he was right) and would mother them all. Eventually, he became the best known and most accessible of all impresarios. Many are the artists who sought out his advice and protection. His early death at 40 years of age caused something like consternation among the hundreds of his friends and colleagues. A picture I cannot get out of my mind is my brother suddenly being summoned by telephone and, some hours afterwards, leading down Maiden Lane a very tipsy and argumentative Tyrone Power, father of the film-star. This great tragedian would slip off the track now and again, but he had so many good and admiring friends that he could always count on being rescued. His magnificent voice and diction made some thrilling records of that day.

FROM ZINC TO WAX

Our artists arrived in four-wheelers and hansom cabs. I remember George Mozart, a red nose comedian, arriving in a four-wheeler and unloading a heavy theatrical wicker trunk. This was dragged into the studio and I asked George to rehearse while I continued my preparations. After what I thought was a rather long lapse of time, I looked into the studio to find him standing before the trumpet in full make-up, complete with red nose, whiskers, and costume. Then I realized the reason for the trunk. Dear, simple George had anticipated television by thirty-five years. With difficulty I explained to him that to record his songs he need not have troubled to put on his make-up.

Again, there arrived in a two-wheeler, dapper, breezy Louis Bradfield. He wore a very effective toupee. His favorite story was about his young son, who would come behind him when he was reading and, lifting up the toupee, would say "Where to, governor?"

Stout was the great standby of our artists in those days. It amazed me to see the number of empties that accumulated at the end of a session. Harry Fay's capacity was six bottles, but Ernest Pike and some of the ladies ran him a close second. Ernest was a silver voiced tenor whose records of popular ballads and especially 'mother' songs were favorites in thousands of homes. Following the tradition of tenors, he was a simple, good-natured lad and the butt of jokes and puns. His father was a cook at Sandringham and thus it came about that Ernest was once invited to sing at the Palace by Royal Command. He was not made of the stuff to carry off such honors and this afforded constant ammunition for the puns and wit of his colleagues, especially Peter Dawson.

I have seen Peter's mimicry and puns rile even such exalted people as Sir Harry Lauder, Chaliapin and Dame Nellie Melba, however. Peter is no respecter of persons and under the name of "Hector Grant" he recorded in perfect imitation Sir Harry Lauder's entire repertoire, a fact which Sir Harry never forgave. Chaliapin was furious when Peter followed him on the platform before hundreds of gramophone dealers and, imitating the Russian's mannerisms of waving his arms and striding along, smiled sweetly and announced in broken English in a deep voice "Number Fifty-Five" and, after a pause, waved to the pianist to carry on. Melba was rabid when, at a recording of "My Old Kentucky Home" with a male quartet, including Ernest Pike and Peter Dawson pressed close round her, Peter gave her that impertinent look of his. She turned on him saying "You're from Australia?"; he answered "Yes, Ma'am." She asked, "What city?"; he replied "Melbourne." Her retort was "What! That town of parsons, pubs, and prostitutes!"

Peter is primarily a record-maker. Oratorio and concert have been secondary lines, although on the strength of his thousands of records he has proved a draw in the provinces and seaside resorts. He also made a phenomenally successful concert tour with Mark Hambourg, also of record fame, visiting Australia and India, where both harvested a small fortune. These two witty men got along extremely well on tour, as may be imagined, except for the bone of contention as to who was the greatest draw of the team! It was the same contention that kept Flagstad and Melchior enemies off the stage but lovers on for so many sold-out performances of *Tristan und Isolde*. The Scandinavians are realists and practical people.

Peter Dawson arrived in England from Australia in 1904 at the age of twenty, and has made records twelve months in every year since then—which is undoubtedly a record. His average earnings for that period must have been close on £2,000 a year. He returned to Australia at the start of the present war and is now a partner in his brother's prosperous can-manufacturing company.

Changing over from zinc-etching, with its limited possibilities, to recording on hard wax tablets marked an almost magic expansion in the gramophone record business. It also sounded the death-knell of the phonograph cylinder as a musical instrument. Now we could give our ambitions freer scope. The wax-recording meant a cleaner cut, less surface noise and the music more faithfully registered. Wax also benefited the routine of matrix making. Then followed the invention of a process of duplicating matrices which made possible the stamping of hundreds of thousands of records from one performance instead of barely a thousand.

All this happened in 1901. Until that time, all these developments of the flat disc recording had been held up by complicated patents in the hands of Emile Berliner, Edison, the American Graphophone Company, and the Columbia Company. The latter was the powerful, wealthy company exploiting the Edison and Graphophone phonograph cylinder patents. Panic-stricken at the rapid progress

FROM ZINC TO WAX

of Berliner's flat disc, they headed him off from using wax as a recording medium by fortunately acquiring the J. W. Jones U. S. Patent No. 688,739—for "a groove of even depth." An injunction brought to a standstill for two years the flat disc business in America. This was lifted in 1902, when the litigants pooled patents and the Victor Company and Columbia Gramophone Company left the starting post neck to neck, to compete hotly for the disc business for the next thirty years. To this pool Emile Berliner contributed "a sound box guided by a spiral groove," the Columbia "a stylus vibrating laterally and engraving a groove of even depth" and The American Graphophone Company "wax as a medium of recording."

Thus, under license of the Victor Company (controlling the Berliner rights) we in England led off with Caruso recording ten titles on wax as the first coup in the battle. In March 1902, armed for the first time with the new recording equipment and wax discs, I found myself in Italy for the purpose of recording a conventional programme of Italian opera, ballads, comics, and bands. It was my second recording trip to Italy and we put up at Spatz's Hotel in Milan. We were allowed to set up our recording equipment in this hotel only because it was a recognised center for singers and musicians. Spatz's son-in-law was Giordano, the celebrated composer of *Andrea Chenier* and the exalted Giuseppe Verdi had been a permanent resident of the hotel, actually occupying the suite on the *Bel Étage*, beneath our third floor apartment. It was in these rooms that he had died a few months before.

My brother Will accompanied me on this trip, and what a thrill awaited us! Our local representative was Alfred Michaelis, a man of enterprise and vision. He lost no time in excitedly telling us that two tenors were creating a furor at the Scala, and that we must record both, or at least one, of them. Their names were Enrico Caruso and Alessandro Bonci. Our first attempt to hear Caruso was not a success. It happened in this way: our then General Manager, William Barry Owen, and his wife chanced to pass through Milan just at the time we arrived and Alfred Michaelis had arranged a box party at the Scala. The programme was *Germania*, an opera by Alberto Franchetti with text by Luigi Illica, first produced at the Scala on March 11, 1902 and published by Casa Ricordi. The cast included Caruso, Sammarco, and Pinto. The house was sold out and

[45

to obtain a box Michaelis had to bribe certain powers. The Scala boxes were all owned in perpetuity by the wealthy and noble families of Milan, so it was to be hoped that the proprietor of the box Michaelis had secured would not show up that evening. We arrived and filled every available seat. The overture had just started and we had settled ourselves for a grand treat, when he heard an insistent knock. Michaelis, greatly annoyed, threw open the door— and there stood the proprietor, Baron de L——, and his guests. In the real Italian fashion, a tempestuous scene immediately ensued. The altercation grew louder and louder as the vestibule quickly filled with attendants, urged on by the disturbed audience to stop the fracas. Michaelis, most humiliated, pointed out that his guests were Americans who would carry back a very bad impression of Italian manners, but this was to no avail and we all filed mournfully out of the box. Michaelis then challenged the Baron to a duel. Cards were passed and my poor brother Will was asked to act as second to his friend. All that night I remained in the company of my very nervous brother, discussing the mode of procedure to be carried out by a second in a duel. However, the next morning calmer tempers prevailed and apologies for the misunderstanding were exchanged by both parties —much to the relief of my brother. Shortly afterwards, armed with good stalls, we really heard *Germania* in peace and comfort.

I cannot describe my transports or the wild enthusiasm of the audience when Federico Loewe (Caruso) urged the students to revolt against the invader, Napoleon—"Studenti! Udite!" This impassioned appeal ends with a wild burst from the crowd singing Weber's popular "Luetzow's Wilde Jagd." In the first act there was a wonderful love-duet with Ricke (Pinto) rich in opportunities for both tenor and soprano, that held the audience spellbound. Caruso was then only twenty-eight and in the second year of his grand career as a tenor. He had originally started as a baritone. Tetrazzini, his life-long confidante, was later to describe the young Caruso to me as follows:

"I remember Enrico as a youth of twenty years, before his voice was yet rounded and the different registers smoothed out. I recall the difficulty he had with even such ordinary notes as G or A. He always stumbled over these and it annoyed him so that he even threatened to change over to baritone, saying that he did not know whether he had a tenor or a baritone voice. In those early days I did not run across him very often and it was some years later, when during an opera season in St. Petersburg I sang with him for the first time, that I saw what progress he had made and realized what a remarkable voice he had. The opera was *La Bohême*, the year 1897. I can hear that velvet voice now, and the *impertinenza* with which he lavishly poured forth those rich, round notes. It was the open *voce Napolitana* yet it had the soft caress of the *voce della campagna Toscana*. There never was a doubt in my mind. I placed him then and there as an extraordinary and unique tenor. From top to bottom his register was without defect. He was then, as he was to the end, a gay, rollicking Neapolitan boy. What merry pranks he used to play! What good laughs we had together! His company was a tonic for all ailments."

Is it to be wondered that I lost my head? I turned to Michaelis and said "Find out what fee he will accept for ten songs." The next day Maestro Cottone, our accompanist, returned with a proposition. Caruso would sing ten songs for £100, all to be recorded in one afternoon. (In reality this was the only free period he could squeeze out of the busy season.) To us in those days, these were really staggering terms, but I transmitted them to London with a strong recommendation, feeling all the time how inadequate were words in telegraphic form to describe the merits of the case. A cabled reply came back quickly: *Fee exorbitant, forbid you to record.*

This was humiliating and I felt it was hopeless to argue with the people in London, as it was only by being on the spot that one could grasp the urgency of the opportunity. I therefore gave the word to Michaelis to go ahead, as at the worst we only needed a profit of 1/- on each of 2,000 records to cover the fee. The die was cast. One sunny afternoon Caruso, debonnaire and fresh, sauntered into our studio and in exactly two hours, sang ten arias to the piano accompaniment of Maestro Cottone. The titles were:

Rigoletto	—*Questa o quella.*
Manon	—*O dolce incanto.*
Elisir d'amore	—*Una furtiva lagrima.*
Mefistofele	—*Giunto sul passo estremo.*
Mefistofele	—*Dai campi, dai prati.*
Tosca	—*E lucevan le stelle.*
Iris	—*Serenata.*
Aïda	—*Celeste Aïda.*
Germania	—*No, non chiuder.*
Germania	—*Studenti, udite!*

Not one *stecca*, blemish, or huskiness marred this feat.

We paid Caruso his £100 on the spot. I was stunned at the ease with which such a vast sum was earned and could not foresee that as a result of this contract, Caruso would earn close to $5,000,000 in the next twenty years and the industry twice that amount. Nor could I foresee that these records would let down all the barriers of prejudice which the great artists held against recording.

The ten precious waxes were shipped to Hanover and processed without one failure. All were issued and I heard the figure of £15,000 net profit mentioned as a result of the venture.

The record "E Lucevan le Stelle" from *Tosca* was regarded as sensational. Mr. Conried, who was then manager of the New York Metropolitan Opera, heard it in Mr. Alfred Clark's office in Paris and carried the record to New York to play for his directors. As a result of their impressions, Caruso was cabled a contract immediately.

Caruso's first appearance at Covent Garden in May of the same year coincided with the issue of these records. Thus, my bold manoeuvre proved very opportune. The argument that the recording might have been better carried out in London does not hold. London is the last place in the world to undertake recording with international artists during an opera season. Their time is so nicely calculated as to leave no loophole for singing for records.

My brother Will was now sharing my duties and this enabled me to volunteer as technical recorder and artistic adviser for an expedition to the Far East. The object was to open up new markets, establish agencies, and acquire a catalogue of native records. Tom Addis, accompanied by his good-looking wife, was the business head, and I had as my helper young George Dillnutt. This trip occupied me from September 1902 to August 1903, and included stops for recording in Calcutta, Singapore, Hong Kong, Shanghai, Tokio, Bangkok, and Rangoon. I returned to London later via Singapore, Calcutta, Delhi, Bombay and Marseilles.

For this expedition I designed and built a successful weight-motor, enabling me to dispense with heavy storage batteries and fragile clocksprings. We loaded our equipment and 600 wax blanks on the good ship *Coromandel*, built in 1868. We sailed from Tilbury Docks on a beautiful September morning, cheered by many artists and col-

FROM ZINC TO WAX

leagues who came to see us off. As we steamed down the channel into the unknown I felt like Marco Polo starting out on his journeys. Here was excitement and adventure enough to satisfy any young man of twenty-nine. Even the old-fashioned East Indiaman with its high poopdeck and mixed class of passengers promised mystery and romance.

The Gramophone

Goes East

CHAPTER IV

The Gramophone Goes East

THE *Coromandel* was of the vintage when shipbuilders could not decide between sails or steam power, and so installed both. It was comfortable and carried only cabin and third-class passengers. In the long list of travellers there were no exalted names from the Civil Service, military, judicial, or the ruling class. This did not mean we thought the less of ourselves. My fellow-travellers quickly divided into sharply defined social groups: tea-planters, railroad and mining engineers and officials, departmental managers, a few young women going out to be married or seeking husbands. Only one thing reduced them all to a common denominator—returning from holidays in England, they were all broke! The Australians getting off at Colombo formed a clique apart. They gambled all day and seemed to resent the superiority of the Anglo-Indians. Of indefinite classification was a friendly, stylish little blonde, accompanied by her two children in the care of a nurse. One child was blonde like the mother, the other was coffee-coloured and had the dark, soulful eyes of an Indian. Her name was Banerjee and she was joining her husband, a brilliant Indian who was one of the few native judges at that time.

Another passenger, courted by all of us far beyond his social merits, was young Bond. He was a jockey on his way to ride in the Viceroy's Cup. Later we all played his mounts faithfully during the races and lost consistently. In the Viceroy's Cup race his horse broke a leg and had to be shot.

[53

THE MUSIC GOES ROUND

By the time we reached Gibraltar all the passengers were accounted for with the exception of a Mr. and Mrs. Norton. Curiosity ran high about this couple as soon as we had seen the very stylish baggage they brought on board. It was only as we passed by Stromboli, then in eruption, that they put in an appearance. They were a strikingly handsome American couple, well dressed and exclusive. Mrs. Norton easily out-distanced in chic and elegance all our ladies, and we men hungrily admired her as the Nortons paced the deck, absorbed in each other.

After a six weeks' glorious but uneventful journey we anchored one morning in the muddy Hooghly River to take on board a pilot. While he carefully navigated us up the crowded jetty of Calcutta, returning teaplanters told stories of the fat fees earned and princely lives led by these pilots. They would have made even Huckleberry Finn envious.

After the quarantine the climax of our journey was reached when we were boarded by an Inspector and a squad of policemen. They had warrants for the arrest and extradition of Mr. Norton, a banker from Philadelphia, on the charge of embezzlement. He had left his wife and children for the lady we knew as Mrs. Norton, a chorus girl!

It took three days to unload our thirty heavy cases and pass the customs officers. Our agent, Jack Hawd, had arranged a location and had asembled a collection of artists who watched us curiously as we prepared our studio for recording. It was the first time that the talking-machine had come into their lives and they regarded it with awe and wonderment. The rains had passed and India's glorious dry season was ahead of us. We entered a new world of musical and artistic values. One had to erase all memories of the music of European opera-houses and concert-halls: the very foundations of my musical training were undermined. I soon discovered that the Anglo-Indians, whom we contacted and who were acting as our agents and factors, were living on another planet for all the interest they took in Indian music. They dwelt in an Anglo-Saxon compound of their own creation, isolated from India. They had their own cricket and tennis clubs, teaparties and bridge, "Sixteen annas to the rupee." The native bazaars never saw them, and even the Eurasians aped them to the extent of tabooing all Indian society.

THE GRAMOPHONE GOES EAST

I met the Superintendent of the Calcutta police, who placed at my disposal an officer to accompany me to the various important entertainments and theatres in the Harrison Road. Our first visit was to the native "Classic Theatre" where a performance of *Romeo and Juliet* in a most unconventional form was being given. Quite arbitrarily, there was introduced a chorus of young Nautch girls heavily bleached with rice powder and dressed in transparent gauze. They sang "And Her Golden Hair Was Hanging Down Her Back," accompanied by fourteen brass instruments all playing in unison. I had yet to learn that the oriental ear was unappreciative of chords and harmonic treatment and only demanded the rhythmic beat of accompaniment of the drums. At this point we left.

We now proceeded to attend a dinner party and Nautch dance in the home of a wealthy *babû*. We elbowed our way through an unsavory alley, jostled by fakirs and unwholesome sacred cows, to a pretentious entrance. The host and his native guests eagerly welcomed the brave band of *pukka* Anglo-Saxons who bestowed such honor on his house. No native women were present excepting the Nautch girls who have lost caste. We Europeans ate at a separate table; not even our host sat with us. After a rigidly European dinner we retired to a large salon and were entertained by the Nautch girls.

The room presented a most interesting sight. At one end were the native gentlemen in their white gowns; some wore strings of pearls and diamonds and valuable rings. At the other end was our small party of Europeans in evening dress. The Singing Girl advanced slowly around the room singing. Following her closely was her band of five musicians, consisting of two *esrag* or Hindustani violins, one tumbler player with a right and left *tamboora* and two *mandieras* (bells) players. Bringing up the rear were attendants for preparing the betel nut and another holding a silver cuspidor. The singer was heavily laden with gold ornaments and bracelets, anklets, and pearl necklaces, and to crown all there was a large diamond set in her nostril. She was a Mohammedan and very popular. She terminated each song with a cleverly executed muscle-dance. I found the performance long and boring and her mouth dyed with red betel-nut offended me.

That evening we heard another celebrated singer, Goura Jan, an

[55

Armenian-Jewess who could sing in twenty languages and dialects. Her great hit that evening was an adaptation of "Silver Threads Among the Gold." Her fee was 300 rupees per evening and she used to make a brave show when she drove at sundown on the Maidan in a fine carriage and pair. Hers were among the six hundred records which proved a firm foundation for our new enterprise.

Her flair for publicity is well illustrated by the feast she once provided for her cat when she produced a litter of kittens. This affair cost her twenty thousand rupees. There were hundreds of guests, so naturally this feline function became the talk of the bazaars.

When she came to record, her suite of musicians and attendants appeared even more imposing than those who used to accompany Melba and Calvé. As the proud heiress of immemorial folk-music traditions she bore herself with becoming dignity. She knew her own market value, as we found to our cost when we negotiated with her. Once, when I reproduced a record of the "Jewel Song" from *Faust*, sung by Suzanne Adams, Goura Jan and her attendants were astonished by the rapidity of those *bravura* scales and trills.

Every time she came to record she amazed us by appearing in a new gown, each one more elaborate than the last. She never wore the same jewels twice. Strikingly effective were her delicate black gauze draperies embroidered with real gold lace, arranged so as to present a tempting view of a bare leg and a naked navel. She was always *bien soignée*. Addis, our sales-manager, and I made guesses at her age. I thought she was twenty-two, he put her down at twenty-five, but we were both wrong. Though she looked like a young girl, she was forty-five.

In my search for artists I attended theatres, parties and fêtes. Never again will I be able to summon up an equal enthusiasm for Indian music, for one indispensable accompaniment to most songs was a simple missionary's organ. The keys were played with one hand while the other worked a bellows. I found it produced a dull and uninspiring sound, and I soon came to loathe the instrument. Only one or two male singers were recommended to us and these had high-pitched effeminate voices. There was absolutely no admiration or demand for the manly baritone or bass, and in the Orient vocalists in these categories would starve to death.

Goura Jan, famous classical Indian singer, with native musicians in a pause during a recording session at Calcutta.

Photograph by the Author

All the female singers were of course from the caste of the public women, and in those days it was practically impossible to record the voice of a respectable woman. The songs and dances were passed by word of mouth from mother to daughter. They began public appearances at about twelve years of age. The clever brainy ones went up to the top and sometimes travelled all over the country in great demand at the wedding feasts of the wealthy. As they began to make names for themselves many of them insisted that the word "amateur" should be printed on the record label. Fees as a rule were very reasonable in comparison with those paid in Europe but recording expenses were heavy, since most of the artists had to be trained over long periods before they developed into acceptable gramophone singers.

Janki Bai was one of the best classical singers and her fee was 3,000 rupees for a recording session. To attend a wedding celebration her fee varied with the standing of the parties; from a wealthy family she would get 5,000 rupees, and the festival on such an occasion would last several days. Dulari was another popular female artist, much more adaptable than Janki Bai though not so good a classical singer. Dulari was willing to learn new songs and was quite a good dramatic artist. Sets of records had a great success for several years. These were mostly fairy tales, legends, and so forth, which were specially written for recording.

Most of the better known artists had their own private bands. The older generation in India had no appreciation of European music, which is said to sound as unpleasing to them as Indian music sounds to us.

The gramophone we brought to India was to enjoy an especially widespread popularity as an entertainer, and was to vie with the umbrella and bicycle as a hallmark of affluence. Even now shoppers in the bazaars demand a large glittering brass horn to dazzle their neighbors. Today the advent of talking films produced in India has started a craze for the theme songs similar to those in European productions. Their popularity all over India has sent up the market value of the singers who introduce them, and their recording fees have gone up proportionately.

Thirty years have elapsed since my first visit to India. We found music there static and after a few years there was very little traditional music left to record. Songs for festivals and weddings were already in our catalogue and new artists were learning their repertoire from gramophone records. Practically speaking there is no written Indian music, and there are no publishers of Indian music. What copyright fees the companies had to pay were on the words or poems of some of the songs which had been published in books. The company therefore founded training centers in Calcutta, Delhi, Lahore, Madras, and Rangoon and engaged musicians to train artists and to set tunes to selected poems. Almost every year thereafter from two to three thousand songs have been recorded in all parts of India, in most of the six hundred dialects and languages. Unique among the principal countries of the world, India has not as yet permitted radio to challenge the supremacy of the gramophone.

Our local sales manager was a young Eurasian named Christensen, whose devotion and hospitality I had difficulty in shaking off. His father was a Swedish sailing-captain and apart from his muddy complexion he looked more like a blond Swede than an Indian. He was married to a wealthy widow, proprietor of an undertaking establishment. They lived over the showrooms, and I shudder now to think of the dinner they gave, preceded by an inspection of their stock of lovely coffins.

My itinerary called for Yokohama as the next stop, and after packing up I had four days to wait for the next direct sailing for that port. I squeezed in a trip to Darjeeling, where I was lucky enough to see a sunrise over the roof of the world from Tiger Hill, with the first rays of the sun lighting up Mount Everest and the monster peaks round about. It was a memory to carry through life.

I easily obtained accommodation at the swank hotel, "The Woodlands." The great shopkeeper Mr. Whiteway, proprietor of Calcutta's large department store Whiteway and Laidlaw, had not been so lucky some years before. During the off-season, he had applied for rooms and had been told, "Sorry, sir, but we are full up." They really meant, "Sorry, sir, if we entertained shopkeepers, our Civil Servants and military officers would leave us." To be sure that such an indignity could not happen again, he later bought out the hotel, lock, stock and barrel, and put an embargo on all snobs.

To show what a distorted value some people have, Christensen, with the idea of doing me honor, met me at the railway station on my

Photograph by Arthur Clarke

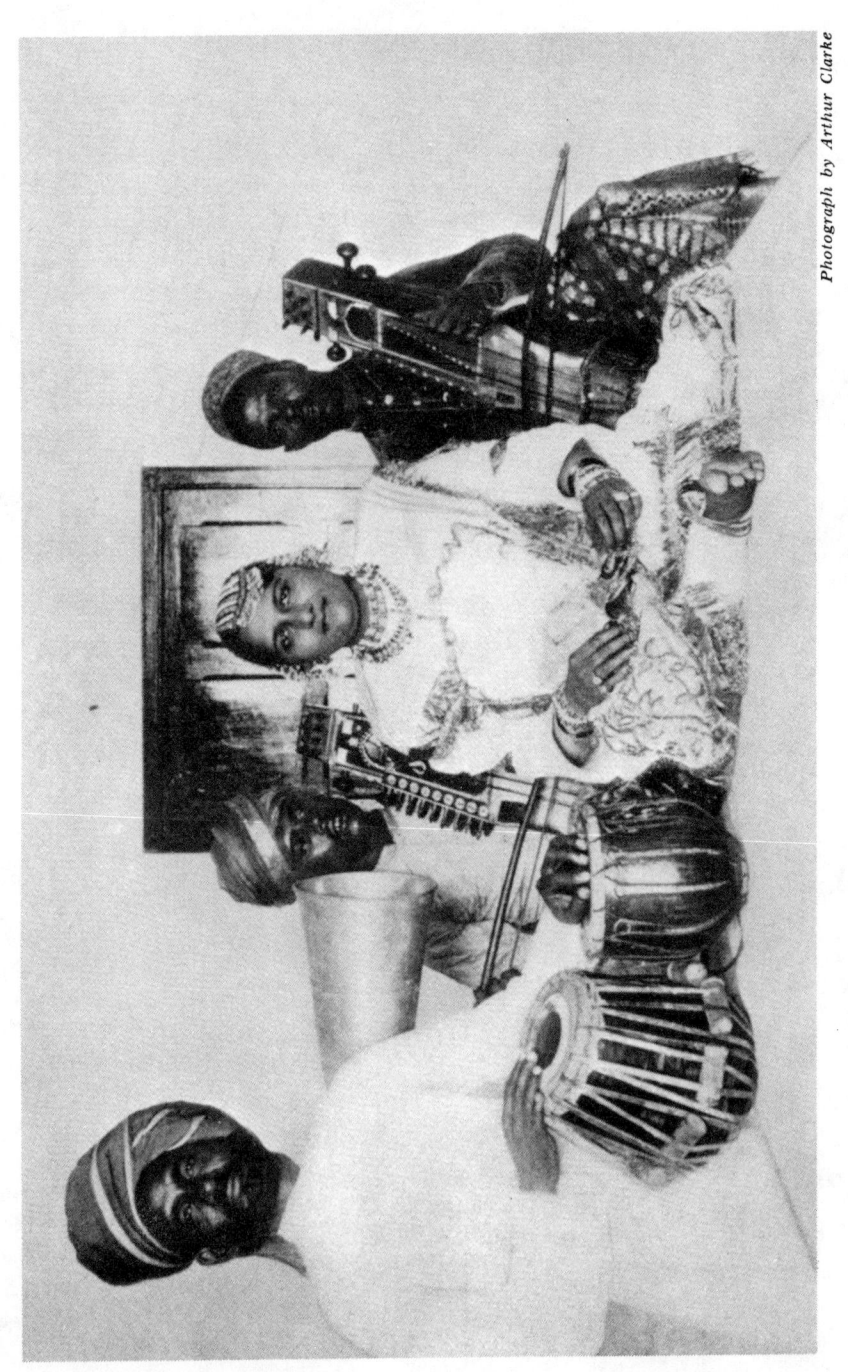

Janki Bai with Indian musicians, in a pause during a recording session at Calcutta.

return from Darjeeling, with a best, Class I, hearse and a pair of fine black horses.

In New Year's week of 1903, we arrived in Yokohama Bay in time to see five Russian warships there, the last ever to anchor in that bay.

A Mr. Black was to help us to find artists and arrange their programmes. He was an Englishman married to a Japanese lady, and had lived thirty-five years in Japan. He was almost a professional story teller. Naturally, as he spoke both English and Japanese with equal fluency he was a godsend to us. Seated at a table, he would relate stories lasting from thirty to sixty minutes, an amusement of which the Japs are extremely fond. Once he was called upon to entertain the Crown Prince of Japan. Thinking a thirty-minute tale would be long enough and would not tire the Prince, he told one of that length. Afterwards the Chamberlain approached him and in the name of the Prince thanked him but requested another story which should be longer. At the end, again the Chamberlain thanked him, but said the Prince would like another story and a still longer one. Altogether Black told stories for three solid hours.

We set up our recording machine in a small European hotel in Tokio. We had already spent two weeks visiting theatres and teahouses and holding auditions, and had drawn up a fairly comprehensive programme of national music. Already I saw that music was a more robust art here than in India. There were signs of a progressive urge and a greater variety of effects were being developed. Some of the instruments were treasures of workmanship with their gold and lacquer ornamentation. Curiously, many of the teachers of musical instruments and of singing were blind men.

In all, I recorded some six hundred titles covering every variety of the national music. It was the nucleus of what was to grow into a large catalogue, for the Japanese quickly developed into great lovers of recorded music.

A copy of a few pages of my diary will give a glimpse of my routine while on a recording trip at this period.

"*February 12, 1903.* Tokio: As today we had the afternoon free we decided to go to the theatre and from there to a Japanese eating house. We paid 14 yen ($7) for two boxes supposed to hold four each. This may be so when one squats down, Japanese-fashion, but they can only accommodate two European chairs. If one wishes to visit the theatre here, one first goes to a neighboring tea-house, in order to procure tickets and make arrangements for the supply of food during the long play, which usually lasts from 10 A.M. to 10 P.M. During the long intervals between acts one can retire to the tea-house to rest.

The stages are on a huge circular turret that revolves, so that while the front half is being used the back is being dressed. Then there is a long aisle, about 4 ft. wide, leading through the audience to the front of the house. This aisle is used for departures and returns from journeys. When using it the actor's footsteps are always accompanied by a wooden clapper to represent retiring or advancing footsteps. The costumes are all real and beautiful. There are no women on the stage; all parts are taken by men and men made-up as women, who are in looks and action perfect counterparts of women. Until recently the men playing women's parts always dressed in women's clothes at home, only wearing men's clothes in the streets.

There is music all through the dialogue and three different bands are required, one for dancing, one for dialogues, and one for interpreting thoughts and emotions. The latter is done by a man chanting, accompanied by a *samisen*. The pathetic scenes are dragged out to fearful lengths in order to give the women in the audience plenty of chance to cry. The emotional acting is excellent. Where our stars saunter up and down the stage soliloquizing and wildly gesticulating, these actors calmly sit on their haunches and barely move even their jaws.

We next went to a fine restaurant for dinner. We had enormous appetites. We took off our boots and went to a pretty little room and sat on the floor. A little charcoal fire in a brazier was brought in. The first course was green tea and cake. Then a tray was brought, containing a bowl of fish and vegetables, and pieces of raw fish, little raw minnows, fish hash, seaweed, and croquettes of game, as well as chestnuts and apple-sauce. Besides this there was a small cup of red salty sauce, in which you are supposed to dip everything before eating. The next course was a beautiful fried fish garnished with plums. Then a sort of custard fish-chowder, *saki* and lager beer. To fill up, a large bowl of rice. We could not eat three mouthfuls, and so after all this grand spread we had to order a few European sandwiches.

During the dinner four geisha girls sang and danced for us and amused us generally. A geisha is assigned to each guest and she literally feeds him and adds generally to the conviviality. Although these geishas are ladies after a fashion and cannot be approached too boldly, when I went to the toilet I was followed by two of them, each with a small dipper full of water ready to pour over my hands to wash them.

Friday, 13th. I am beginning to like their music a little. Today we had in the studio a geisha band, and to see these little women with big European band instruments was the funniest thing imaginable. This band played on both Japanese and European instruments. I made a photograph of them.

We also had some male singers who are favorites of the Emperor. In fact, they are the interpreters of the only class of music he likes. They do a kind of impassioned declaiming, using the full power of the voice and going from the lowest pitch of their voice to the highest. The volume they produce is tremendous and before starting they wrap with many turns a broad band tightly around the abdomen. They use no accompaniment. To me it sounded like a donkey braying.

Over half of the artists we have had are blind men. The blind all seem to go in for singing and performing on musical instruments. They play the *kyoto*—a large flat harp-sounding instrument, and the *samisen* (banjo played with a large piece of ivory) particularly well.

The fees we paid ranged from 10 yen ($5) to 60 yen ($30) a session, per artist. The last figure we only paid to one artist, 40 yen being our usual top price.

We always have tea and cakes in the afternoon and even the most dignified artist, if he doesn't want to eat the cake at the time, will wrap it up in some of the crêpe paper they always carry and take it home. It is always the custom when giving a dinner to wrap up in a piece of paper or a box all the food your guest cannot eat and hand it to him. Or if your guest has accepted the invitation to dine and at the last moment is prevented from coming, you wrap his portion up and send it to his home."

I had already met signs of the great transition from Oriental to Western music that was to take place in Japan and surprise the world thirty years later. But I could hardly foresee that a European musician like Heifetz would one day give a series of twelve recitals in a month to sold out houses, or that 100,000 records of Beethoven's Ninth Symphony would be bought by Japanese gramophone enthusiasts. Since 1936 two record selling society schemes have been flourishing in Japan, known as "Gems from the Great Masters" and the "Record Lovers' Society." Each has over twenty thousand subscribers pledged to buy each month the record chosen by a selection committee. Those subscribers completing the year receive free an album and a brochure of analytical notes. Sometimes the sale of forty thousand copies of certain favorites has been reached. The very high standard of the choices shows a fine sense of discrimination among Japanese music lovers.

To this very day I have not been able to account for the Japanese gluttony for Western classics. It may be a cult adapted by the younger generation, who feel that not to possess a library of Bach, Beethoven, Haydn, and Schubert means loss of face.

Chaliapin, Renée Chemet, Jacques Thibaud, Heifetz, Kreisler, and Weingartner were all lionised on their concert tours to Japan and brought back handsome profits. Weingartner's records of the "Choral Symphony" reached an unprecedented sale.

It is significant that no Japanese instrumentalists or vocalists have attained the highest standards set by the Western world, despite their industry and enthusiasm. As composers they have produced nothing outstandingly original. They have simply grafted our culture on their tree and not even made use of their own national idioms for a new growth combining the two colors. After all, their classic music and literature come from China.

We had cold snowy weather during the greater part of our sojourn, but as the train carried us to Kobe, our port of departure, we had a perfect view of the snow-capped Fujiyama looking every bit as beautiful as the colored post-cards. We now transferred our base of operations to Shanghai where the important music-house of Moutrie & Co. were to help and advise us in the first gramophone recording in China. I will again quote a few pages from my diary, written during those glorious days:

"*Monday, March 16th, 1903:* We have made arrangements with a George Jailing (or his Chinese name Shing Chong, of Honan Road) a *comprador* ('go-between') to arrange with artists.
Tuesday, March 17th: We secure a room in a Chinese hotel run on the European plan (that is, only European *chow* is furnished). The Chinaman is very fond of Western eating and in Foochow Road are a great number of European restaurants. By accident I happened to wander into the kitchen and the dirt and smells which greeted me put me off ever attempting to have meals there.
Wednesday, March 18th: We made our first records. About fifteen Chinamen had come, including the accompanying band. As a Chinaman yells at the top of his power when he sings, he can only sing two songs an evening and then his throat becomes hoarse. Their idea of music is a tremendous clash and bang: with the assistance of a drum, three pairs of huge gongs, a pair of slappers, a sort of banjo, some reed instruments which sounded like bagpipes, and the yelling of the singer, their so-called music was recorded on the gramophone.

On the first day, after making ten records we had to stop. The din had so paralyzed my wits that I could not think."

THE GRAMOPHONE GOES EAST

Up to the 27th of March we made 325 records for which we paid $4 each. To me, the differences between the tunes of any two records were too slight for me to detect. On one occasion a dirty beggar was singing a lamentation and a visitor (Capt. Daniels of the SS. *Chuzan*) asked our *comprador* if it wasn't a love song. The reply was, "No, he is singing about his grandmother." As with the Japanese, there is no romance or love sentiment. Their pathetic or sentimental songs would be about the death of a parent or grandparent or some other ancestor, or perhaps of a son.

Our hotel in Shanghai was on a street generally used by funeral and wedding processions, and almost every day two or three would pass by, clashing cymbals and playing pipes. The two are very nearly similar, except that with a funeral white is the predominating color for the mourners and the coffin, whereas in a wedding procession the gaudy palanquin containing the bride is the characteristic feature. The funeral procession of a mandarin which we saw one day was a grand affair. In line were Chinese mounted soldiers, banner and umbrella bearers, a long line of offerings comprising three or four pigs roasted whole, a number of roasted lambs, sheep, and kids, as well as fruit, prepared dishes, and flowers. The coffin was borne by ten stalwart porters followed by the son of the deceased behind a square white screen. As I watched from a window above I could look over and see the son dressed in common white cloth, walking barefoot. He was sobbing with violent grief, and supported on either side by two friends. The rest of the mourners followed in carriages, palanquins, and rickshaws. Often professional mourners were employed whose business it was to cry and rave in a most pathetic way during the whole progress of the funeral.

In Hong Kong I again set up my equipment in a Chinese hotel and recorded another 200 songs. This time the artists were principally tea-house girls. Their bound feet made it impossible for them to walk so they were carried to our improvised studio on the shoulders of giant coolies. These girls were lacquered and painted and dressed in embroidered silks, and looked like expensive doll-babies. I have reason to remember their long, colored fingernails. Their voices have the sound of a small wailing cat, and while I was attempting to push one singer closer to the horn she turned on me like a viper. At the same time the big coolies also attacked me. Evidently I, as a foreigner, in touching the lady had committed a *faux-pas*. After that I was more discreet in dealing with the tea-house girls.

Outside of the Treaty Ports, the gramophone never achieved in China the vogue it enjoyed in Japan. Among the Chinese of America, the Malay States, and Australia, however, there was a large sale of records, proving it was largely a question of affluence and accessibility. No one doubts that the Chinese are a musical race. In my native city of Washington of a Sunday one could not pass any of the numerous Chinese laundries without hearing Wu Lee singing to his friends.

After a visit to Canton I continued my pilgrimage to Bangkok, Singapore, and Rangoon, recording a large assortment of Siamese, Javanese, Malay, and Burmese gramophone records for the first time in history. Only the recording I carried out in Burma lingers in my memory. There was a charm about the people, the country, and its music that made a strong appeal to me. Compared to the anaemic music of India it had vigor and color. These bright people have an entertainment called a *zat*. The basis of the drama, which is interspersed with songs and ballet, is the age-old story of a prince and princess. About forty players, mostly young and pretty girls, take part dressed in bright, costly gowns. The acting consists of exaggerated poses and postures. Poe Sein was the most popular actor and he always took the rôle of an heroic prince. His opera company travelled up and down the Irrawaddy River in their own barge and paddle-steamer, something like the show-boat troupes of the Mississippi. The boats are used for transport and living quarters only, however, as the performance takes place in the village theatre or in the open air. It starts at 9 P.M. and goes on all night. The band is composed of bells with mellow-sounding scales, and of percussion instruments consisting of pieces of bamboo struck with a hammer. Complete *zats* of forty records formed a very profitable part of my programme of Burmese recording.

Everywhere the invention aroused the greatest interest. The native and European press interviewed us and printed many columns about this amazing expedition. In my spare time I gave dozens of gramophone recitals to audiences who heard recorded sound for the first time. My selection of European records was worn to the bone before I returned to London in the autumn of 1903. On several occa-

THE GRAMOPHONE GOES EAST

sions my path crossed those of the Bandmann and Brough travelling theatrical companies and I learned to appreciate the great boon and blessing these lifelines brought to England's exiled sons and daughters. I often wondered why a Minister of Fine Arts did not have a stroke of genius and acquire immortal fame by subsidizing these hard-put wandering minstrels who do so much to keep the home-ties unbroken.

The War Years

CHAPTER V

The War Years

THE First World War naturally played havoc with an international business like ours. The company had the major part of their matrices stored in the Hanover factory in Germany, which supplied most of Central Europe, Scandinavia, and the Balkan States with records. Hardly completed was the transfer of all master-shells from Hanover to the Hayes pressing plant, started in 1908. This plant was intended to house the central archives for all master-negatives. A large factory in the friendly Hanseatic town of Riga had just been completed in 1913, and was capable of supplying all Russia with records.

At that time Riga was a premier city for manufacturing on modern lines, and its products were the equal of any in Europe for price and finish. The Lettish workmen were the most intelligent and disciplined to be found in all Russia, but once in a while they would go out on the loose. The Letts were commonly supposed to have a distinct Mongol strain in their blood. Contact with their Teutonic and Slav conquerors has also left its mark. From one side came a fine feeling for machinery, from the other a light-hearted way of looking at life. Our matrix plant personnel consisted of five skilled workmen. One weekend they purloined from the works, for home consumption, a demijohn of denatured alcohol. On the following Monday we received a deputation from their widows.

In the spring of 1915, I happened to be in St. Petersburg when the order was given to evacuate the machinery from our plant and destroy the building. We searched St. Petersburg and Moscow for a suitable location to which to transfer our large stock of thousands of copper matrices and our pressing-plant. St. Petersburg itself was threatened at the time by the German armies, and Moscow had just undergone a most destructive pogrom in May which left the most modern of its buildings in ruins. Even railway stations, schools, and churches were filled with wounded soldiers retreating from Warsaw, the parks and boulevards taking the overflow of refugees and their belongings. It was the search for these factory sites that opened my eyes to the terrible housing conditions then only too prevalent.

I remember driving to the outskirts of the city where we were shown a loft. On opening the door we were nearly knocked over by the stench. Lying body to body were two rows of snoring droshky-drivers. There was no ventilation, and no light of any kind except our torches, which revealed walls crawling with vermin. Bad as it was and badly though we needed the premises, I declined to give the word to the agent which would have sent the occupants packing. Our next visit was to a brewery that in normal times produced a brew which held its own with the finest on the European market. It was most depressing to see such a splendid, up-to-date equipment of aluminum and copper vats and electrical apparatus being wantonly sabotaged.

On November 14, 1914, I started on the first of the journeys I was to make to Russia during the war by way of Bergen, Stockholm, Trondhjem and St. Petersburg. With my American passport I had very little trouble, and I received a royal welcome from our marooned agents, Albert Lack and George Cooper, when I arrived in St. Petersburg. I shared a flat with Cooper in a newly built apartment house of vast dimensions; the walls were three feet thick and the foundations were built like a concrete vessel to float on the marshland upon which the city of St. Petersburg stood. That winter there was no fuel to feed the great central-heating system, so our rooms were as cold as a refrigerator. Four months after the War broke out I saw the birth of that pathetic and unhappily permanent feature of Russian life, the queue. What can ever compensate for the billions of hours weary women and children have so patiently endured in cold and rain, standing in those dismal processions?

By 1917 only were we able to collect the scattered segments of our plant and set up in Aprilerka, outside Moscow, twenty or so presses

—in fact, just in time to be taken over by the revolutionaries. To the best of my knowledge this factory is being operated even today by the U.S.S.R.

As in England, I found there was a great increase in the demand for records from both soldiers and civilians. The hits of the war period were "Gai-da Troika" (Hey there, Troika), "Ochi chorniya" (Black Eyes), and so on, and are actually the songs made popular by the thousands of Russian refugee-artists since 1918 in the cabarets and theatres of Paris, London, Rome, Shanghai, and Constantinople. They were not copyrighted, and the composers and publishers could claim no royalties on the millions of copies sold throughout the world, as Russia was not a party to the 1912 Berne Copyright Convention. There was a copyright law in Russia and our copyright department decided that "mechanical rights" were payable on all arrangements. Faced with this decision, Mr. Suk, our artists' manager of that day, founded a shadow publishing firm and I soon discovered that it claimed every popular and folk song as its copyright because of some inversion of chords or other simple change.

It is quite a different thing to adapt a folk-song as Chaliapin did with the well-known "Volga Boat Song," which was only used as a chorus number when I first heard it in 1908. Even sung by the well known St. Petersburg Male Quartet it had a very small sale in disc form. It was I who first brought the melody to Chaliapin's notice when, in 1922, he was seeking to extend his concert répertoire and wanted a climax song for the first part of his programme. Chaliapin objected that *Oiy Ouchnem* had just one verse and was only sung as a male chorus. But I persisted and together we produced two more stanzas and conceived the idea of beginning the number softly, rising to a *forte* and fading away to a whisper, to picture the approach and gradual retreat of the haulers on the river banks.

There was only one composer to whom Chaliapin would entrust the job of making an arrangement, and that was Koenemann, then at the Moscow Conservatory. He was told to get on with it, and submitted various drafts before Chaliapin selected the one now on the records and published in England by the house of Chester. Chaliapin offered to accept £600 down for the mechanical rights of his "Song of the Volga Boatmen." That the offer was rejected was

THE MUSIC GOES ROUND

fortunate for him, since the royalties earned have reached nearly £3,000. This was one of his best paying investments in a world of collapsible values.

Among the artists recorded upon my arrival in St. Petersburg was Maria Michailowa, whose record of Gounod's "Ave Maria" had become world-famous. In my pocket I had a commission from Lionell Powell, the concert impresario, to engage her for a concert tour of England if my impressions upon hearing and seeing her were favorable. My friends in Russia marvelled at my enthusiasm for her, since she had remained only a second-line artist at the opera house and had never made a concert tour even of Russia, in spite of her successful records. Indeed I received a shock when I met the dumpy little creature, then over fifty, after the picture my imagination had painted from hearing her golden records.

Passing on to Moscow I had two unusual records made that had enormous popularity. I had often visited the Kremlin, where the guides showed you the biggest bell in the world and impressed on you that Moscow was a city of a thousand churches. This encouraged me to make a record of Moscow bells. In the open the cold was far too severe for our waxes so I had to arrange for the bells to come to us. One morning a well-known bell-founder brought a peal to our hotel. The largest, weighing several tons, being unable to pass through the door, had to be hoisted up through the window. When these five monsters were installed in the room our concert began. Heavens, what a din! Their vibrations almost brought down the house. These records had an immense vogue with Russian soldiers, mainly perhaps because they reminded them of the familiar echoes of their village chimes.

The other unusual record was one of The Lord's Prayer, sung by the priest, Rosoff, with the Uchoff Choir. The soloist, a magnificent creature, tall and massive, with long wavy hair and a patriarchal beard, had a pedal-bass voice recalling the tones of a 32 ft. organ stop. He began the first phrase, "Our Father Which Art in Heaven," on the lowest note of his voice, gradually ascending, semitone by semitone, with steadily increasing volume until the high C was reached, and with that the choir burst out into harmony with "For Thine is the Kingdom, the Power and the Glory for Ever and Ever, Amen." It was a superb climax.

THE WAR YEARS

Rosoff was proud of his breath control and would lie at full length on the floor and invite me to stand on his diaphragm. Then, taking a breath, he would easily lift me up seven inches in the air. This priest and his choir made a good thing out of blessing homes, new shops, and factories, besides accompanying the "Holy Picture" to the bedsides of those *in extremis*.

Three times during 1914-15 I made the long land journey to Russia by skirting the Gulf of Bothnia. It all seems so futile now, because the records made and the assets piled up were eventually lost in the revolution.

It was when I succeeded, after a struggle, in finding a place on the train that was to carry me to Baku and Tiflis that I realized what chaos one year of war had produced, and I began to have doubts of ever being able to travel back again. The train was crowded, packed tight to overflowing—which means the passengers were even clinging to the platforms and roofs, quite a normal state of affairs since the war. As it was summer the heat, dust, and stench were overpowering. Our locomotive burnt wood, so it had to stop after every twenty miles and raise its steam pressure. Then begging peasants appeared with outstretched hands, not aggressive like professional beggars, but with the mute appeal of a sick animal. The station restaurants would still serve travellers with simple food. These people were friendly and naive. Sitting at the table, eating a bowl of borsch, a neighbor would take from his pocket a wooden spoon with which every one travels, exclaiming, "Ah, *tovarich*, your borsch smells very good; is it as good as it looks?" He would then help himself from your bowl and add, "Ah, yes, it *is* good soup."

The farther south we went the hotter and more uncomfortable it became, and we suffered from thirst in a country where, because of cholera epidemics, one was warned against drinking unboiled water. I was joined at Baku by my old friend, Fred Tyler, who was glad enough to see me. Everything was at a standstill but food was more plentiful, and I must put it on record that I enjoyed a Persian melon that was my reward for all the hardships I had undergone. These melons are actually grown in Russian Turkestan and are known as *Tcharjui* melons, from the name of the town where they are chiefly produced. They weigh about fifteen pounds each and are transported across the Caspian Sea, each hung in an easy-riding straw basket. They ripen in this position and will not keep in any other way. Despite every effort it has not been found possible to grow them successfully in any other part of the world. I have heard that even in the fertile dry plains of Texas all attempts to grow them have failed.

I was surprised to receive an urgent note from a Mr. Leslie Urquhart to come and see him. Full of curiosity and flattered to be taken the slightest notice of in such strenuous times, I went to the imposing office building of a large petroleum company and was shown into an up-to-date office that might have been in New York City. Urquhart was a business man on the grand scale, as his modern office equipment would indicate, but there he was stranded with all his technicians called up for military service and his intricate dictating phonographs and calculating machines gone wrong. He had heard of my arrival at the club, where I had been described as a "Talking-Machine Expert." Here, he thought, was a chance to have his machines put right. It was ironical to see this high-pressure businessman trying to carry on in spite of war and famine with no helpers; but I could do nothing for him.

In the beautiful town of Tiflis I set up my recording equipment and in company with Fred Tyler proceeded to collect our artists for recording. Mrs. Tyler and her children were summering in the Kajorie Hills, a zigzag climb of three thousand feet above, beginning virtually at the front-door of Tiflis itself. He and I worked in the sultry city and lived in his deserted apartment, but made pleasant weekend trips to visit the family. There, judging by the food Mrs. Tyler prepared for us, we might have been in Lancashire. Only the bread was the unleavened flat biscuit, baked in a pit heated by glowing embers of wood ashes. Whether it is in Alexandria, Moscow, Bombay, or Paris I have always been sure to enjoy good Lancashire cooking, even down to the "hot-pot," when a guest of Mrs. Tyler.

Most of the recording in the Caucasus was done in Tiflis where we found Georgian, Armenian and Tartar artists, but we also used Baku, Kutais, Petrovsk for Daghestan singers, and Georgievsk in the northern Caucasus for Tcherkess artists. We also recorded in Tiflis the choir of the Viceroy's bodyguard of Cossacks—a fine body of men with some remarkable soloists. The Viceroy at that time was Count Vorontseff Dashkoff who preceded the Grand Duke Nicholas. This recording was carried out in the Orient Hotel in Tiflis. With the Hotel Europe in Baku, owned by Mme. Carpentier, another Frenchwoman, this was the best hotel in the Caucasus at that time. For the recording of the Cossack Choir we arranged a huge side table laden with *zakuska* (hors d'oeuvres), which rapidly disappeared during the intervals, washed down by copious draughts of vodka. In fact, the last few numbers must have been taken in the proper atmosphere and no doubt registered the true Cossack spirit.

After completing recording in the Caucasus I packed up and despatched records and equipment to Moscow. I should think they are still shuttling between Baku and Batum because we never saw them again.

My journey back was a repetition of the discomforts I had already experienced, but this time I knew what to expect. In Moscow Chaliapin offered me hospitality, as the hotels had been taken over by the government. We dined regularly at the well-known Hermitage Restaurant where he seemed to command the best in the house. He had just finished the film *Ivan the Terrible* and together we witnessed a run through. It was long and tiresome. His acting made no compromises with film technique and so was too long drawn out and impeded the action of the story. He brought the five tins containing the five acts to England, where they were held up by the Customs. Then he placed them in bond and carried them to New York, hoping to dispose of the film there, but as the duty demanded was excessive, he finally took them with him on his return journey to Europe and threw them overboard in midocean, hurling an imprecation after them.

Only two years before, after the brilliant Drury Lane opera season, he and his family had crossed the Channel and begun a motor tour of France and Switzerland. They were swept up in the French mobilization and lost baggage and car. Thirty days later they managed to reach London with the greatest difficulty, and one afternoon, returning early from my office, I found them camped in my drawing room. They were still dazed by the swift change in their fortunes and for the next few days I busied myself expediting their return to Russia by the long northern route. Now they were truly happy and cheered to see me so soon again, after giving up all hope of ever setting eyes on anyone from the outer world until after the war.

I was still able to return to England by way of Finland. At the frontier I was searched and relieved of thirty gold sovereigns, for which I received and still possess a cheque on the Imperial Bank of Russia for 450 roubles. This secret reserve of gold I had carried in a belt worn next to the skin. I had not intended to declare it, but the presence of bloodhounds sniffing around, and the warning of a fellow traveller that every passenger was being stripped, made me hastily change my mind. Other passengers less discreet were detained. They lost the train and their money as well.

Once in a sleeping car between Belgrade and Budapest, when most stringent controls at the frontier were in force to prevent the escape of capital, I was asked if I owned some thousands of dollars uncovered by the frontier guards between the mattresses in the adjoining compartment. My American passport led them to saddle me with the ownership. The occupant of the compartment, an Austrian Jew, denied that they belonged to him but I could see him turn a sickly gray as the officers took possession of those lovely dollars.

The Finnish railway ended at the small town of Tornea, and the gap of some twenty miles to Hapahanda, the Swedish railhead, had to be made by rickety country carts in summer, or in winter by small low sleds drawn by little shaggy horses and carrying one passenger each. Wrapped from head to foot in folds of sheepskin robes, the traveller reclined cosily in the cradle of the straw-filled sleigh. The feeling of comfort lasted about ten minutes until the zero cold penetrated your protection. Just about the time you felt the numbness that precedes freezing to death, your driver stopped and bundled you out at the jolliest and warmest of inns, built of wood and smelling of pine-log fires. Another perfume was that of coffee. The sight of good things to eat, spread out on a long buffet, turned you into a ravenous wolf. In fact, this one moment compensated for all the trials endured in Russia.

A twenty-four-hour journey on the single track railroad skirting the Gulf of Bothnia, dodging in and out of pine forests, brought me to the flourishing city of Stockholm and the realization of the absolute chaos I had left behind me in Russia. A week later when I arrived in London I acquired the reputation of a prophet among my friends by foretelling a revolution in that unhappy country.

After a holiday spent in America during 1916, no easy journey to make in wartime, I made a second trip to Italy. Owing to Italy's lateness in entering the war, business was flourishing. Only the lack of materials from England prevented a boom in records. I reached Milan in the spring of 1917 to carry out the recording of war songs and to make contracts with artists, and also to erect a local pressing and matrix-making plant. The Southampton-Havre route was open for civilians during the first three years of the war, so although the passport control hesitated and ransacked their index-cards, they passed me through with the usual careful search and a final rubbing of lemon on my bare back, which I really enjoyed. My experiences in Russia had so tempered me that although Italy was literally scraping out the corners of her grain bins I found the scarcity of food endurable. The staple diet of *pasta* and *pane-unico*, dark and full of straw bits, was palatable if eaten with morsels of tunny fish, hare, or horse meat on the side. The glorious water from the mountains and the ever abundant grapes, peaches, tomatoes, cheese, and chianti were obtainable in season at reasonable prices.

I enjoyed the excitement of creating a pressing plant out of parts scavenged from the junk heaps of the Porta Magenta. Since new machinery could only be had for armaments and hardly a scuttle of coal for raising steam could be found in all Milan, some ingenuity had to be used before I could press records in the summer of 1918 in our first Italian factory. But I saw a good deal of Tetrazzini and helped her to entertain Major Mackenzie Rogan and the Coldstream Guards on their visit to Italy.

The full bands of the Guards and the band of the Garde Républicaine, totalling over two hundred players, had been sent to Milan and Rome to cement goodwill and friendship between the three countries. At their open air concert in the Piazza del Duomo, in company with the band of the Carabinieri, also a hundred strong, and at their concert at La Scala they were a grand sight and made most inspiring music. Tetrazzini organized a reception on a lavish scale for them. It must have cost her a pretty penny, but it went a long way towards fostering a goodwill with her English admirers and its value was reflected in the very successful series of recitals she gave in England after the war.

In the spring of 1918, I made a contract with the twenty-eight-year old tenor, Beniamino Gigli, who, dressed in the uniform of a private in the infantry, sang his first ten records. Our house maestro, Carlo Sabajno, was also in uniform as a flautist in the band. I think they were both only perfunctory soldiers, as Gigli was singing regularly at the Scala and Carlo was busily engaged recording and foraging around for tins of bully beef and white bread and butter. He would exchange records with the American soldiers for these precious eatables, which they seemed to have in abundance.

Of war work I also had an opportunity to do my share. Lord Northcliffe, extending his scheme of propaganda behind the enemy lines, had sent Colonel Baker to work on the Italian front at the Isonzo, where the Slavs, Jugoslavs, Croats and Serbs, Hungarians, and Czechs were manning the mountain trenches on the Austrian side, sometimes a few hundred feet from the Italian lines. I was sent to Vicenza whence I would make excursions in army lorries, under military escort, to various prison camps. Deserters of those nationalities would record their folksongs, dances, and spoken words, urging their listeners to desert without fear as friends would receive and care for them. These records were played back at points in the trenches opposite the places where those nationals were known to be posted and, according to Col. Baker, resulted in a fine harvest of deserters.

Those days will live in my memory for two things: the reckless untamed driving of the Italian chauffeurs who seemed bent on imitating the comic films of motor racing, and the blood-curdling mountain thunderstorms with their blinding flashes of lightning and torrents of rain. Still, I survived and managed to return to Milan with a mixed booty of bully beef and white bread and butter, exchanged for gramophone records with a section of English gunners.

One can safely say that the four war years were not productive of any advance in music or the recording art. It was a sterile period of suspended animation. At best it left the appetite whetted for a feast—a feast that came with the big boom in gramophone records in 1920-1922. Those years produced a veritable harvest for the various companies and their artists.

The amazing appetite for music and entertainment immediately after the war can be gauged by the average earnings from record royalties in 1923. Three top violinists each averaged $78,000, two sopranos each $89,000, two contraltos each $32,000, three baritones each $22,000. Of course the average earnings of two celebrated tenors of that epoch far exceeded $150,000.

The partiality for voices and the violin in those days is reflected in these figures. Five years later a swing to symphonic, choral, instrumental, and piano music was to come about, when electrical recording produced such a miraculous improvement in sound reproduction.

In England during the war the cheap portable machine became all the rage and proved a boon to the soldiers, as it broke the monotony of their routine existence in the dugout. Popular patriotic songs were recorded and distributed in thousands; the gramophone was encouraged by the military authorities of both sides, who looked upon it as a vital necessity. In contrast to the sterility of song writers in the present war, a fine crop of martial ditties appeared to keep the pressing plants busy and to pile up the fortunes of song writers and publishers. The vast quantities of cheap gramophones available to the Tommies were later to be found in thousands of humble homes and so paved the way to a wonderful post-war boom. Estimated sales of songs like "Keep the Home Fires Burning," "Pack Up Your Troubles," "Mademoiselle from Armentières" and "Tipperary" amounted to anything up to half a million discs each.

Negatives stored in the archives of the Hanover factory were returned to the English company under the terms of the Versailles treaty. Even so, some valuable "masters," like those of Willy Hess, Leopold Demuth, Leo Slezak, as well as important Russian, Arabic, and Turkish matrices still remain untraced. After unsuccessful efforts had been made to repurchase our subsidiary German company, known as the D.G.A., my company in 1926 founded the Electrola Company in Berlin. Its managing director was Leo B. Curth who had previously been manager of the D.G.A. Swept upwards on the boom of electrical recording, the Electrola quickly became the leading gramophone company of Germany and by the time the Second World War broke out it was to be responsible for a great share of the marvellous library that made the decade of 1930-1940 the golden age of recorded music in spite of the prevalent tension and unrest.

The Procession Passes

CHAPTER VI

The Procession Passes

THE gramophone has now become a household word, in some homes almost a household god. With the piano it has long been a symbol of culture even in the humblest family. But in the early days its technical perfection was far from complete. At first we had to choose our "titles" so as to obtain the most brilliant results without revealing the defects of the machine.

First of the most successful instruments to record was the human voice, because its range of frequencies was within such a limited compass. This was what made it so practical for our crude system of recording.

Next in order came military bands with their brass, wind, and percussion instruments. Therefore in pre-1914 catalogues you will find that vocal and military band records predominate. Today symphonic and theatre orchestras, jazz and swing bands compete keenly for the space allotted to instrumental records in our monthly lists. Seldom more than one record of a military band appears, though in the old days the military band used to occupy one-third of our issues.

The Band of the Coldstream Guards appeared to me to answer the requirements for gramophone records completely, so I hunted out the leader, Lieut. Rogan, in his Streatham home and started him on his long career of recording which spread the fame of the Coldstreams to the ends of the world. Time passed and the young subaltern secured well-deserved promotion. As Major Mackenzie Rogan he was in command of the five bands of the Brigade of Guards on their memorable visit to Italy in 1918, already described. When dressed in his full regimentals Rogan was a fine figure of a man and topped over seven feet in his busby. I was fortunate to assist in the celebration of his fiftieth year of service in the army, much of it spent in India and Burma. Later he became Lieut. Colonel Mackenzie Rogan, the highest rank ever attained by a bandmaster in the British army. My brother Will, short and stout, was particularly fond of his company and I enjoyed watching them set off down City Road bound for the Athenaeum Club in Stratford Place, where these two *bon vivants* knew the best food and wine in London could be obtained, and where one might even run up against Nikisch, Richter, Ysaÿe, Van Rooy, and Franz Schalk.

Rogan was not a great musician but he was the greatest bandmaster in the British army. Brought up in the hard school of the army since his sixteenth year, he was, as can well be imagined, a strict martinet who never relaxed before his men. I can sense even now the solemn tension that reigned in the recording studio while Rogan, seated on high, transfixed by forty pairs of silent eyes, indicated the start and finish of a record, never raising his voice above a whisper. During the entire three hours he was the only one permitted to speak. One felt that it would be a catastrophe involving nothing less than punishment by death for a player to sound a wrong note.

At one time, our catalogue contained over one hundred titles of records by the Coldstream Guards' Band, so great was their vogue. Even today, notwithstanding a musical experience that should have made me more discriminating, I am still carried away by military band music. No wonder this superb band was selected to carry out so many good will tours to Australia, Canada, France, and Italy. When I first came to London, Earl's Court was the shop window for military bands and I always think it was there that their music sounded best and they reached their greatest glory.

Stringed instruments we recorded by a subterfuge. We substituted the Stroh violin for violins and violas, for a 'cello we used a bassoon, and for the doublebass a tuba. The Stroh violin was invented by the late Augustus Stroh. Its four strings are stretched over a diaphragm-resonator to which is attached a horn.

Augustus Stroh was a British subject of German extraction. In turn he had been the chief mechanical designer for Tyndall, Huxley,

Wheatstone (the father of electrical measurements) and Sir William Preece, for whom he built from instructions cabled by Edison a duplicate of his phonograph. It was this phonograph which Sir William played before the Royal Society in 1878 to illustrate his lecture on the phonograph. This historic instrument is in the Gramophone Company's museum at Hayes.

In some ways acoustic recording flattered the voice. A glance at the rich catalogue of that period will show that it was the heyday of the singer. Long lists of records after great names fairly tumble from it. One has only to mention Caruso, Melba, Tetrazzini, Alma Gluck, Destinn, Michailowa, Plançon, De Gogorza, Journet, Scotti, and John McCormack in this vocal cascade. Strange to say the velvet tone of Kreisler's violin, for some unknown reason, was best in those old records and has never been recaptured by the electrical process.

The inadequacy of the accompaniments to the lovely vocal records made in the Acoustic Age was their great weakness. There was no pretence of using the composer's score; we had to arrange it for wind instruments entirely. The articulated tuba tone was altogether too insistent. Though marked advances were made in the technique of manufacture which reduced the surface noise on the disc, nevertheless the artist and the selection had invariably to be selected with care so as to cover up all instrumental deficiencies. Only full, even voices of sustained power could be utilized, and all nuances, such as *pianissimo* effects, were omitted.

There has always been a healthy competition in the record industry. This reduced itself eventually to a rivalry between two great concerns for the dominance of the world markets. They were the Gramophone Company (with its affiliated company the Victor) and the Columbia Graphophone Company. The race resulted in giving the public a wider range of artists and music. But in the end the 1930 slump made a reduction imperative in the hundreds of artists' contracts and the glut of monthly record issues. For this reason the two interests were merged in England into Electric and Musical Industries Ltd., but only after two rich and comprehensive catalogues of records had been built up. The annual printing bill for each of the companies for the English catalogue alone amounted to thousands of pounds and to this must be added the foreign reprints.

The story of how Louis Sterling saved his company, Columbia, from being frozen out of the electric recording business constitutes an epic of the talking machine industry. To my knowledge it has never been told before.

No secrets are more carefully hidden than those worked out by the research laboratories of the big American corporations. The radio, talking films, and electric sound-recording emerged in rapid succession in the early twenties. All were based on the Fleming amplifying valve. The Western Electric Company, a subsidiary of the American Telephone and Telegraph Company, did much research work and their acoustic studies had already become world famous. By solving the problem of talking films and electrically recorded discs they added still another brilliant chapter to their achievements.

Acoustically recorded sound had reached the limit of progress. The top frequencies were triple high C, 2088 vibrations per second, and the low remained at E, 164 vibrations per second. Voices and instruments, especially stringed instruments, were confined rigidly within these boundaries, although the average human ear perceives from 30 to 15,000 vibrations per second and musical sounds range from 60 to 8,000 vibrations. Electric recording encompassed this and more. A whisper fifty feet away, reflected sound, and even the atmosphere of a concert hall could be recorded—things hitherto unbelievable.

On this revolutionary sound recording system the Western Electric people were secretly at work. One of the most alert of talking machine personages of that day was the old pioneer, Frank Capps, inventor and associate of Edison. Like a good general, Sterling retained Capps as a scout and adviser, receiving from him regular reports on the industry in America. He and his friend Russell Hunting were then in charge of the Pathé recording plant in New York City and to this plant the Western Electric people arranged to send their wax records for processing. Capps and Hunting were curious enough to play over the sample pressings before sending them to the Western Electric people. What they heard coming from the records took them completely by surprise. For the first time they heard sibilants emerge from the trumpet, loud and hissing!

Louis Sterling received from Capps sample pressings of electrical recordings (how these were obtained was never disclosed) and a letter worded in the most urgent terms. Part of the news intimated that the wealthy Victor Company was negotiating with the Western Electric for the exclusive rights in the new process. This decided Sterling and he sailed on Boxing Day on the *Mauretania* cabling to delay matters until his arrival. The truth was that a draft contract for the exclusive use of the system had been in the hands of the Victor Company for over a month, but owing to the illness of E. R. Johnson, their Chairman, it was still unsigned when Louis Sterling arrived in New York.

Louis Sterling put in a busy week and hammered away so convincingly at the Western Electric on the fallacy of granting a monopoly of their valuable process to one corporation that they withdrew their proposals to the Victor Company. The outcome was a victory for Louis Sterling, as both companies were offered a license on an equal basis.

One day in the autumn of 1924, I received a telephone call. It was from Russell Hunting, who had just arrived at the Hotel Imperial, Russell Square. He said, "Fred, we're all out of jobs. Come down here and I'll show you something that will stagger you."

When I reached his rooms he swore me to secrecy before playing the records. They were unauthorised copies of the Western Electric experiments and, as Hunting predicted, I saw that from now on any talking machine company which did not have this electric recording system would be unable to compete with it. Louis Sterling has since told me that this was his conclusion, as well. He added that it was the one thing, after two years of slump, that the record industry needed to rescue it from ruin.

Emile Berliner on his last visit to England in 1935 told me he was responsible for passing on to the Victor Company the information about the Western Electric's experiments in electric recording. This led to their opening up negotiations to acquire the rights. When passing through New York City, he had happened to pay a visit to the Western Electric laboratory to renew acquaintance with his former colleagues of telephone days. Whilst there, they demonstrated to him their experiments in electrical sound-recording.

In the postwar boom there was keen bidding for the services of celebrity artists, but it was not until the early electric recording boom of 1926-28 that the bidding reached its highest point. I remember being sent to the Vienna première of Puccini's *Turandot* in 1926. Artfully prepared propaganda paved the way for the début of a young tenor who, it was claimed, would be a greater singer than Caruso. This was Kiepura, the 24-year-old Pole. I was one of half a dozen talking machine scouts who converged on Vienna to hear and bid for him. He was a keen bargainer and played one company off against the other. He carried my offer of £1,000 annual guarantee to our rivals. A competitor secured him at a high fee, but it was not from opera arias that they got their money back: they had to wait for talking-films to come five years later. The film song "Tell Me Tonight" was the nugget that was to repay them; its sales were over 40,000.

To my mind Kiepura was a genius in publicity and audience psychology. Even in an opera performance he would make sure that a piano was ready in the wings for accompanying him as he rushed out to take his encores—all, of course, irrelevant to the opera. Only once did I see him dismayed. This was at his Albert Hall début one Sunday afternoon. There was unpleasantness at the rehearsal when Kiepura behaved in an arrogant way towards Sir Landon Ronald without offering an apology. The orchestra noted this and quietly bided their time for redressing the slight. At this concert Kiepura sang the big aria from *Carmen* where there is a silent pause after the dramatic high C. One of the brass players chose this moment to utter a most resounding and embarrassing "raspberry."

The dodge of securing a guarantee was frequently made use of by artists and their managers. Kreisler's contract with the Victor Company ran out at a critical moment when powerful interests were trying to break into the record industry: the acquisition of such a tremendous name would have meant valuable prestige. To retain him the Victor Company had to guarantee royalty earnings of $750,000 over a period of five years. This is the largest fee yet paid to any instrumentalist, but Heifetz, Elman, Rachmaninoff, and Cortot cashed in earnings during that same period which were almost as large.

Sometimes, to have one artist exclusively meant dominating certain markets. Miguel Fleta, the tenor who created the part of Kalaf in the La Scala première of *Turandot*, was one instance of this. In him we had a difficult man on our hands, but as he was the key to the

Spanish market we humored him. He had a fine manly voice and had acquired the art of spinning out a high note to the finest thread. This never failed to bring down the house. He would even introduce this specialty in his opera arias, much to the annoyance of the conductor, who had to wait with arms upraised until Fleta finished. This led to many fights with conductors but he knew how to play to the gallery and so always won out, except with Toscanini who could discipline even a Chaliapin. In Latin countries on the opera stage Fleta was a spellbinder and a law unto himself. He would respond to a *bis* with encore after encore of popular songs which had nothing to do with the opera. Outside of Spain and Italy his fame was built up on the number "Ay-Ay-Ay," a steady seller from 1922 when I first recorded it in Milan. It easily passed the 100,000 mark and during the last five years of Fleta's life (he was only 44 at his death) it was to be his main source of income. How are the mighty fallen!

In boyhood he had served his apprenticeship as a bull-fighter, and the swagger he acquired in the ring no doubt helped to endear him to the Spanish public. More than once the orchestra waited in vain for him to appear at our Madrid studio. On one occasion I actually went to his home to fetch him and even then he escaped me by stopping at the flat of his lady friend for more than a few minutes, leaving me waiting in the taxi. Her attractions were evidently more potent than those of the recording session, for he did not appear again that afternoon.

For fifteen years he was always in demand for opera and concerts, earning £200 to £300 per performance, yet he was to know want before he died. The story is the same with singer after singer of world reputation. Somehow or other instrumentalists generally seem to fare better in this respect; apparently they hold on to their earnings longer than singers, and survive crashes and slumps notwithstanding their weakness for poker and bridge.

There are exceptions to this rule. Chaliapin lost a fortune in Russia and made another in the last fifteen years of his life, dying comparatively wealthy. Battistini died a millionaire. Tamagno died at 54 and left his natural daughter a large fortune, the result of a life so frugal as to be a joke among his colleagues. As he prepared his own macaroni over a gas-ring in his modest New York hotel room during his Metropolitan Opera seasons, I wonder whether he dreamed that a dozen years after his death his vast fortune would disappear and his heirs become largely dependent on his gramophone royalties.

Singers, by the way, when at the full maturity of their art should record their repertoire with a first class company, thus securing not only a mirror of their attainments but also a sure safe deposit for their income when their voices begin to fail.

Our recording scoop of the year 1903 was this very Francesco Tamagno. Alfred Michaelis carried out with stubborn persistence the negotiations with Tamagno's lawyer, and the document eventually signed was the first to give the artist a royalty on the sale of each record, a stipulated selling-price of £1 each, and a distinctive colored label. In addition he received a cash advance of £2,000—a great sum for those days—plus a royalty of 4/- per record. He only lived a few years after this and the resulting records, I regret to say, can be considered only a faint reflection of that extraordinary voice.

To carry out this recording my brother, as Tamagno's guest, spent a week in his mountain home at Sousa in the Mont Cenis pass. In his own music room overlooking the valley the apparatus was erected, as stipulated by his contract. Tamagno was the son of a rural innkeeper near Turin, and to his active outdoor life he doubtless owed his splendid physique—that great chest and iron throat which produced those wonderful *robusto* tones for which he was noted.

At 36 years of age he was lifted to the highest pinnacle of fame when Verdi chose him to create the title rôle of his immortal opera *Otello* at La Scala. After that he was in demand at high fees all over the world. My friend Chaliapin told me that in his student days in Milan he heard *Otello* from a seat in the gallery of La Scala. Never could he forget the thrill of Tamagno's mighty voice as it overwhelmed both chorus and orchestra with the high C of "Esultate!" He said it was always followed by such a burst of applause, *bravos* and *bises* as to resemble a riot, but he added that, for him, the greatest moment in the opera was Tamagno's fine acting in the death scene. He maintained that the world would have to wait long for an Otello who should combine a fine robust tenor voice with uncommon acting ability and such a handsome appearance as Tamagno possessed.

I was fortunate enough to hear him at the Vienna Konzerthaus a few months before his death—an experience I shall always treasure.

THE PROCESSION PASSES

In the autumn of 1906 I made notes about the recording of another legendary figure of the Victorian age, Adelina Patti. I feel justified in quoting them at length because of the importance accorded to her advent on records and the fact that these were among the few records thought worthy of being included in the archives of the British Museum and the Paris Opéra.

I have always instinctively felt that Patti was the only real diva I have ever met—the only singer who had no flaws for which to apologise. No doubt she had so mastered the art of living and protecting herself from the public gaze that she could plan her appearances for just those moments when she was at her freshest and brightest. The year she celebrated the fiftieth anniversary of her début was the year she consented to make gramophone records.

When my brother and I went to Craig-y-Nos Castle we travelled by a narrow gauge railway to Penwylt, now called Craig-y-Nos. Here a bus met us and we drove to the sombre and imposing edifice where the singer lived. There we were greeted at the door by her agent, Mr. Alcock, and his wife. We soon discovered that every provision had been made for receiving us: two large bedrooms had been cleared and were placed at our disposal. Here we assembled our recording machine. We had a curtain over one of the doors, and through a hole projected the recording-horn. The piano was placed on wooden boxes and when Madame Patti entered the room she was terribly intrigued as to what was behind that long horn. She had the curiosity of a girl, and peeped under the curtain to see what was on the other side.

It was an ordeal for her to sing into this small funnel, while standing still in one position. With her natural Italian temperament she was given to flashing movements and to acting her parts. It was my job to pull her back when she made those beautiful attacks on the high notes. At first she did not like this and was most indignant, but later when she heard the lovely records she showed her joy just like a child and forgave me my impertinence.

Do not imagine for a moment, however, that when we set up the recording machine Madame rushed into the room to sing. Not a bit of it. She needed two full days to get used to the idea, during which she simply looked in every now and again and saw the ominous preparations for immortalising her voice. She did not know whether

[91

to be glad or sorry. To reward us for this long wait she would say: "Those two nice gentlemen—let them have champagne for dinner tonight to make up for their disappointment."

She was used, in a queenly way, to rewarding any services or kindness that people showed her. She had a large and noble heart, but was decidedly temperamental; she would be calling everyone "darling" one minute and "devil" the next. But perhaps a woman who had sacrificed so much for her art and for her friends and relatives could be forgiven all these outbursts of temper.

It was in the days of her second husband the tenor Nicolini that her castle was at the height of its merriment and could fairly be called Liberty Hall. Wonderful performances of operas took place in the private theatre, particularly *Roméo et Juliette* and *Faust*, with Patti and Nicolini playing the principal parts. They were a loving couple both on and off stage. Later Nicolini financed Paganini's Restaurant, Great Portland Street, which was to become the haunt of so many famous musicians in the nineties.

I feel that the week we spent at Craig-y-Nos brought joy to Patti's then somewhat retired life, and after we left she no doubt settled down to a rather humdrum existence. When we were leaving she commanded the butler to give us braces of pheasants and masses of flowers from the garden, which we took back to London as trophies of our visit.

Another bright spot was when we brought these records for her to hear some weeks afterwards. Again the hospitality of Craig-y-Nos was placed before us and we saw what a charming host her third husband, Baron Cederström, could be. The records we played to Patti and Cederström we could truly say were exceptionally good, and Patti was not disappointed in the sacrifice she had made to carry out this recording. In most of them she was accompanied by Sir Landon Ronald, who was instrumental in carrying out the negotiations. In a few she was accompanied by her nephew, Mr. Barilli from America, who happened to be her guest at the time.

Madame took a keen interest in her records and whenever visitors came to the castle she proudly showed them off to her admiring listeners. We can only regret that the present improvements in recording were not at our disposal when her records were made but, such as they are, they give a very fair idea of the vocal reserves of

Patti even at the age of sixty-three. Remembering that this lady started her public career at the age of nine you can imagine that her voice was not in its prime. Few other sopranos had a career of over half a century, however.

I heard later that when my brother and I arrived Madame instructed her friend, Mrs. Alcock, to take a peep at these two suspicious characters and report to her what they were really like. When Mrs. Alcock returned and said we looked like harmless young men, she said, "Well, look after them well."

I can vouch that we were royally treated. They set before us not only the reserve of their gardens and hothouses but also the choice of the winecellars. A master-hand knew the vintages which Nicolini had so intelligently laid down and we drank many toasts to the health of the house. Occasionally Patti would look in on us and would make some passing joke; she was always ready to share a laugh. One of her treasures was an orchestrion of the type which was in vogue in the big country houses of those days. Hers was supposed to be the biggest in England. With one blast it would resound through those old walls in a most odd way. At least 60 instruments were represented and she had 120 music rolls for it. The instrument itself was a Freibourg costing £2,500 and the rolls cost £11 each.

One of the truly great gramophone artists, the length of whose career was only rivalled by that of Patti, was my dear friend Mattia Battistini. Shortly before his death he celebrated the fiftieth anniversary of the commencement of his active career as an opera singer. Battistini made his début in Rome in *La Favorita* when he was no more than twenty years old. Unlike most singers, who continue to give concert recitals when they are too old for the physical exertion of stage performances, Battistini even a few months before he died was still singing in opera at Budapest. We first recorded him in Warsaw in 1902, and his last records were made in Milan, conducted by his great friend and adviser, Maestro Carlo Sabajno, in 1925.

His was a fine example of a successful career of singing in our own times. He made song his life work and was courted in the highest aristocratic and artistic circles. Battistini offers the rare instance where a singer's social career was as distinguished as his professional career. He was exceedingly sensitive on the point of his artistic prestige, so much so that it almost amounted to a mania. An instance of this occurred when, before signing his gramophone contract, he insisted on a special Battistini label to distinguish his records from those of all other artists. To balance this harmless vanity, he was a man of great charm and distinction of manner, generous to fellow artists and a lavish host at his home in Rieti. His endowments of elegance and distinction led naturally to a marked preference for rôles in which he could play the part of a cavalier or noble seigneur, such as Don Carlos in Verdi's *Ernani*, Rodrigo in *Don Carlos*, the Marquis de Chevreuil in *Maria di Rohan*, or Don Giovanni.

Undoubtedly one of Battistini's greatest assets was the admiration and esteem in which he was held by the ladies, an admiration which the rôles he selected tended to augment. As a vocalist he was pre-eminent. To demonstrate that his position in the world of song was not easily gained, it will be sufficient to give a short outline of the régime which he strictly observed from day to day, even during his annual summer vacation. During this holiday it was his practise to retire to his beautiful estate at Rieti, between Ancona and Rome, in a country of woods and mountains quite isolated from the world, where he lived in truly patrician style. Here, throughout the three months of his vacation, he received a continuous stream of visitors and admirers, among them ambassadors, princes, and cardinals, from St. Petersburg, Madrid, Paris, Budapest, Vienna and other capitals. Battistini married the Baroness Romanones, a cousin of the King of Spain.

His day would start at 5.30 A.M., when he went for a two hours' ride in his park. At 7.30 A.M. he took a cup of coffee, after which two hours were spent in his office dealing with correspondence. From ten until noon two whole hours were passed in singing. In addition to practising his regular exercises for the voice he used to sing as many as twenty to thirty arias. From noon till two was his interval for lunch, after which he took a siesta. Again from four until seven in the evening three hours were devoted to singing.

This was his daily régime which his guests knew and respected. They were at liberty to wander through his beautiful estate where horses and carriages or automobiles were at their disposal.

When on tour, however, Battistini's régime was modified: he saved up all his energy for his public performances, rising only at midday after a kind of reception held at 11 A.M. in his bedroom, recalling the royal *lever* of Louis XIV. Still in bed, he drank his chocolate and offered refreshments to his guests. At these affairs one could always be sure of meeting highly placed personages of whatever country he was visiting.

Battistini himself himself used to tell a story which illustrated the esteem in which he was held in the Russia of the Tsars. A certain Grand Duke, a great admirer of his, was very desirous of securing the sword he wore in the opera *Ernani*, which was of beautiful Toledo workmanship. Battistini knew that the Grand Duke wanted his sword as a souvenir, and one day called on him to present it. "Here it is," said Battistini, "but may it please your Highness to remember it not only as a personal souvenir but as a reminder to make good the lines I speak in Act 3, '*Perdono a tutti.*' "

It so happened that a friend of Battistini's had been condemned to death for some political offence; the efforts of his family to save him had been in vain and the higher courts of appeal were closed to him. No other resource remained but to solicit the personal intervention of someone in power. Battistini had undertaken to do this on behalf of his friend. The sequel was that the Grand Duke accepted the gift of the sword and assured him that he would secure a pardon for the prisoner.

Battistini only once went to America and until his dying day told the harrowing tale of that voyage with amusingly realistic gestures. It is doubtful whether it was any worse than the average sea voyage, but he would never risk the ocean crossing again. He made a vast fortune, chiefly in Russia, probably amounting to some twenty million lire, and his wife brought him a dowry of equal amount. It is believed that when he died his estate was worth over half-a-million sterling, in spite of the regal manner in which he had lived and spent his money. Battistini died on November 7, 1928, at his Villa di Colle Baccaro in his native city of Rieti.

Some of his contemporaries also died wealthy—for instance, the tenor Marconi whom I remember recording in his beautiful *palazzo* in Rome. But then Marconi was a very close spender and never squandered money when travelling, as so many singers do. A rich man also was the genial tenor Angelo Masini who retired the year I made my first records in St. Petersburg, where he had amassed a fortune and where his name became a legend. For many years his principal haunts were the gallery of Milan's La Scala and the cafés of its bright Galleria where I often met him surrounded by his cronies. When he retired he remained "put" and, to my lasting regret, waived aside all our blandishments to record.

His only appearance in England was when he sang in the première of the "Requiem" at the Albert Hall under its composer Verdi, His quarrel with Colonel Mapleson is an example of how a short-sighted impresario can deprive a nation from hearing the greatest tenor of his age. In my dealings with celebrities I have adopted the attitude that be they ever so stupid or unjust I, the mere mortal, must bow down to the god.

Battistini's last London appearance in opera had been in 1901, and it looked as if England would not again hear one who was considered to be the greatest exponent of *bel canto* of his day. My enthusiasm for this artist was so great that I made every attempt to interest the English impresarios in promoting concerts for him in England, but I could make no progress until I ran across L. G. Sharpe and we came to an arrangement to go fifty-fifty in the expenses and profits. Three Queen's Hall recitals were given in each of the years 1922, 1923 and 1924. Their artistic and financial success was very gratifying to us, but beyond this there was the satisfaction of having our convictions substantiated. Battistini was then over 65 years of age and the press filled enthusiastic columns with praise of this great artist and his demonstration of the authentic Italian school of singing. I am certain that to many young singers and teachers those performances were a revelation. There was no assisting artist, and the programme consisted of up to twenty of the most difficult arias and romances ever written for baritone voice. The baritone seemed to get better as his voice warmed up and the remarkable thing was that he finished each concert absolutely fresh. Afterwards he would relax and say, "Now I will indulge my one remaining vice." He would then produce a large Havana cigar, light this up, and lie back luxuriously in perfect ease and contentment.

This suggests the life of sacrifice and self-denial that an artist like Battistini, in fact that every great artist whom I have ever known, has had to practise, notwithstanding the gossips who prate about their self-indulgence. Battistini was rigorous in the discipline of life. He was punctual in all his habits, most abstemious in eating,

Lunching at Frascati, Italy. Marconi the tenor, and the author (left).

drinking, and the other pleasures. He might look longingly at the fruit but he would not touch it.

It can be said that Battistini lived for song. His whole life was given to it, and he used to say that if he could not sing he would die. Even a few months before his death he came to his great friend, Maestro Sabajno, and announced to him that he was about to start on an opera tour which included Prague, Budapest, Bucharest, Warsaw, and Berlin, and he would certainly have gone on with this project if the Maestro had not warned him that it was an unheard-of undertaking in view of the condition of Europe and of his advanced age. Battistini thereupon cancelled all except the Budapest appearance. It was not money alone that he had in view, although his fees for these performances were probably the highest he had ever received in his life. The man had to sing to live: he never retired. He had a strong constitution and in a career of over fifty years he rarely missed a performance through illness.

The quality of his voice was of the kind one finds only in Italian baritones, with a dulcet, silvery timbre, almost approaching that of a tenor. His remarkable range enabled him to sing easily a top G or even an A-flat in full voice. Listening to his records one realizes the ease and fluency of his production no less than the richness of the tone, while as an interpreter there is a high intelligence at the back of every phrase that he sings.

His greatest pride and hobby was a collection of some eighty expensive and carefully selected costumes, unequalled by those of any contemporary singer. In fact, so proud was he of his wardrobe that when he died he left it in its entirety, together with the trophies of his long career, to the Commune of his native town, Rieti.

Some of the most beautiful renderings among his records are the arias, "Il mio Lionel" from *Marta*, "O Lisbona, alfin ti miro" from *Don Sebastiano*, "Eri tu" from *Un Ballo in Maschera* and "Pari siamo" from *Rigoletto*. After a performance of *Don Carlos* in Vienna not long before his death, a leading critic wrote: "This septuagenarian is an incomprehensible miracle whose splendid voice is almost wholly untouched by age. He can compete, as to brilliance and power of singing, with the youngest vocal celebrities whom, however, he surpasses in musical culture, artistic mixture of registers, and technical perfection. Physically also, this incomparable artist has preserved his freshness and elasticity, whilst histrionically he always fascinates and moves his audiences."

It is interesting to contrast the career of Titta Ruffo with that of Battistini. The former had a short one, but of meteoric brilliance. In an age when the worship of the tenor left almost all other types of male voice in comparative obscurity, he was successful first of all in the modest rôle of the Herald in *Lohengrin* at the Costanzi Theatre in Florence in 1889. From that time until the outbreak of the World War he rapidly built up a splendid reputation. His forceful and intense acting overshadowed even his singing but undoubtedly the unsparing demands he made on his voice curtailed his active career. It has been said that the rivalry between the four great baritones, Titta Ruffo, Pasquale Amato, Antonio Scotti and Dinh Gilly, rang the curfew on all their voices.

It was in the season of 1908, at the Teatro dal Verme in Milan that Ruffo gave a series of eight performances of Thomas' *Hamlet* to sold out houses which established his fame and resulted in contracts for South America and with the Philadelphia-Chicago Opera Company which were unique in the tremendous guarantees he received. Incidentally, that season he also began to make gramophone records, receiving the largest fee ever paid to a baritone.

Titta Ruffo confined his activities to Russia, Spain, Italy, and North and South America, and was never heard at Covent Garden in important rôles. Indeed, Covent Garden at that time was ruled over by impresarios whose policy was to concede high fees only to *prime donne* and tenors. Because of this Battistini, Titta Ruffo, and Chaliapin were excluded from London until Sir Thomas Beecham broke down the barrier with his brilliant season of Russian Opera in 1913 at Drury Lane.

During his short period of fame Titta Ruffo amassed a fortune which enabled him to achieve that greatest ambition of all Italian singers, namely a *palazzo* in Rome. I have visited many of these homes, for instance that of Cotogni, the celebrated baritone, whom I recorded in Rome in his eighty-sixth year; that of Francesco Marconi with its terraces of palms and azaleas interspersed with fragments of Roman and Greek sculpture; that of Tetrazzini also with its figures and pergolas, and that of Beniamino Gigli at Recanati on the Adriatic with its well laid out park and charming Florentine villa overlooking the valley of the Tiber.

I remember being with Chaliapin in the old Waldorf Astoria Hotel on his return to New York when Titta Ruffo was announced. Chaliapin was suffering from laryngitis, which had forced him to cancel his engagements, and in an agony of self pity he was quite unlike himself. Titta Ruffo breezed in like sunshine from heaven and for two hours they exchanged stories. I sat there spellbound and realised that these two overgrown schoolboys were probably the greatest *raconteurs* living. They were entirely satisfied with the effect they were producing on one another and as the stories became more and more ribald they gesticulated to each other until in the end Chaliapin had to get out of bed to illustrate his points. I remember in particular one story he told about a drunken man wandering into a ball-room searching for the *retirati*. Titta Ruffo excelled in Tuscan dialect stories. I can never forget the richness of those two magnificent voices—even in speech. They were simply trying to impress each other, and had they been paid a fee of a thousand pounds for their performance they could not have been more assiduous in their anxiety to create an effect.

Here Comes

the Prima Donna

CHAPTER VII

Here Comes the Prima Donna

OF ALL female voices the one easiest to record and most appreciated by the public is the soprano. At all times there has been a reigning queen of song at each important centre of gramophone activity. Sometimes they overlapped and then jealousies would have to be composed. This adjustment would have to be diplomatically carried out by our publicity departments. From 1908 to 1914 the roster of favorites according to countries read somewhat as follows:

England	— Melba
Italy	— Giuseppina Huguet
France	— Maria Barrientos
Austria	— Selma Kurz
Germany	— Frieda Hempel
Russia	— Neshdanova
U. S. A.	— Geraldine Farrar

The best records of this group were made before the war by the acoustic process, which was particularly favorable to this type of voice, seeming to lend it body. After 1918 many of the coloratura sopranos who held top place in the opera, concert, and record fields came mostly via America. They included Amelita Galli-Curci and Lily Pons, but Italy also produced Toti dal Monte and Lina Pagliughi, both light sopranos of the more robust order that gives the listener intense satisfaction through sureness of *fioriture* and reserve power. None of these later divas had the requisite gifts to make the great career of a Tetrazzini or a Melba. Their records of the coloratura repertoire never failed to thrill one by their brilliance, and the divas themselves were first-class publicity material.

The importance to my company of these ladies made it necessary for me to make them my special study and care. The pleasure was mutual, and thus the human side of their lives, usually hidden from the public, became an open book to me and I enjoyed acting as their adviser. I found no great difficulty to steer a middle course between their interests and those of my company. As a class, vocalists were more prone than instrumentalists to open their hearts to a sympathetic ear, once you had gained their confidence. This tendency, I am afraid, caused many to lose their life savings during the various crises of the past twenty years. An instance occurred among those artists attached to the Chicago Opera and the New York Metropolitan who followed with blind faith the advice of such bankers as Samuel Insull and Otto Kahn to play the market. With singers it was generally a case of "Easy come, easy go."

However, bad advice was not the reason Tetrazzini, the maker of many fortunes, died penniless and had to be buried by the state. As will be seen, she was headstrong and acted on her own impulses which, through lack of business experience, were often at fault. By 1914, twenty-six years before her death in Milan, she had completed her effective opera career, which she began at sixteen. That she was adventurous and courageous was shown by her many combats both in and out of the law courts. She was good hearted into the bargain, for on one occasion she shouldered the entire financial burden of an opera company touring South America when their manager had absconded.

When, in her eighteenth year, a soprano celebrates her fiftieth performance of *Lucia* with a gala night it is something to boast about, but when in addition each performance is sold out and at every one of them the President of a great republic is in the audience, it is enough to turn any singer's head. This is what happened to Luisa Tetrazzini in Buenos Aires in 1890. It must have spoiled her a bit, because when she could not find an impresario bold enough to tour her in the provinces and follow up her success, she stubbornly formed her own company, went barn-storming and reaped a harvest. Her self-confidence dates from the day when, as a girl of sixteen, she sang the important rôle of Inez in *L'Africaine* at short notice in the Fenice at Florence. So genuine was her success that bigger rôles followed in the Rome season.

The scene shifts to Buenos Aires. There, by great luck, she found no reigning diva in occupation. She created a furor at $7,500 per month and was the talk of the town for five years. Supposed love escapades and adventures, even involving the name of President Saenz Peña, added spice to her sojourns in the Argentine. During most of these years her favorite sister Eva was also a member of the troupe and tried to look after Luisa. Eva, nine years older, was a lyric soprano of established reputation. She became the wife of the celebrated conductor Campanini, and the sisters remained great friends all their lives. In fact, Eva was the only confidante whom she completely trusted.

The brilliance of these years can also be gauged by the fact that Tamagno was one of the Company, and with him she sang in *Les Huguenots*, Bertha in *Le Prophète* and Matilda in *William Tell*. The baritone Sammarco, a great actor and friend of Caruso, and Borgatti, Italy's greatest Wagnerian tenor, were other members. Campanini was in charge.

The roaring nineties were the days when money dripped from the pampas-grass of the Argentine, the rubber of the Amazon, and the nitrates of Chile, and the fortunes of many Italian artists were built up from their engagements in those countries during that period. Tetrazzini often related to me the story of those hectic days and of her rapid advance as measured by money:

$17,500 per month for second year—18 years of age
$22,500   "   "   "   third   " —19   "   "   "
$27,500   "   "   "   fourth   " —20   "   "   "

These figures give one some idea of her popularity. She was loaded with gifts and jewels. Her dressing room was always filled with masses of flowers, and on gala nights to keep up a good old custom the students would unharness the horses and pull her carriage from the theatre to her hotel. Once she paid the captain of a steamer 100,000 francs to help her escape from the two impresarios who were fighting over her.

The scene shifts again, this time to St. Petersburg. There she

[105

found a rival diva in possession—the wonderful Sigrid Arnoldson, then at her zenith. The twenty-five-year-old Tetrazzini had her days of glory there, however, when she sang opposite the Rodolfo of a young tenor of the same age, Enrico Caruso. This began a great friendship which lasted until his death. Further fruits of this Russian period were her friendships and active collaboration with that fine tenor, Masini, and with Battistini the magnificent—both idols of the Russian public. She only tarried one season in Russia, as the rival prima donna was too firmly entrenched among the people who mattered to be easily dislodged.

So the next few years find her principally in South America and Mexico, managing her own opera company and mopping up the millions. Mexico, with President Diaz for dictator, had always been an ideal firmament for opera stars, and on her previous visits she had completely established her position when touring with her own company. By all these successes and rewards it can easily be understood why for her there was no financial inducement strong enough to lure her to England, Europe, or the United States. Even in Italy after those first two years she rarely sang again. It was not until the war years that the wanderer returned to appear at a series of Red Cross charity concerts.

At the end of her Mexican tour in 1904 she went direct to California, travelling overland, and came under the management of one Dr. Lehay, an impresario of great enterprise, from whom she learned valuable lessons in modern publicity methods. He made a fortune arranging her appearances in California, and she remained loyal to him for all her Pacific Coast visits, where she was always a firm favorite.

Lehay hit on a bright idea to launch her first concert in San Francisco, billed to take place on Christmas Day. For some reason he was denied the usual big hall. The papers took the matter up, and to the reporters Tetrazzini announced that she was going to sing even if it had to be on the streets. This gave Lehay his cue and he applied to the mayor for permission to give a free open-air concert. The mayor readily consented and the press gave the enterprise a big boost. It was a warm, sunny day and some 250,000 people attended. The affair was so successful that reports of it were telegraphed all over the States, and it established a custom which has persisted up to now in that city—a free open-air concert is still given in San Francisco every Christmas Day.

Tetrazzini had the voice and could deliver the goods. The public went away satisfied that they had heard the greatest diva of all time. Throughout her career she pursued *réclame*, and for this reason she was better known to the man in the street than was any other prima donna. Why, even the maid in the pantry heard of Tetrazzini as a songbird, whereas she would be a bit dubious over Melba's classification. Lionel Powell, the English impresario, pursued the same policy during the many years he managed her tours in the British Isles. She was news and therefore her press conferences were well attended. She always asked me to act as interpreter at these affairs, and I found them great fun. One had to serve up discreet news and guide the scribes away from private affairs which sometimes seemed the only things that interested them.

The stock question was, "What do you think of London?" They might better have answered it themselves, since the diva lived hermetically sealed, for the duration of each visit, in her private suite at the Savoy. Her only outdoor experience was the journey to and from the Albert Hall in a closed conveyance. The lady reporters would ask her views on English cooking when they might have known that she remained faithful to her Italian dishes. To another question, "What do you think of Englishmen?" she might have truthfully answered: "Apart from my manager and my accompanist, Ivor Newton, I have never met any."

Only at the end of a tour could she risk going to a film or a variety show. She did very little reading, loved to be busy in the kitchen, and prided herself on her macaroni triumphs of which she partook freely. Her whole day pivoted around the visit of her accompanist, the inimitable Ivor, when for one solid hour she would practise her repertoire and study new songs. The impresarios found her very reliable and she rarely had to postpone a concert. On her last tour, when past her prime, laryngitis caused her to cancel a few appearances. Once when she was in Scarborough a hurried call was sent to Harley Street for an eminent throat specialist. But even his great skill could not enable her to fulfil her engagement, which had to be cancelled, with all money refunded. In spite of this, the specialist duly sent in his account, which worked out at a guinea a mile and amounted to over £300. This was disputed, but eventually they came to a compromise.

In 1922, I helped her with her book *My Life of Song* but felt, as she related the various episodes of her crowded career, that she was only showing the façade to the gaze of the world. As is the case with most Latins, it was of vital importance for her to preserve "face."

In Italy the family is closely knit and works in complete harmony. It is easy to see how, in this particularly united family, the precocious Luisa assimilated almost without effort all the soprano rôles from Eva while she practised. Actually she had only one year at the Florence Conservatory, where she studied merely the rudiments of music. As a singer, she was a "natural" and so never had the drudgery of placing the voice and ironing out imperfections of registers. She was no great musician but had an impeccable ear. Most of her rôles were hammered into her by a *repetiteur* during her 'teens, and there they stayed put. Like Patti's, her voice had the body of a lyric soprano with the range and flexibility of a *leggiero*—just the type demanded for such dramatic rôles as Lucia, Violetta, and Amina in *La Sonnambula*. Those are the three parts in which she excelled.

At the full maturity of her art, she made her début in London where Melba was then predominant, and never doubted her power, when once heard, to conquer and retain the English public. It was in the Autumn and not the Grand Season, otherwise it is doubtful whether the managing director, Harry Higgins, would have braved the wrath of Melba who at that time was the reigning prima donna at Covent Garden. Higgins first heard of her through Campanini. He signed her up for ten performances during the autumn of 1907. Before the ink was dry he wanted to call the season off, and when she refused he offered her £300 to cancel the contract. Tetrazzini stood firm and threatened legal proceedings. Higgins then decided to go ahead with it.

Hearing about this engagement of a new soprano, my directors cabled to Carlo Sabajno, our Italian maestro in Milan, to secure the lady at once for record making. So he obtained an appointment and presented himself at the Tetrazzini apartment, hat in hand, only to be told that Her Ladyship was still occupied with her toilet. It was a humiliating experience for a maestro to hang around, waiting like a lackey, and he made some remark to that effect which the maid repeated to her mistress. Whereupon he left, slamming the door after him. I once asked Tetrazzini why she always refused to let Carlo conduct for her, and she told me that she seethed with anger when she heard that message from the maid and vowed she would get her own back. This trait of never forgetting or forgiving was most pronounced in the lady.

A month later she was in London. She had never sung there before and was still unheard of in England. Even to Higgins she was X, the unknown quantity, and his tilt with her naturally prejudiced his outlook. One foggy Saturday evening in November she made her début in *La Traviata* before a half-empty house. One could barely see the platform, so dense was the atmosphere. The few bored critics of the Sunday press opened their eyes in amazement when they heard her wonderful singing, and next morning the papers went wild about her. On Monday, bright and early, our manager was on her doorstep, awaiting her pleasure. She made him wait. She had not forgotten the Sabajno episode, and took it out on us not only by keeping our representative in the cold but also by dictating her own terms for recording. In due course cordial relations were established and she became and remained one of our most valuable artists. To his dying day, Higgins considered her the greatest prima donna of his time. He said nothing ever excelled the brilliance of her attack and the *abandon* of her cadenzas. Of this her gramophone records alone are proof enough.

She had a genius for lending herself to occasions of a kind that had definite publicity value, and her temperament was just the right one to ensure their success. It was she who, in January 1911, laid the cornerstone of the huge "His Master's Voice" cabinet-factory at Hayes. Later she paid visits to the factory to sing to the working girls during their dinner hour. She and they thoroughly enjoyed these visits, which were well staged. The streets leading to the works were always hung with banners and streamers.

Many years have passed since I last saw the great singer. It is my lasting regret that I could not meet her again to recall the old days of our happy association. For two years during the first World War, however, I was marooned in Italy where I was frequently her guest in Rome and Milan. I can take the credit for arranging her return to the English concert platform and was also responsible for fixing up her first broadcast in England. For that début at the microphone the fee was far in excess of those paid to any other artist, at all events by the B.B.C., in those days. As a relaxation on her last visit, I took Tetrazzini to hear Gracie Fields in a revue at the London Coliseum. Tetrazzini's is one of the celebrity heads painted on the striking curtain of that theatre, and this pleased her immensely. Gracie played in a sketch where, as a charwoman on her knees, she is supposed to be scrubbing the opera house stage. She says: "I want to be an opera singer and sing like Tetrazzini," and proceeds to burlesque a prima donna with those comic cadenzas of hers. Tetrazzini laughed so loud that she could be heard all over the house. The audience, who had recognized her, proceeded to give her a warm reception. After the show we went on the stage, and Gracie and Luisa met for the first time. They were two congenial souls in complete sympathy. I am sure that Gracie will remember that evening.

To complete this appreciation, I should refer here to a coincidence which has once more placed the name of Tetrazzini in close juxtaposition to that of Caruso. During our experiments with the comparatively new electrical re-recording process which I touch on in the last chapter of this book, we found that these two golden voices lent themselves most readily to that method of superimposing a modern orchestra on the old acoustical record.

Tetrazzini died at the age of 68 on the 28th of April, 1940.

What Emmy Destinn was for many years to the world of Covent Garden, Celestina Boninsegna was to La Scala, Milan. She carried all the great dramatic soprano rôles in Italian opera. Her voice was so smooth and velvety and of such even registers that recording was no effort; the results obtained were always thoroughly musical and therefore gave intense pleasure. Those harsh places expected in any record by a dramatic soprano were conspicuous by their absence. Boninsegna was a fine big woman of generous stature with a temperament to match. She simply exuded good nature. She never spared herself, and in consequence her voice could not stand the wear and tear of constant work. Thus her career was meteorically short. I like to dwell on the memory of her superb cooking and can still taste that dish of *tagliatelli bolognese*, a specialty to which I have become a lifelong addict.

While she was in the kitchen her big husband played the host, bouncing on his knee a baby boy, appropriately christened Hercules, who looked for all the world like one of Michelangelo's massive cherubs in Saint Peter's. In "Pace mio dio" from *Forza del Destino*, Boninsegna showed off her voice to even better purpose than did the rest of her many fine records. I freely admit that Destinn was the greater of the two artists under review, not only because she had the drama in her voice for the most exacting emotional rôles but also because she was a really brilliant linguist. However, to my intense chagrin I was less successful, by the crude recording process then in use, in bringing out the best of her qualities. Even so, the records indicate a great reserve of voice and an inexhaustible supply of breath.

Like Tetrazzini, Melba was more than a prima donna. She was in the diva class, and well she knew it. About her reams have already been written so I will confine myself to her activities as a recording angel. For long she doubted, or pretended to doubt, our ability to reproduce her voice successfully on the wax. Overtures were started by Landon Ronald, our musical adviser, in 1906, and continued over a long period. They involved a visit by our sales manager, Sidney Dixon, to Monte Carlo, where Melba was starring in opera. For one whole month he courted her with flowers, speeches and dinner parties; still she would not be convinced. Finally she fell to a ruse. While she was dining in her apartment with the great composer, Camille Saint-Saëns, Dixon in the next room played a Caruso record. Saint-Saëns was enthusiastic, which had the desired effect on Melba. She capitulated.

In those early days we had no studio worthy to receive such a celebrity, so she made it a condition that a test recording should be carried out at her home. Our equipment was set up in the beautiful drawing room of her mansion in Great Cumberland Place. Like Tetrazzini's house, this room was filled with treasures and trophies. Landon Ronald had charge of the arrangements and also conducted the orchestra of some 45 players whom we somehow managed to crowd into the room. The recorders were working at great disadvantage, and our nerves were keyed up to the highest tension.

Melba's first selection was "Caro nome," and I shall never forget the thrill of that first phrase when the test was played back. It was a great adventure for those pioneer days and far from satisfying, but enough was achieved to convince Melba that, under favorable conditions, the engineers could make successful records of her voice.

Later, in the same drawing room, we made the historic recording of the Bach-Gounod "Ave Maria" with Kubelik playing the obbligato—a landmark in the steady progress of gramophone music. Thousands of copies were acquired by music lovers who regarded this title as a treasured possession. Afterwards the diva came to us and entered into a life contract with "His Master's Voice." She was an astute business woman. Final negotiations for her contract had to be carried on through secretaries and solicitors. When the documents were at last completed they were of imposing length.

One of the tensest moments I have ever experienced in any recording studio was when, at City Road, Melba had just completed a charming record of "Caro nome." As the operator lifted the wax from the turntable his hands trembled so much that he let the disc fall and it rolled along the floor on its edge. Everybody was aghast, silently watching its progress and wondering on which side it would come to rest. If on its face, the wax would be ruined. Luckily it fell on its back. Then Melba's pent-up feelings were let loose in a tirade in which she told the poor operator in the plainest terms just what she thought of his clumsiness.

On another occasion we were going to do the Quartet, "Bella figlia del amore," from *Rigoletto* at City Road. Melba and Sammarco arrived on time. Kirkby Lunn, somewhat late, received a Melba reprimand. But John McCormack, later still—about half an hour—was whipped by the diva with a truly cutting remark. And then was released such an exchange of the choicest Irish and Australian compliments as made even the engineers grin. After a few minutes the sun shone again and they all sang like angels. The last record we made of Melba's voice was during her farewell performance at Covent Garden on June 8, 1926. The record also reproduced her last speech, made before the footlights. That throb in her voice, when she was overcome with emotion, was clearly audible. It gives one a queer feeling to listen to it today.

HERE COMES THE PRIMA DONNA

I sometimes wish that other great singers would do as Melba did, fix a definite date for their farewell appearances in public and in the studio and keep to it. It is a difficult problem to break the news to singers that they are prejudicing a magnificent past by outstaying their welcome when their voices are no longer fit for reproduction.

Though she made and kept a hard bargain, there was nothing mean about Melba. Indeed, she was a model of generosity and possessed numerous musical protegées, many of whom made good. She was intensely patriotic, and her fine work in giving numberless concerts during the war earned over £100,000 for charities and for herself the coveted title of Dame of the British Empire. In later years Melba became an ardent gramophile, and once sent her father in Australia the best instrument of the day with a special recording in which she offered him birthday greetings and sang a short song.

I follow Melba with her protégée, Toti dal Monte, because Melba mothered her on the Tait-Williamson Grand Opera Australian tour of 1924. It was at this point that the two great protagonists clashed, as told with little attempt at disguise by Beverly Nichols in his book and play *Evensong*. When Toti dal Monte, one of the greatest modern exponents of florid coloratura, first rose above the operatic horizon in Italy she began as a lyric soprano and created no immediate stir. It was originally intended that she should be a pianist, and she had nearly completed her studies in Venice when she strained a tendon in her left hand, which meant farewell to her ambitions as an instrumentalist.

Our negotiations with Toti dal Monte took on the aspect of a dogfight. On her side, she called in her family and relatives. They were not going to let their one valuable possession, Dal Monte's voice, pass out of their control without exacting the best possible terms. They proved to be tough nuts to deal with. After dragging on for two or three months, negotiations culminated in Paris. On her side she produced her managers and lawyers; we also were well represented. It was only after many arguments and compromises that she finally signed an exclusive contract. Although they had rigged the market thoroughly, the price we paid did not prove exorbitant since there has been a nice margin of profit for all concerned. She came to London for her début at a Sunday afternoon concert at the Albert Hall, equipped only with a prima donna's evening dress which would have been ill suited to the occasion. It was late on Saturday afternoon, but I and the impresario, the late Lionel Powell, dashed to Berwick Market, off Wardour Street, in the hope of finding something more appropriate. Being barely five feet tall and rotund, she was not easy to fit. It is doubtful whether the blue gown eventually selected was an entire success, but at the concert what she may have lacked in costume she more than made up for in coloratura.

Tait and Williamson, for their great Australian venture, had also engaged the tenor, Enzo de Muro Lomanto. His fine voice and acting also helped to make a triumph of this first Australian tour of Italian opera to be given after the war. The two young artists met for the first time at rehearsals, and were married halfway through the tour. To celebrate the event, a belated but highly spectacular wedding breakfast was given at Melbourne at a cost of over £1,000. The joke of it was that Dal Monte imagined the management were paying for this as a publicity-stunt. Toti was swiftly disillusioned when she was presented with a bill. But she paid up like a little gentleman. After the tour she returned to her home in Trieste where before long she became the mother of a fine baby girl. She has since declared that her expensive wedding was well worth the outlay. Later I travelled to Trieste and had the pleasure of giving her *bambino* a gramophone.

Little Toti, smiling and good-natured, held first place in Italy and the Latin Countries in the twenties, nor was this surprising. In such operas as *Lucia di Lammermoor*, *La Traviata*, *La Sonnambula* and *Rigoletto* the listener was given utter satisfaction by the security of her singing. Her voice had the roundness and volume expected from a dramatic soprano, yet withal there was that innocence of timbre and clean technique which one associates with a boy's voice. No wonder her appearance in Australia during the 1924 season created a riot which meant crowded houses night after night in Melbourne and Sydney, making the Tait-Williamson tour one which will go down to posterity as the most successful in many years.

Melba also made personal appearances during the Tait-Williamson Season, thereby challenging comparisons with her protegée, Toti—comparisons which were more odious than ever. In her sixtieth year and on the verge of retiring, Melba tried bravely to play the part of benevolent patron to the younger woman. To have done so to a rival of mediocre calibre might have been possible, but Toti was just too good, and the crescendo of demonstrations, night after night, was more than Melba could endure.

Then came another coloratura. Amelita Galli-Curci was lucky to arrive in the United States during the lean war years when the concert headliners were becalmed in Europe. She had been appearing in South America with Caruso and Titta Ruffo, but America, hard-hit by the War, seems to have overlooked her success in the Latin Republics. So she had to start right from the beginning. At the end of her resources she landed in New York, and by great good fortune Campanini offered her a couple of trial performances with the Chicago Opera, little thinking she would prove the sensation of the season. This was followed by a bid from New York where she appeared at the Lexington Theatre on January 28, 1918 in *Dinorah* (Meyerbeer). My opposite number in the Victor Company, C. G. Child, grabbed her and hurried her to the recording studios where, strangely enough, a surprise awaited him. Usually a coloratura soprano offers little difficulty. But Galli-Curci's handicap was a tendency to go above the note. She was naturally used to singing in large halls and opera houses, and was plainly cramped in the confines of a small studio, hence she was prone to force. She might therefore have to repeat a number as many as twenty-five times before a satisfactory "master" could be obtained. However, the phenomenal sales of her records in America and England more than warranted all this trouble. When in 1924 Lionel Powell announced her début at the Albert Hall, the house was sold out three weeks before the concert. For many years subsequently the same thing happened. Like Tetrazzini, Galli-Curci was a fine subject for our publicity department, who revelled in her sunny disposition and willing cooperation. Among other stunts, they staged state visits to our factory as well as to some of our most important accredited dealers throughout the country.

She is of mixed parentage, with an Italian father who was in the banking game, and a Spanish mother. She was born in Milan, and at the age of four played the piano well enough to impress the composer Mascagni, who urged that she should have the best tuition procurable. By the time she was sixteen she was an exceptionally gifted player and had won a prize at the Milan Conservatory. At this stage, when her prospects looked bright, her family met with financial reverses, and she had to help them by giving pianoforte lessons for very low fees. And here reality sounds more like romance, for Mascagni, who never lost interest in her playing, heard her warbling one day in her simple artless manner, and was struck with the quality of her voice and her easeful production. Once more he advised her to study, but this time for an operatic career.

"I had no teacher in those days," says Galli-Curci. "I had to learn to sing by the aid of my piano and the birds." In time her financial difficulties were overcome, and after a short course of training the young girl went to Rome to seek her fortune as an opera-singer. The work was hard and discouraging. She began very modestly until, after many set-backs, she was engaged to understudy a soprano at the Costanzi in Rome.

She made her début as Gilda in *Rigoletto* and, as a result, received a three years' contract at six dollars a performance. This engagement began in 1910 and gave her valuable experience which paved the way for her future triumphs. We soon find Galli-Curci singing in places as widely separated as Barcelona, Buenos Aires, and Petrograd. She became the idol of Spain, then of the Americas.

Another glorious singer who, had she been born a generation later, would have sent all Hollywood clamoring on her doorstep, is Maria Jeritza, or Baroness Popper. In her heyday, Jeritza was a most attractive woman with a head of real flaxen hair, and had a superb dramatic soprano voice which she exploited particularly well in *Tosca* and as Princess Turandot. Jeritza reigned supreme in Austria in 1914 when the Vienna Opera was the first in Europe, and among her admirers was His Most Catholic Majesty, Emperor Franz Josef.

Her name was forgotten in England after the war because as Baroness Popper, the wife of an Austrian nobleman, it had naturally not been mentioned during hostilities. In 1920 I was the only one who still knew her when she arrived in London on a visit with her husband. By frantic telephone calls I managed to get Harry Higgins along in time to discuss plans with her. The result of that meeting is now history. Jeritza gave a splendid performance as the

Princess in *Turandot*, the Puccini opera, when it was first heard in England three months after the composer's untimely death. She was a sensation as Tosca because of her intense acting and because in the second act she sang the great aria "Vissi d'Arte" as she lay prone on the floor, face downwards. A link with her family has lately been broken by the death of Blanche Marchesi, the famous singing teacher, daughter of the still more famous Mathilde. Blanche was the mother of Baron Popper.

What a fine colorful work is *Turandot*, Puccini's swan-song, with its rich orchestration and matchless stage-settings! The part of the Princess requires a dramatic soprano voice of tremendous carrying power to penetrate through the oriental clash and din of the orchestration and calls for a real musician of colossal endurance to survive the ordeal. Another ideal Princess was that sterling Lancashire singer, Eva Turner, who began in a small way with the Carl Rosa Opera Company, rose to stardom at La Scala, and finally returned to her native land to shine at Covent Garden. Frankly, there was nothing of the diva about her. Working her way up from the chorus she became so accomplished a prima donna that her mastery was acknowledged by critic and public alike. But not without a struggle did she finally win recognition from the opera pundits.

These gentlemen, whether in New York or London, are a queer lot at the best of times, but not half so queer as some of the exotic queens of song who appear in hopes of capturing another throne. Only too often they wish to be taken at their own or their agent's valuation, which is occasionally a bit steep. Harry Higgins, the husky Edwardian, was never tired of telling the story of goodness knows how many prima donnas. "Would you believe it," he would say, "she actually asked two hundred pounds a performance, so I said 'My dear woman, I only want you to *sing*.'"

When I told a journalist friend that I was working on my first book, he said I should include some sensational stories about prima donnas. One international artist whose memoirs have already appeared omitted this saucy episode, in which she played the rôle of misleading lady.

Imagine a gala night at the end of a brilliant opera season. Many floral tributes were taken to the apartment of the leading star, who was giving a supper party. In the course of the evening she succeeded in encouraging her husband, the conductor, to drink until he was so overcome that he fell asleep. Whereupon she and her lover, a handsome basso, laid him stretched out on the floor, surrounded him with masses of flowers, and, like La Tosca after bumping off Scarpia, placed a lighted candle at each end of him and a crucifix on his breast. Then they eloped together. Eventually the betrayed husband caught up with the lovers at Buenos Aires, and accepted a monetary consolation of some size from the misconductor to resign his claim on the lady. I never heard the sequel.

As will be seen, I have not placed my prima donnas in strict chronological order, for this book does not profess to be a history and dates are of no paramount importance. So now let us take a glance at that attractive creature, Grace Moore. Miss Moore is the perfect type of artist for today, at home both in the film world and in opera. By a combination of qualities, converging at the right moment, she was lifted to international fame and fortune in Hollywood. As an opera singer alone it would have taken her years to have achieved such distinction. I remember when she sang at Covent Garden what an anxious moment it was, following her great success in the film *One Night of Love* and the tremendous advance publicity she received. Her début was as Mimi in *La Bohème*, and the house was sold out solid for weeks beforehand. She carried a great weight on her shoulders, great things were expected of her, and she made good, thanks in part to Maestro Bellezza who knew just how to suppress her film instincts and bring out all that was most operatic in her. Some folks are inclined to underestimate Grace Moore's ability as an opera singer on account of her notoriety as a movie star, but Beniamino Gigli confidently asserts that she is a born singer with the potential equipment of a legitimate prima donna.

The procession passes. Here comes Rosa Ponselle. Tall, with a graceful carriage and finely cut features, she sweeps along. So striking is her appearance that you could never miss her in a crowd. During her short reign, this opera queen was perhaps the most perfect *lirica spinta* soprano that ever lived. She first came into prominence when Caruso discovered her and her sister Carmela during the war, singing in vaudeville, and obtained for her an audition with Gatti-Casazza. This led to her withdrawal for serious study and coaching. After which she began almost immediately as a prima donna at the age of twenty-two in Verdi's *Forza del Destino* with Caruso at the Metropolitan Opera House. Each year thereafter she would add but one opera or so to her repertoire, never swerving from the principle laid down by her teacher, Romano Romani, to take a year or two to master a rôle before trying it out on the public. In her portrayals of Violetta, Norma, Luisa Miller, Giulia in *La Vestale*, Leonora, and Gioconda, she has no equal. I will go further than this and hail her as the greatest actress singer of our time. Allowing for intelligent visualization, I consider the study of her records of excerpts from these rôles will substantiate my claim.

I remember how, when she was putting in two years' hard work on Violetta in *La Traviata*, I visited her retreat on the Lago di Como and observed the clever way she mapped out her day to concentrate on her studies. Her recreation was cycling through the Italian villages and generally "going native," dressed in shorts and with a bandana round her head. Because of her dark, swarthy complexion she was indistinguishable from the peasants of the country. A good meal is a gift from the gods, not to mention the divas, and I recall even now that savory dinner of *pasta al sugo*, a macaroni preparation, and lake trout, which she set before me that day. Cooking is the glory of every Italian girl; they are so practical in the kitchen, and how they enjoy it!

Rosa Ponselle's first appearance as Violetta, her greatest rôle, was made in London in 1930 with Gigli, and proved an instantaneous success. It was a *tour-de-force*, and I doubt if there will ever be a Violetta in our day to come up to her. She had the right stature, temperament, figure, costume, and voice. She kept a supreme vocal "line." To crown all, she invested the character with her own magnetic personality. In every rôle she assumed, she took peculiar pains to dress the part, and never for one moment appeared costume-conscious as was the case with other artists I could name. Of course she made money, plenty of it, but then she was a definite draw. Unhappily, a large percentage of her profits was lost in the crash in Wall Street in 1930-31. At that time her gramophone contract alone was worth £7,000 a year.

There is a human side to her character which calls for special mention. Once Rosa, my friend and colleague the late Trevor

Osmond Williams, and I escaped from a superheated salon in the Savoy Hotel, London. This was in the middle of a lavish supper party to which she had invited us. While we were taking the air on the Embankment my poor friend, already ill, collapsed. For half an hour Rosa, seated at the base of Cleopatra's Needle, bathed his head and soothed him until he recovered. There was an air of tender solicitude and pity in her nursing that I shall never forget. Rosa is commonly rated as a good scout—indeed I don't suppose she has an enemy in the world. Not long ago she was married, and I wish her every joy and happiness that should be the reward of one who has sacrificed so much to her art.

"Terribly temperamental, these prima donnas," says your average citizen, and why shouldn't they be? It would be strange if it were otherwise. For so many nights and matinees they must live in a land of make-believe, completely at the mercy of their public. No allowances are ever made for the state of their health or their domestic troubles. They are expected to be always keyed up to concert pitch when, in fact, the singing voice is more often below par than above it. In truth, the chances of a perfect performance must be only one in ten. But if the backers always conceded a prima donna's desire to postpone a show they would soon go broke. No, she has simply to learn to sing over a cold and carry on.

To the music critics I would say with James Clarence Mangan, the Irish poet, "If you're wise, be merciful." One word more on this absorbing topic. Apparently, adiposity is the prima donna's besetting sin. Mass gives tone. As with an instrument, so with the voice. You cannot possibly have a grand piano without a grand frame to show it off.

Chiefly Wagner

CHAPTER VIII

Chiefly Wagner

AFTER the first World War there was a period of four years before musical activities resumed their stride. It might be said that the Covent Garden opera season of 1924 started music once more on the up grade. For that season a company of comparatively unknown artists was collected from Central Europe and the Wagner famine was relieved with a diet of truly superior performances given by an exceptional cast of singers. We heard the greatest Wotan, Brünnhilde, Sieglinde, Fricka of our generation: Friedrich Schorr, Frida Leider, Lotte Lehmann, Maria Olczewska, besides an ideal Octavian and Sophie in Delia Reinhardt and Elisabeth Schumann. For *Der Rosenkavalier* we had in Lotte Lehmann perhaps the finest Marschallin ever heard. The greatest *heldentenor* of our times, Lauritz Melchior, was to join the galaxy of immortals a few years later. To these add Germany's best opera conductor, Bruno Walter, then in his forty-eighth year, in charge of that youthful company eager to give London its first German season in ten years. It was a feast for the gods.

I was kept busy at the Garden and became very friendly with all of them, including the managing director Harry Higgins and, a year later, Eustace Blois. Both were delightful and charming men. The Gramophone Company did not neglect this happy opportunity of beginning an uninterrupted programme to build up its catalogue of operatic music. Elisabeth Schumann, whom I had met in 1922 while crossing the Atlantic, was my sponsor and as her dressing

[123

room was usually the meeting place for the whole company, we quickly became acquainted. Elisabeth was and still is the chum of Lotte Lehmann. I think such a genuine friendship between two prima donnas is a rare thing. They are both clever and broadminded women and consult each other on all business and family affairs. They made their début together in Hamburg as pages in *Tannhäuser*. Each artist had a three-year contract. During the first year Schumann sang small rôles and received 150 marks a month, or about $40. For the second year she got 250 marks, and the third year 400. Then she arrived. The next year saw her engaged at 18,000 marks for a nine months' season. It was soon evident that the house would be sold out whenever she was announced to appear in rôles like Susanna, Cherubino, Zerlina Pamina, or Eva and of course her greatest part of all, Sophie. But only after 1921 did she begin to receive really lucrative engagements and lay the foundation of a small fortune. The same applies to Lotte. These two were always happy when sisterlike and relaxed in their homes they exchanged intimate confidences. "Wir spielen keine Theater," Elisabeth told me. She played the part of Sophie in 1911 in Hamburg under Gustave Brecher, when Katharina Fleischer-Edel sang the Marschallin and Edyth Walker the Rosenkavalier. Lotte later assumed the rôle of the Marschallin in Vienna.

At the opening performance of *Rosenkavalier* during the Covent Garden season of 1938 Lotte once more essayed her great rôle but in the middle of Act I she broke down completely and staggered to the wings. It was a sad finale to the hundreds of Marschallins she had played and our hearts went out to her in sympathy. She has since sung the part again in America, I believe.

After the war Richard Strauss, then 57 years old, and Schumann toured Europe and America, Strauss himself accompanying her recitals of his lieder. On the S. S. *Adriatic* I played poker every evening with them, together with Chaliapin and Lucrezia Bori. Egged on by Elisabeth, who tipped us off about Strauss' parsimony, we all played against him one evening. The "ante" was only five cents and every now and again she would flick one of the coins from his pile into hers. This would go on until he spotted her. Then the game would be interrupted while he laboriously counted out his money. The smoking-room, led by the boisterous Chaliapin, would rock with laughter. Strauss is not witty but he has a sense of humor and when he laughs his nose goes white. This peculiarity would set us off again.

Elisabeth contributed to our hilarity by disclosing her odd gift of imitating bird-calls without moving a muscle of her roguish face, so that it was almost impossible for the hearer to trace the source of the sound. If she had not laughed we should have persisted in thinking there were canaries in the salon. A few years later, much against Schumann's will, I utilised this gift of mimicry and made her record Zeller's charming "Viennese Nightingale's Song" in which she whistles the refrain. This happy thought not only netted her several hundred pounds but endeared her to the masses.

A few years ago I had lunch with Strauss and Elisabeth Schumann in the grillroom of the Savoy Hotel. Strauss had come over to conduct for the B.B.C. and said that for this visit he was going to insist on being paid on the gold basis instead of in depreciated sterling. This was no joke, for he went on to tell Schumann then current in Vienna. "We shall soon all be begging in the streets," said the optimist. "From whom?" asked the pessimist.

When I visited her in her Vienna home Schumann proudly showed me a Strauss manuscript and told me its story. He asked her to sing for some guests portions of the just completed *Aegyptische Helena* for their criticism. He sent her a hastily copied voice part, the notes looking like pinpoints. She complained that they were so small as to be illegible. He replied, "Never mind, I'll play the piano accompaniment." Afterwards she demanded the manuscript as a souvenir and he wrote on it, "Meiner ersten Helena." Strauss always fancied her cold boyish voice for his Salome and offered to rewrite the part for her. Nikisch, under whom she sang in many Gewandhaus programmes, had a weakness for her canary bird imitation and once Furtwängler declared to me that for him Schumann was his favorite singer because she not only sang the music but felt what was behind it.

When Strauss went to the Vienna Opera in 1919 he insisted that they should engage Schumann, and so she made her home in that city. After that contracts with the Munich and Salzburg festivals as well as for the Covent Garden spring season followed regularly for many years.

Elisabeth had a comfortable apartment in the courtyard of the Spanish Reitschule, famous for its pure-bred white Arab horses imported from Spain over a hundred years ago. It was part of the acres of buildings forming the Hofburg, the Vienna residence of Emperor Francis Joseph. The dainty little horses stopped at the door as they passed through the courtyard on their way to exercise every morning. Among them was an old mare of over thirty-five who would bend her knees to receive a lump of sugar from Schumann's hand. Among many other treasures found in her home were a manuscript of *Fledermaus*, a present from the widow of Johann Strauss, a letter of Goethe, and Wagner's celebrated "Absage an Hanslick" letter, in which he reveals that Hanslick was the original of Beckmesser.

About twenty minutes by car from her friend, Lotte Lehmann lived in an expensively simple châlet called "Hinterbrühe," overlooking Vienna and the Danube. In this cosy retreat one summer day Lotte gave a luncheon to Lauritz Melchior and his wife Kleinchen, Elisabeth, and myself to celebrate the successful recording of the complete first act of *Walküre*. Our conductor, the ever busy Bruno Walter, could not spare the time to enjoy this Arcadian feast—that was his loss. The excellent Austrian cooking and Tyrolean wine which Lotte's mother supervised were fully appreciated, but it was when coffee and cherry-brandy were served on the terrace overlooking Vienna bathed in sunshine that our joy reached its climax. That was our last reunion in Austria.

In those days Vienna as a music center could not be ignored, but it was living on the momentum of its past glories and was as poor as a churchmouse. Its wonderful Philharmonic Orchestra and Opera had the character and authority of a prophet in rags. The succession of great men who fought to conduct them is significant: Richard Strauss, Franz Schalk, Felix Weingartner, Bruno Walter, Furtwängler, Toscanini—they form an imposing array. The intrigue and politics of the Schalk and Mahler factions, the Walter and Weingartner partisans, were the staple conversation of the Ring cafés. It started with the Wagner and Brahms controversies, and I believe Mahler and Bruckner music flourishes side by side only because neither partisan would give way to the other. The slogan of both factions was "No surrender." It was like a prize-ring, and every conductor had to be a great musician and a great fighter into the bargain.

In the thirties it was deplorable that the great Vienna Opera House should have been made a cockpit for party strife. It was even worse that these famous conductors, guiding its destiny, were coerced into showing their political colors despite their protests. This unhappy state of affairs was due, of course, to Hitler.

For a time the Vienna State Opera was under the joint direction of Franz Schalk and Richard Strauss. Owing to differences Strauss withdrew in 1924. The indefatigable Schalk continued to dominate until his death in September 1931, but his influence could still be felt years after. Even recently the question was asked why a certain baritone of small talent was singing important rôles. A wit replied, "Oh, he's under Schalk's protection."

I carried out many recording sessions in Vienna with the Philharmonic Orchestra and found them in general a cynical lot, snobbish and blasé. The only one who really had them tamed was Toscanini—they ate out of his hand. How those veteran players, many of whom had reached pension age, survived his régime I don't know; he certainly revitalised them though he left them panting at the end. They seemed to respect Bruno Walter and gave him of their best, yet after two hours' unsatisfactory rehearsal in the Ländler Movement of the Mahler Ninth Symphony an old second-violinist sidled up to me once and said: "He can't conduct it, he's only following the orchestra."

This Ninth Symphony I recorded three months before the Anschluss at an actual performance in the old Musikverein. Schuschnigg and most of his Cabinet were present that Sunday morning: it was a page of history. The photograph in this book of Bruno Walter was taken in the famous greenroom that morning. His daughter, who later committed suicide, and her husband were present.

That same bleak January week in the historic Imperial Hotel I dined with Alexander Kipnis and his American wife and just around the corner at Meisl and Schadn's I lunched with the newly wedded Mr. and Mrs. Herbert Janssen. These great singers had just started in at the Vienna Opera under a new contract, having both found Berlin under Hitler too uncomfortable. A few weeks later they were to leave Vienna hurriedly for the same reason. Many others had also to depart precipitously, leaving their jewels and treasures behind; but all my friends, as long as they could sing, could flee without property and yet contrive to fall into comfortable niches in America.

Weingartner at the age of seventy signed a five years' contract with the Opera but because of the factions and intrigues had great difficulty in carrying it out. Nevertheless he refused to capitulate and resign. I recorded some very important works with him and the Philharmonic Orchestra, while he treated them with a frigid detachment and they responded with grudging correctness. I remember essaying a comparatively new concerted work. Again one of the cynical players whispered in my ear, "He'll never get through it."

Like a damsel in distress these people sometimes farmed themselves out to wealthy amateur conductors and then they were really funny. At rehearsals they were complacent and unctuous and affected deep admiration whenever the young gentleman would explain at length some new approach to Beethoven's Fifth Symphony. They would noisily rap the backs of their fiddles with their bows—the strings' way of applauding. Once my friend Anton Weiss offered me tickets for one of these affairs, and when I asked, "What's he conducting?" Weiss replied, "I don't know, but we're *playing* the Fifth." When I entered the hall the hundred men arranged on the platform favored me with knowing winks, and as the conductor took his place on the dais the greeting from the orchestra might have announced a Toscanini.

Weiss told me another amusing story about this restless amateur. His valet, distressed by an untidy entrance of the strings at one of his concerts, apologized for his master after the performance, saying, "I can't understand how it happened, because he's been playing that Toscanini record and rehearsing before a mirror every morning for the last six months." They might be a hardboiled lot, but the Vienna Philharmonic can never be the same without the familiar faces of Arnold Rosé, Mairecker, Buxbaum, Starkmann, Anton Weiss, and Burghauser. Their names recall the academic atmosphere which surrounded this ancient and august body.

The doughtiest fighter of all was the late Franz Schalk. Nothing could shift him; he died there in harness at the age of sixty-eight. He was distressed because he had not been invited in recent years

Bruno Walter. From a photograph by the author taken in the greenroom of the Musikverein, Vienna, two months before the Anschluss, 1938.

CHIEFLY WAGNER

to conduct in London where, before the war, he had made such a good impression. A few months before his death the invincible white-haired warrior sought me out in London and we arranged a guest performance which, I regret to say, never took place.

To record Friedrich Schorr, Richard Mayr, Maria Olczewska, and Elisabeth Schumann on their native heath was simplicity itself; organisation, tradition, and authority were there on tap for me. One could always arrange a time and there was a choice of fine halls with good acoustics like the Konzerthaus and the Musikverein. I mention this because finding a favorable location for recording was always a difficulty in Latin countries and in England. These artists were my friends and with true Viennese hospitality threw their homes open to me and arranged to make me persona grata at the Opera House. When they came to London for the Grand Season or a concert tour I was able, in my turn, to be of great assistance and encouragement to them.

Operagoers will recognise the debt they owe to Frida Leider during those wonderful dozen years from 1924 to 1937 when her Brünnhildes and Isoldes were the very keystone of the Wagnerian structure. Those German sopranos seemed to have perfected a new school of singing; their restraint and voice control showed that the only effective reply to the Wagnerian orchestras was to husband resources. In looks rather sombre as if continually harboring a grievance, I found Leider hard to negotiate with. Finally she came out with a decision: "My brice is one hundred pounds a song, *AB-SO-LOOTLY!*" Naturally we nicknamed her Madame "Absolutely." In business she was cold and exacting but, that finished, she could be a charming hostess and a true friend. I have never heard her utter an unkind word of a colleague. Dramatic sopranos are seldom an easy proposition to record because they are expected to go all out for their high notes. However, Leider was an exception because of her perfect control of emission. She was pitilessly intelligent, and I would have liked sometimes to surprise her into giving her candid opinion of some conductors, many of whom she has rescued from humiliation by her solid musicianship and coolness in a dilemma. I asked her once if it was true that she had intended to become a doctor, but she laughed it off. She started as an accountant in an office and for a time attended a school for typewriting. Her début in opera was modest: she sang the "Cry behind the Rocks" in the Hamburg Opera House for an elderly Brünnhilde who could not reach the high notes.

I am proud of the fine list of records made by Leider because I think she will go down in history as the finest Wagnerian soprano since Ternina. The standard of performance she maintained in those gruelling rôles over a period of more than twenty years was exceptionally high. It was upon artists of her calibre that the success of those great Wagnerian festivals of Berlin, Bayreuth, Covent Garden, the Teatro Colon in Buenos Aires, the Metropolitan in New York, and Paris solely depended. What a responsibility! Her records will always be treasured by future generations of singers.

The proper place for Lauritz Melchior is between the two Isoldes he so manfully supported in Europe and America—Leider and Flagstad. For many years Melchior sang opposite Leider and I can vouch for it that they were really trusty friends and staunch colleagues, although towards the end when the amazing Flagstad swept across the firmament a rift was started that was hard to close. One thing is certain, never was his rivalry with Leider so marked as that which developed between Flagstad and Melchior—a story to be told later in this chapter.

The pivot around which Wagnerian opera revolves is the *heldentenor* or heroic tenor, and since the première of *Lohengrin* in 1850 the search throughout the world for this rare bird by opera managers and conductors has been going on. Any presentable young man who can sound only a few good upper notes can easily obtain an audition and, if at all promising, will be able to secure a patron or a syndicate to back him during the three or four years necessary for training. Then, whereas the ordinary singer has the greatest difficulty in obtaining a hearing by responsible directors, the mere mention of a dramatic tenor quickly opens all doors. This was so in the case of Lauritz Melchior. He certainly made records as a baritone for the Danish Gramophone Company, singing the usual popular ballads whilst he was completing his musical studies at the Copenhagen Operascool. He was terribly poor after the War, having a wife and two children and no work, and in 1920 he slipped over to London to try his luck. I recollect frequently meeting him at the stagedoor at Covent Garden, waiting for an audition as a baritone. He found the going hard in those days and certainly looked it.

Later, I remember him singing at the Promenade Concerts in London, with Sir Henry Wood, still as a baritone. This was a most fortunate début, for in the audience there was an observant musician who made up his mind that here there was potential material for a Tristan or a Siegfried. His excuse for seeking out Melchior in the artists' room was an article in a French periodical which commented adversely and unfairly on Melchior's singing. Hugh Walpole—for he was the man—offered his assistance by replying to the article. That was the beginning of a friendship which endured until Walpole's death. He learned that Melchior was consumed by the ambition to change his voice in order to sing dramatic tenor rôles. Being handicapped with a family and by lack of funds, he was not in a position to do so, however. Walpole offered to back him and paid a visit to Copenhagen where he met the Melchior family and discussed the pros and cons of the project. The offer was accepted and Melchior returned to London to study with the late Victor Beigel, who was responsible for training so many of our English Wagnerian singers.

The Covent Garden Opera Syndicate heard of this through their scouts and engaged him for their spring season. Actually he first sang there as a tenor in 1924, in German. As so often occurs when the need is urgent, he was rushed in and sang *Walküre* under Bruno Walter without any orchestral rehearsal. This goes to indicate the usual famine of Wagnerian tenors, for in spite of his lack of experience in great rôles, the Covent Garden Syndicate were willing to put up with his imperfections whilst he was appearing in the Grand Season.

Melchior's association with the New York Metropolitan Opera began in the autumn of the next year. From that moment he has continued to be a steady visitor to Covent Garden and to the Metropolitan Opera, and holds what is virtually a worldwide monopoly of Wagnerian tenor rôles.

One can judge how vital was the demand for Melchior's voice to sustain the Wagnerian cult when it is realised that since 1929, when he first began to keep a record of his appearances, he has sung each of the rôles of Tristan, Siegmund, both Siegfrieds, and Tannhäuser over a hundred times, and the other Wagnerian tenor parts hardly less often. Meanwhile, he has also sung other parts, such as Otello and Rhadames, as well.

That he is gifted with a wonderful constitution is proved by the fact that since 1925, when his first two appearances at the Metropolitan Opera in New York were cancelled on account of influenza, he has never had to postpone or cancel a single performance or concert in New York or at Covent Garden in London. As an example of an active season, in 1937-38 during a period of eight and a half months he fulfilled 110 opera, concert, and radio engagements in France, England, America, and Canada.

I cannot claim to have discovered him; that honor belongs to Sir Hugh Walpole, but I did at least realize that he was the only Wagnerian tenor who could help us to build up the vast series of Wagnerian opera records which the newly discovered electrical process made possible, and I acted promptly. Melchior and I have worked in complete harmony to achieve this great library of Wagnerian classics. We found that we had at last got a tenor who could sing and rehearse record after record without stress and without his voice going husky or becoming strained. The risk of this happening is no joke with a Wagnerian orchestra of one hundred men, costing £200 a session, and expensive singers as well. Imagine the recording of the Quintet from *Die Meistersinger* with Melchior, Schorr, and Schumann, conducted by Barbirolli, with some ten rehearsals and three attempts to make a satisfactory record. It takes a voice of iron to stand the strain and costs over £600 in salaries and expenses.

I frequently visited the Melchiors at Covent Garden during the long pause between the 1st and 2nd Acts when, to while away the time, the artists exchange visits or play bridge. "Kleinchen" (Mrs. Melchior) always presided and distributed refreshments. She is a wonderful foil for the tenor and her infectious good humor and ready laughter attract many friends. These comprise members of the English and Danish royal families, who were always amongst the first to greet them when they arrived in London or in Copenhagen before the present war.

In "Kleinchen" Melchior made a fortunate and happy choice. She was a filmstar in Munich, noted for her daring exploits such as parachute-jumping from a balloon, walking on the edge of roofs,

Lauritz Melchior, the tenor, with his wife, "Kleinchen," outside Londonderry House. From a photograph by the author.

and similar feats. They met while Lauritz was studying in Munich. He declares she fell into his backyard when carrying out a film stunt. In any case, she took complete charge of his upbringing, his social and stage deportment, his German, and his acting. Her critical analysis of his performance after every act has certainly played a great part in his development.

It sometimes amuses Melchior to tell of the first fee he ever earned. He and a young friend on an excursion had overstayed the time limit of their return tickets and were without funds. About that time Denmark was negotiating the sale of her West Indian possessions, the Virgin Islands, to the United States. The boys heard a negro stump-orator haranguing a crowd and urging them to prevent the transfer, and it occurred to them that they might be able to do a stroke of business with the Negro by entertaining his audience. They retired into the woods, prepared a short singing act, and then put their suggestion to the Negro, who promptly agreed to pay them 4/— each for their turn. This enabled them to purchase railway tickets and get home safely.

Melchior's first Covent Garden fee was £40. His present fee is "anything the traffic will stand." He has already accumulated sufficient means to acquire a 3,000 acre hunting estate, situated some fifty miles from Berlin. There before the war I have gone out with him in the early morning to see him bring down a deer and a brace of ducks before breakfast. During his stay study and music were taboo, and opera houses and conductors were not to be mentioned in the hearing of Lauritz. The hunt and food were favorite pastimes and topics of conversation. The table, continually set on the verandah overlooking a large lake, was always groaning under a load of good things to eat and drink. Although Göring often hunted in Melchior's company, yet he steadily refused the Marshal's request to sing in Germany, and is today an exile in America.

I remember him planning his second hunting-expedition in the Canadian Northwest, in British Columbia, in September 1938. The party was to include guides, Indian hunters, and cooks, and would take no less than thirty packhorses. Sport was promised with moose, bear, elk, and mountain sheep. "Kleinchen" said that he would be sure to boast all the winter to his colleagues, Richard Crooks, Lawrence Tibbett, Nelson Eddy, and Bodanzky of the great beasts he had shot, and would show them some badly cured and smelly trophy which had been shipped 4,000-odd miles to his New York apartment. Meanwhile it would be her task to make apologies for it to the neighbors and servants.

I am telling all this to support my conviction that it is the storing up of health and strength, during these open-air holidays, that enables Melchior to withstand the long and arduous seasons of musical work year after year without flagging. Caruso might have taken a leaf out of his book. I remember Chaliapin, the great Russian bass, telling me once that he had heard that Caruso was contemplating adding the exacting rôles of Jean in *Le Prophète* and Eléazar in Halévy's *La Juive* to his repertoire. Caruso was then forty-five years of age. Chaliapin sought him out and had a confidential talk with him, warning him that this would ruin his health. That was what actually occurred, for the great tenor was never the same after assailing those terrific rôles. In fact, had Caruso lived through his last illness, it is doubtful whether he would ever have sung again —and what a tragedy that would have been for him! Chaliapin added that it was by the mercy of Providence that Caruso died at the height of his power.

It was the teamwork of that great soprano Kirsten Flagstad with Lauritz Melchior that made *Tristan und Isolde* a best seller in New York. The Metropolitan Opera House was helped out of a slough of depression and neglect when, in 1935, people began to queue up once more to see opera and *Tristan* was given ten times that season to full houses—an unheard-of thing. It was all because chance brought two fresh and beautiful voices together.

Flagstad often announced her retirement when she was dramatically discovered by Gatti-Casazza while he was scouring Europe for artists in the summer of 1934. She had almost retired from a musical career in which, although she had achieved prima donna rank in her native Scandinavia, outside—in the opera world of Germany—she was only a small-part soprano. The lack of enterprise thus shown in finding potential operatic genius is a standing reproach to the opera-scouts of the world. Eventually Flagstad agreed to return to the stage. Once she told me that she would sacrifice three years to Art, then retire again.

I have found that magnificent bass and baritone voices hail from almost every land, notwithstanding that legend about Russia producing the finest basses. The same applies to tenors and Italy. Certainly she holds the blue ribbon for the lyric and light type of tenor such as Caruso, Gigli, Bonci, De Lucia, and Schipa. Not since Tamagno has Italy produced a dramatic or *heldentenor* to equal Lauritz Melchior or Leo Slezak or Ernst Kraus. But there may be a physical reason why the snow-covered mountains and pine forests of Scandinavia produce so many fine healthy mezzos and dramatic sopranos, Junoesque women with a talent for acting. Representing less than a twentieth of the European population, the land of the fiords has certainly produced more than its quota of great singers. Without delving into books of reference I recall Jenny Lind, Christine Nilsson, Aino Ackté, Sigrid Onegin, Sigrid Arnoldson, Eide Norena, Kerstin Thorborg, Nanny Larsen-Todsen, and now the diva, Kirsten Flagstad.

When on December 12, 1938 the Metropolitan Opera commemorated Madame Flagstad's twenty-five years of opera career by a performance of *Götterdämmerung* in which she sang her greatest rôle, Brünnhilde, Lauritz Melchior, with whom she has sung so many times, did not unfortunately fill the rôle of Siegfried. Between them a difference had occurred difficult to overcome. Flagstad's husband opened his heart to me and said that she was terribly unhappy about this bitterness between old colleagues. With all the other fellow artists with whom she was associated, there always existed the happiest of relations. This state of affairs spoiled my hope of recording in Europe the second act of *Tristan* complete with the two greatest Wagnerian singers of the day, an enterprise we had often discussed and agreed on. I have since learned that the basis of their quarrel was the question of who deserved greater credit for the extraordinary success of their joint Wagnerian performances. The point seems childish beside the catastrophe of the new World War; but I was happy to see that they were again working together in the same programmes in America and had even recorded for the Victor Company a part of the Love Duet from *Tristan*.

As to Flagstad's health, her husband told me that she once sang Isolde at the Opéra in Paris on a certain Thursday evening, and was up at 6 A.M. on the Friday to catch the first train for London. She arrived at Victoria Station at 3.30 P.M. and sang at her Queen's Hall

Recital that night as fresh as a daisy. He added that in the twelve months commencing in the autumn of 1937, she sang over a hundred performances without abandoning a date or having a day's illness. This period included an Australian tour on which he accompanied her. Besides having a tremendous success there she enjoyed the trip as a holiday. What a prodigy of endurance!

About the persistent rumor that Flagstad was going to retire I have said little or nothing. Perhaps her husband did not want to accept the moral responsibility of withdrawing this greatest of all Wagnerian Brünnhildes and Isoldes. In any case, it took the war to make her return to Norway and abandon the stage of the Metropolitan.

The teachers who had the greatest influence on her training were a lady in Norway called Jakobsen and a teacher in Stockholm named Gilles Bratt. The Flagstad family are talented musicians. Her brother, Lasse Flagstad, is a pianist of the first order and an extremely good accompanist. A younger sister is a first-class vocalist of the light opera or operatta stage and has film ambitions. However, Kirsten Flagstad's daughter, now living in America, apparently has no gift or enthusiasm for music.

To complete a chapter mainly devoted to Wagnerian giants, a story about the recording of the Bayreuth Festival may be new to most of my readers. With the advent of the electrical process, certain recordings of popular Wagner selections like the Overture to *Rienzi*, Prelude to *Die Meistersinger*, the *Siegfried* Funeral March, and Rhine Journey sold in tens of thousands. Consequently, when Siegfried Wagner and his wife, Winifred, came to London in April 1927 to raise money to carry out the Bayreuth Wagner Festivals, then in difficulties, the various companies were ripe and ready to overrate the commercial value of the festival records. Incidentally, the visit was linked up with an orchestral concert which Siegfried conducted, rather surprising the critics by his supine deportment and somewhat apathetic gestures. I secured one recording session, the programme being of course the Siegfried Idyll which is still carried on the Gramophone Company's catalogue. After this we adjourned to the Langham Hotel for luncheon and to discuss the Bayreuth proposition. This was that we were to have the exclusive rights to record at Bayreuth, the terms being a royalty on the sale of each record plus a substantial guarantee. Siegfried agreed to everything and seemed most pleased, but we soon spotted that the last word was with his wife. She had already started negotiations with Arthur Brooks of the Columbia Company, and withheld her reply until Brooks could obtain from his director, Louis Sterling, then in America, his company's confirmation.

For three years the Columbia sent an expensive recording equipment to Bayreuth, where for six or seven weeks they sought from the tired artists a spare moment between festival performances and rehearsals to make a few records. Of course, no one could deny the publicity value of the coup but technically these records have always been a disappointment.

Brooks told with gusto how during this period he cabled to London for an urgent shipment of further "waxes" and then sat down patiently to await their arrival. Days passed and there was no sign of them. On telephoning to the factory he discovered that they had been despatched to Beirut, Syria!

In a way, the old law of Germany, limiting the duration of copyright to the life of a composer and thirty years after his death, was partly to blame for the chronic indigence of the Wagner family. For this reason they found it so difficult to finance the Bayreuth Festival. Wagner having died in 1883, all his copyrights expired in 1913. It was the plight of the Wagner family and the Brahms estate, Brahms' music having come into the public domain in 1927, that doubtless prompted the Reichstag in 1934 to extend the copyright to fifty years after a composer's death. This extension puts Germany on an equal footing with France, but she still lags behind Italy. That country adds on another twenty years, but during that period the proceeds of all performing rights are earmarked for the endowment of national opera and music schools. In this particular respect we might do worse than follow Italy's example. It is estimated that from the sale of Wagner records alone during the period 1920 to 1933 the Wagner family might have received close on £50,000 had the new German law been in operation.

Conductors and

Their Sorrows

CHAPTER IX

Conductors and Their Sorrows

WITH the introduction of the new electrical recording process symphony orchestras and their conductors became of paramount importance. The instrumentalists composing an orchestra and the conductor controlling it now began to engage my close attention. I often marvelled at the patience of the men in the orchestra when drill-sergeants like Mengelberg, Klemperer, Karl Muck, Koussevitzky, Furtwängler, and Toscanini put them through their paces for a steady three hours on end. Equally one must wonder at the endurance of the conductors. Yet I don't think we need waste too much sympathy on these doughty drivers. They seem to thrive in spite of their strenuous living. I recorded Weingartner when he was over 75, also Franz Schalk and Kajanus, Karl Muck, Toscanini and Koussevitzky, all when they were approaching 70. Every time I was called in to record these veterans I was amazed at their stamina and freshness after a session. At the Maryinsky Opera the septuagenarian Nápravnik once boasted to me of having conducted over three thousand opera performances in his capacity of chief conductor for over forty years.

Observe that the names above are those of men noted for their intolerance—men who demand a hundred per cent every minute of the hour. I remember Elisabeth Schumann's terse remark when I reported on a certain conductor. I said, "He's a fine fellow, all the men like him," to which she replied: "Then he can't be much good."

Madame Melchior and I were waiting in the dressing room at

Covent Garden while Furtwängler was rehearsing Lauritz in the first act of *Walküre*. I still smile when I remember Melchior's flushed face as he burst into the room, sarcastically shouting, "Furtwängler's a funny man, he does not rehearse, he calls me to the theatre for an orchestral rehearsal, and then wastes our time in pleasantries. Furtwängler doesn't like rehearsing." Amazed, I looked at Lauritz, knowing what a devil Furtwängler was for drilling. When Kleinchen burst out laughing it dawned on me that her husband felt sore after the gruelling rehearsal and just had to let off steam. I know that Furtwängler was trying to crowd six hours' rehearsal into three, but perhaps he also took a sadist's delight in pricking a fat man.

I remember a joke I played the modern Waltz King, Marek Weber. This brilliant *tapeur* after coming from his native Poland to Berlin had never really mastered the German language, but couldn't he make the fiddle sing! He became the most popular recorder of light music in Germany. He employed a small orchestra of fifteen well trained musicians with which he made Viennese waltzes and operetta potpourris. The rehearsal preceding each record was like bedlam let loose. Such cajoling, urging, threatening, cursing, praying in Yiddish, Polish, and German must be heard to be believed. I recorded this rumpus without his knowing it, and whenever I wanted to call a halt so as to get on with our recording, I would play it back into the studio. Weber and the men would find it irresistible and burst into roars of laughter. Later on Marek developed the very acceptable practise of arriving at the sessions with pockets stuffed with neckties or other souvenirs, which he would distribute to his men after a particularly successful session.

After the fashion of old Johann Strauss, he always conducted with fiddle and bow in hand. He used a wonderful Strad that he cuddled like a babe, and was always asking us, "Wie klingt die Geiger?" ("How does my fiddle sound today?") just as an anxious mother might ask, "How does baby look today?" For many years he conducted his band at the Adlon Hotel in Berlin and was really loved by everyone. Wisely, he left Germany in time in 1933, however. Later he flew from Chicago, where he had migrated afterwards, to spend a week with me at the New York World's Fair of 1939 and was proud of his newly acquired United States citizenship, although his vocabulary now consisted of equal proportions of

Polish, Yiddish, and German, spiced with Chicago slang which he had picked up from his bandsmen.

To illustrate Weber's keen Polish nose and to lay the legend that musicians have no business sense, I must add that on my return to London he was one of the first to greet me there. To my surprise he explained that the European situation was developing so fast that he had shipped his bank balance of £20,000 to America only the previous day. Later that same week, I noticed that the Bank of England had placed an embargo on shipping gold abroad. By that time Weber was on his way back to New York rejoicing.

In Washington on Saturday afternoons in the spring and summer the Marine Band formerly gave concerts on the lawn in the grounds of the White House. In the eighties John Philip Sousa was the band's conductor. I was one of the music-mad youngsters who hovered by his podium and never missed a concert. On windy days his music used to become unmanageable, and he would turn round and beckon to me. It was my pride then to stand beside him to turn over and hold down the music.

John Philip Sousa made history in several ways. He was the first bandmaster to receive a commission in the U. S. Army, and he was also the first conductor to rivet the attention of his public on his vigorous gymnastics. The musical critics condoned his methods, for they produced remarkable performances from his magnificent band. What had started with him as a mode of expression natural to his Latin temperament became a "stunt" which made him as famous as did his marches, his Sousa Band (with which he toured Europe) and his medals. The Sousa school of conducting became popular with the public and was copied all over the world.

The first band records I ever made on the phonograph were recorded by his U. S. Marine Band. Thousands of the famous Sousa records occupied the early gramophone lists.

In my youth I also sang in Sousa's choir, which was organized for Sunday evening concerts, and I attended rehearsals in his then modest home in the Navy Yard in South Washington. He patted me on the head and made quite a pet of me. He was a modest, serious man with an extremely orderly and precise mind. He was fastidious in his dress and proud of the decorations he received. His persistency obtained for him by a special decree of Congress a commission as

Lieutenant in the U. S. Army—the first time this was ever conferred upon a musician. He was of Portuguese extraction.

I remember that he was a good family man and devoted to his charming wife and child. I can still see the small room that one entered direct from the street, and a very old "tin-panny" square piano from which he conducted rehearsals. In hot weather the front door used to be left open and a circle of negro children would surround the entrance, silently enjoying the music we made.

Later on, Sousa became a very wealthy man and received a fortune in gramophone royalties on his music, especially on his celebrated marches which I consider to be, of their kind, as good music as the waltzes of Johann Strauss.

Many variety artists copied his conducting antics to the huge delight of their audiences. I saw one of the most absurd developments of the "Sousa stunt" in a great Berlin café. A long-haired, wild-eyed conductor, calling himself "Meschugge" (i.e. "The Madman") drew huge audiences nightly. The high spot of his performances was his "Grosses Kriegs-Potpourri" (Great War-Potpourri) which was received with howls of delight. For this he dropped the bâton and took up an army rifle, going through the Manual of Arms to the time of marches and patriotic tunes. Suddenly the lights would go down and battle music and fanfares would burst forth from the orchestra, punctuated by wallops on the big drum and crashes from the cymbals. The climax was reached when "Meschugge" discharged his rifle and a play of red spotlights disclosed him lying on the platform "dying a hero's death." The turn was so gruesome and at the same time so absurd that it sent everyone even in militaristic Germany into raptures of applause.

My first experience with a great symphonic conductor was in 1912, when Artur Nikisch and the London Symphony Orchestra, fresh from a grand concert tour in Canada and the United States, recorded a part of their touring programme. It was virtuoso playing which was unique at that time and doubtless set a standard which men like Stokowski and Beecham were to emulate later on. Nikisch, a trim, dapper little man, exuded a magic which made the players anxious to obey his slightest behest. He set about his rehearsals in a quiet yet whimsical way. The men nevertheless knew that sooner or later he would let fall one of those steely, satirical remarks for which

Group outside the recording studios at Hayes, Middlesex. The three men toward the right are the author's brother Will, Artur Nikisch the conductor, and L. G. Sharpe the impresario. Surrounding the group are five of the famous "His Master's Voice" dogs.

he was famous. Such was his phrase concerning the jealous quarrels amongst the musicians, that "The only time they are united is when they are united against me." He mixed with his players in a comradely way yet always had their respect as well as their love. This was in great contrast to a certain famous conductor in America who remained so much aloof and detached from his men that he is even said to have designated them by numbers. If, for instance, a flute made a wrong entry, he has been known to stop the rehearsal and say, looking in quite the opposite direction: "Number 32, you came in at the wrong time. If it occurs again you will withdraw and hand in your resignation." That would happen notwithstanding the fact that the unfortunate flautist might have been a member of his orchestra for some fifteen years.

Members of the London Symphony Orchestra pay high tribute to Nikisch's quiet manner at rehearsals and concerts. Only once have they known him ruffled and really angry. It was on their great American tour. At one city, Boston, the home of the great Boston Symphony Orchestra, where they wished to make their deepest impression, they arrived after a tiring journey of twenty-four hours. The train was late and the members of the orchestra had to go direct to the concert hall unfed and without having rehearsed. One of the double-bass players, well-known as a rebel, got his revenge in the very soft *pizzicato* passage which separates Tristan's Prelude from the Death of Isolde. There should be the faintest *pizzicato* on the double-bass. This rebellious fellow gave a terrific "plunk" which mortified the conductor and made him really angry.

When we recorded the "Hungarian Rhapsody," for which Nikisch was famous, one of the players reminded him that Dr. Richter always took a certain passage quite differently. He replied: "Richter was a German-Hungarian; I am a Hungarian-Hungarian."

Nikisch used to explain to his men, when he attempted an extremely extenuated *rubato*, that he permitted unlimited license but always within the framework of the bar, and he insisted on maintaining throughout the strictest rhythm. He will go down to history for his wonderful readings of the Weber Overtures which he made into jewels. Records of some of these are still obtainable.

I have often spoken to players, singers and agents who were associated with Nikisch and find that he left on them a deep and lasting impression amounting almost to worship. All agree that no conductor obtained such unstinted cooperation from his men with so little apparent effort. With few words and motions, he studied with them only the more difficult parts of a score. He always conducted from memory. He would commence the *Oberon* Overture by merely raising his eyebrows and frequently gave directions by a nod. It was not his custom to carry his own orchestral parts and he usually doubled up the brass sections.

An idea of the fees Nikisch obtained can be had from the disclosure that he received £150 for each of two performances of Holbrooke's *Children of the Don*. Of this work he said that it was "clever in parts."

Dr. Wilhelm Furtwängler succeeded Nikisch as conductor of the famous Gewandhaus Orchestra at Leipzig; he received a doctorate from the University of Heidelberg.

I first recorded him in the Beethoven Fifth Symphony after protracted negotiations which had lasted more than eight years, and I journeyed to Potsdam to play over to him his first records. He lived in a quiet retreat known as the "Faisanderie," or Pheasant-breeder's Lodge, in the heart of the dense forest of Potsdam. At the rate of speed (usually terrific) at which Furtwängler motors it was twenty minutes away on the motor highroad from the Beethovensaal in Berlin. The house was built by Frederick the Great as a hunting lodge of the Sans-Souci Palace and is ideally situated for the study and preparation of Furtwängler's programmes. It was here that he composed the great Piano Concerto which has had such persistent success in the hands of Edwin Fischer. In such perfect surroundings and with the ideal acoustics of Furtwängler's music room my records gave fine reproductions and met with his enthusiastic approval.

When demonstrating records to the great conductors for their approval of the day's results, I often wondered what standards they apply or what particular effects they are on the watch for. I have come to the conclusion that they are never thinking of the public but rather of what other conductors will say when they hear the record. Everything else must go by the board. A careless attack by choir or strings, as the case may be, they detest above all things.

In 1938 I spoke to Furtwängler about the deep impression his recordings with the Berlin Philharmonic Orchestra had made:

CONDUCTORS AND THEIR SORROWS

"Prelude and Death of Isolde," "Prelude and Good Friday Music" from *Parsifal* and Beethoven's Fifth Symphony, and I said that I was doubtful whether he could obtain such results with any other orchestra. He thought that he could do so with the London Philharmonic Orchestra, and said that his experience in working with that combination during the past season had convinced him that he could. I remarked that there were many envious conductors who would like to know his secret. He replied that, if he had one it was that he paid particular attention to molding the mass of players into harmonious form by beating *ahead* of the sound produced, guiding and pulling the players and not letting himself be pushed by them. He would indicate to them the *crescendo, rubato,* and so forth and seemed actually to make his baton and his hands sing the notes, but always ahead of the players so that they could follow him. He spoke of the futility of a conductor's calling out "*Cantabile*" and singing along with the players. His own beat anticipated every note. He conducted the orchestra; the musicians did not conduct him.

There was something modest and boyish about Furtwängler which made his company a delight. This naïveté of his struck one the more when he persisted in making approaches to Toscanini at Salzburg or to Bruno Walter in Paris, almost in spite of a certain rebuff, simply because he felt that he had honestly tried to keep himself and his art apart from politics.

I spoke to Furtwängler about the symphonies of Bruckner. He told me that he believes in Bruckner because there is something sincere and spiritual in these symphonies which will make them live for ever. He said that a few years ago, when touring Italy with the Berlin Philharmonic Orchestra, he played Bruckner's Eighth Symphony. Later, a friend told him that the audience was visibly bored and that on all sides there were cries of "*Basta! basta!*" The next year he again visited Florence with the same orchestra, and the same symphony was listened to with the utmost enthusiasm and enjoyment.

Concerning Bruckner, Dr. Furtwängler told me the following anecdote:

Bruckner was a well known though shabby figure in the concert-hall in Vienna. So modest and diffident was he that the players were a bit careless in their behavior towards him. On one occasion he was taking a rehearsal and stood on the platform with his arms uplifted, patiently waiting to get their attention. Finally Rosé (the *Konzertmeister*) asked, "What are you waiting for, Maestro?" He replied: "I am waiting for them to get down to business." The tone of apology in this reply goes a long way to explain his feeble resistance to those well-meaning patrons who took it upon themselves to rescore his symphonies, often to their detriment.

From amongst the many present day conductors who were pupils or apprentices of Nikisch during his long reign as conductor of the Gewandhaus at Leipzig, Albert Coates stands out as the one Englishman who achieved international fame.

I was recording Chaliapin in our studio in St. Petersburg when the exuberant Albert Coates breezed in with, "Oh, I heard that an English firm was running this show, so I thought I would look in. You don't mind, do you?" In those days he was first conductor at the Imperial Opera House under the eighty-year-old Czech Nápravnik, and he stood every chance of becoming a dominating force in the Russian musical world. He was a tall magnificent fellow of undisputed genius, with the gift of making staunch and faithful friends. I can see him now conducting *Prince Igor* at the Maryinsky Theatre with all-embracing gestures of those sweeping arms, and with his features glowing with pleasure and excitement. That was in 1912. He had Russia within his grasp then, and had the war not occurred I could imagine an Englishman becoming for the first time an international conductor of consequence. Anyone who dominated the musical world in the Russia of the Romanoffs was, with their backing, a power indeed. That youthful, talented giant could have done it.

In 1925 Coates, who was recognized as England's great conductor of Wagner, joined with me in the endeavor to satisfy the eager appetite for Wagner music which had gone unsatisfied throughout the War. He is responsible for a valuable nucleus of records of *Tristan, Parsifal, The Valkyrie, Götterdämmerung* and *Siegfried* in English which to-day remains without equal. We have made together literally hundreds of recordings, and each one of them recalls an episode of some excitement. Certainly, with him no recording can be prosaic.

Albert Coates made many valiant attempts to recapture his contact with Russia, for which country he has never lost his affection, as his many engagements there since the Revolution bear witness.

From the very commencement of my Milan days thirty-six years ago, the name of Toscanini was dinned into my ears. The Gramophone Company's "house conductor" was Carlo Sabajno, a *maestro sustituto* for Toscanini when the latter was conducting at the Turin opera house. Sabajno worshipped Toscanini and based his deportment and his professional attitude towards an orchestra upon his example. I learned a great deal about Toscanini from Sabajno: how he studied his scores until the early hours of the morning in order to commit them to memory; how he castigated the orchestra and the singers; his tireless demands on the artists, his autocratic rule over the opera house staff, the house, and the lighting. If displeased at rehearsals he would tear up a score or throw it on the floor. But sometimes some member of the orchestra, when attacked, would hit back. I remember, at the Scala, the smashing of a violin and the sopranos in tears, one after the other, at his protests. At that time every young Italian conductor copied the tactics and behavior of Toscanini.

It was wonderful what Toscanini could make of an artist when he felt that he had in his hands intelligent material. It mattered less that an artist should be endowed with an exceptional voice than that he should have a responsive intelligence. Consider, for instance, those supremely intelligent artists Stabile, the baritone, and Pertile, the tenor, both of them glories of the post-war period of the Scala Theatre.

I was happy when at length I was able to establish contact with Toscanini and this led to his taking charge of the B. B. C. London festivals. On his arrival in London I gave a small luncheon party at the Savoy to which, by an inspiration, I invited the young London conductor John Barbirolli, Toscanini's successor at the New York Philharmonic Orchestra. Toscanini was wonderfully kind in giving helpful advice to young Barbirolli. An instance of his extraordinary memory came when he recalled that Barbirolli's father had played the viola under him at Brescia some forty years previously.

Our recording experience with Toscanini showed that he was, quite honestly, bored by it. Nevertheless some good results have materialized as is shown by the long list of his recordings now in the catalogue. It must not be imagined that we always had a smooth pathway in obtaining these. I remember one session which we arranged in our own studio. We assembled the full B. B. C. Symphony Orchestra and anxiously awaited Toscanini. When he arrived we detected dark clouds on his brow. We escorted him to the podium, but he would not ascend it. He just stood there, obviously unhappy. At length he took his place and signalled the orchestra to begin, but halted the musicians after twenty bars or so and said: "I do not like the placing of the instruments and the acoustics . . . If I conduct records today I shall not be able to conduct your concert tomorrow . . ." And in a flash he had got down from the podium and was motoring away before we could recover ourselves and think the matter over. We then reasoned out that he was right about the acoustics and the placing of the instruments. Perhaps his motive was to administer a salutary medicinal draught. For my part I am certain it was beneficial although at the time it seemed drastic.

It must not be imagined that Toscanini regards the gramophone as a negligible quantity or that this is the reason for his aversion to recording. On the contrary, he is a real gramophone-fan and knows every record made by the most eminent of his colleagues. He listens carefully and can point out most of their shortcomings.

Of all the London Symphony Orchestra conductors, the late Sir Landon Ronald has been the one most closely associated with me, and since it was I who discovered him for the gramophone I take the greatest pride in his brilliant career. I recollect the evening of March 1, 1900, when I attended a performance of *Floradora* to hear Florence St. John, and sat just behind the conductor. I was impressed by his alertness and the brisk way in which the show went forward. I reflected that here was a practical man as well as a musician, and on making inquiries I learned that, young though he was, he had already had considerable experience in opera and also as a pianist. Not everyone took the gramophone as seriously as I did then and though my ambition was to add the great names of Patti, Melba, and Calvé to our list, when I thought of approaching them I felt that only a musician of standing could command their confidence—someone like Landon Ronald, perhaps.

The outcome of my reflections was that Ronald joined our forces and he brought to us not only the three great divas but also many other great artists, such as Plançon, Renaud, Kubelik, and Elman, all of whom we recorded. Some of those early records are still available and are eagerly sought after by record collectors. As England's most polished conductor, with his own Albert Hall orchestra, Landon Ronald contributed the best orchestral records of the pre-electric days, and his readings have been proclaimed unique for their high musicianship. So they should be, for his masters were Nikisch and Richter. I always felt that his devotion to the Guildhall School of Music robbed him of the possibility of attaining international fame as a conductor. His musical talents were great, and in addition he had a wit and gift for storytelling which made him popular in all sorts of society. Nobody could preside over a banquet with so much ease and charm.

He could even tell a joke against himself. When attending banquets at a certain famous hotel he always marvelled at and was flattered by the manner in which the cloakroom attendant remembered him. This man used to take his hat without giving him any ticket for it and return it unfailingly. One day, however, Sir Landon Ronald found in his hatband a slip of paper on which were the words "Big Nose," evidently intended as a means of identification. His confidence in his fame became somewhat diminished after that!

It is interesting to review the various ways in which some famous conductors were launched on their careers. Most people know, for instance, that Toscanini began his active life as a 'cellist and that his first great chance came when he was fulfilling an engagement in that capacity during the opera season at Rio de Janeiro. The audience vehemently protested at the manner in which a certain performance was being conducted. This led to Toscanini's colleagues turning to him to save the situation, for though he was only a young 'cellist, they knew that this serious youngster was not only capable of playing his own 'cello part without notes, but that he spent his spare moments in studying the opera scores and had committed every note and every word to memory. All he needed was the opportunity, which resulted in his appointment as conductor of the orchestra in place of the offending individual.

It is noteworthy that the best English conductors have been wonderful accompanists, to think only of Percy Pitt, Hamilton Harty, Albert Coates, Landon Ronald, and Malcolm Sargent. An exception is John Barbirolli who prides himself on having started his career, like Toscanini, as a 'cellist. Koussevitzky, whom I have recorded as a bass viol virtuoso and also as a symphony conductor, does not play the piano at all. When he wishes to study new music he gets the composer to play the score over on the piano whilst he follows it at a desk. In this way he covers the maximum of ground in the minimum of time. I remember approaching his home in Paris one day in the summer. The windows were open, and through them there came the thunder of a piano. I looked in, and there was Prokofieff at the piano, playing one of his latest works, and Koussevitzky at a music stand following with a baton. That was his way of mastering the work.

I remember the efforts I made to be present at the entire series of Koussevitzky's open air concerts in the Petrovsky Gardens in Moscow when he surveyed from memory all the important piano concertos up to 1912—a really great feat.

The story of how Koussevitzky got his chance is full of interest. Nikisch used to go every winter to Moscow to conduct operas and symphonies. It was at one of his performances of *Lohengrin* at the Bolshoi Theatre that Koussevitzky, who was playing the double-bass, was noticed by a beautiful lady in one of the boxes. She was the wealthy Natalia Ushova. Koussevitzky had personality and charm, and music was the lady's consuming passion. She saw that he had genius and only needed greater scope in order to develop his powers. Natalia Ushova took an opportunity to make the acquaintance of his wife and told her that her husband's genius was being wasted. In the end an arrangement was come to, and with the financial assistance of Madame Ushova an orchestra of sixty men was organized and placed at Koussevitzky's disposal. Taneiev became his tutor of harmony and thorough-bass, and Scriabin his musical adviser. Such was Koussevitzky's training. With his natural gifts and good memory he made rapid progress, for he had already learned a great deal from Nikisch. Two years later a steamer was chartered for a cruising-tour of the towns lying on the Volga River, made in the company of the best musical critics of Berlin and of Russia. Scriabin was also a guest on the boat. The idea of a symphony orchestra touring the Volga on a luxurious river boat was so novel and turned out so successfully that it was the talk of Russia for years afterwards.

Madame Ushova's family were wealthy tea merchants, and her union with Koussevitzky, to whom she was married some years later, was a happy and fortunate one for both parties; for the wealth of the Ushova family in great part disappeared and eventually the big fees earned by Koussevitzky as conductor supported the family exchequer. His wife Natalia, who died recently, was said by all who knew her to have been responsible for much of his success.

I happened to be at the Koussevitzky home in 1924 when the manager of the Boston Symphony Orchestra was there to conclude their first long-term contract with him as conductor. The Boston Symphony Orchestra had held pride of place in America prior to and during the war, right up to 1918, when its greatest conductor Dr. Karl Muck was dramatically interned on an unproved charge of refusing to play the National Anthem. It was the only non-union symphony orchestra in America, was well-endowed and had a sound pension-fund. Its record after the war and until Koussevitzky took over had been dismal. It was only after various well-known conductors had been tried out without improving the situation that he was approached and asked to state his terms. Though these were drastic, involving autocratic powers, the removal of more than twenty-five of the older musicians and the combing of Europe and America for substitutes, the manager wisely accepted. The result has been remarkable, for the orchestra has regained its undoubted preeminence. Now Koussevitzky has a life contract with them.

Besides his orchestra, Koussevitzky had one other hobby until the present war, his music-publishing house, the firm of Éditions Russe de Musique. Both the orchestra and the publishing firm will go down in history as his finest creations. As a music-publisher he carried on the tradition of that great patron, Belaiev, who rescued from oblivion the composers who established Russia's national music, Borodin, Moussorgsky, Rimsky-Korsakoff, and the rest.

In 1933 at his first rehearsal with the B. B. C. Orchestra he was much displeased with the deportment of the men and stopped the music frequently to discipline them. Finally, throwing down the stick, he left the platform saying it was impossible to continue as he could not get a proper response from his men. He went to his hotel and packed, and it was only at Victoria Station that an official of the B. B. C. succeeded in heading him off and bringing him back to a very contrite orchestra, resigned to do anything to avert a scandal. In 1935 he took charge of their festival with marked success after they had failed to secure Toscanini. I signed him for the autumn of that year for a solid week of recording with Beecham's newly organized London Philharmonic Orchestra. We were together most of the time, and it was for me a delightful experience to study at close quarters this bright and agile mind.

John Barbirolli's father was a native of Padua, whilst his mother was from the South of France, though of Italian extraction. To me he boasted that on his father's side there was Jewish blood in his veins, and it is most certain that from that side he inherited his musical ability. The parents settled in London in the nineties, and the father played the viola almost continuously in the Alhambra Music-Hall orchestra, though at one time he had his own small combination and gave after-dinner concerts on Sundays in the Leicester Lounge. He used to show me a programme in which John McCormack's name appeared, telling me that he paid him one guinea for the engagement. That was in 1905. I remember him as a quiet man, absorbed in music, his memories of Italy, and his son John. To be near their parents the Barbirollis lived in Bloomsbury. The family is so closely united that I can only liken it to the modern theory of the atom which scientists are unable to split. His father watched his every step and there can be no doubt that the coaching John Barbirolli obtained from him proved a solid foundation for his musical training. His mother, whom he idolizes, cared for his health and organized a home where quiet and study were possible. I can see her now, beaming with delight and pride as we sat down to a meal of her own preparation—and jolly good it was, too.

I pursued John Barbirolli assiduously as I needed a first class orchestral accompanist for opera as well as concerto recording. I knew that in him I had found a gifted and practical man. He was elusive in negotiations and I very nearly lost him, as my terms were below those offered by a competing company, which, however, could not give him the worldwide publicity that I was able to offer. Eventually, the contacts that I made for him with such great celebrities as Heifetz, Rubinstein, Elman, Kreisler, Schnabel, Chaliapin, and Melchior brought him to the notice of Arthur Judson, manager of the New York Philharmonic Orchestra. Naturally, his great work with the Scottish Orchestra was a big factor in determining his selection to succeed Toscanini as conductor of the New York Philharmonic Orchestra.

Many of his London friends were skeptical of his ability to hold the arduous position of conductor of the most venerable and important orchestra in America, and when, in the autumn of 1936, they saw him set out alone for New York they were filled with misgiving. It seemed just like David setting out to slay Goliath. They could point out dozens of candidates who appeared to be more eligible. When I heard these people talk I used to chuckle to myself, though I refrained from attempting to explain just why John Barbirolli was the right choice. They would never have understood.

For years Bruno Walter, as permanent conductor of the Vienna Philharmonic Orchestra, chose that body to make his gramophone records, but in the spring of 1938 the political upheaval caused by the Anschluss forced me to seek elsewhere for an orchestra to carry out recordings scheduled for publication.

Neither Bruno Walter nor I enjoyed the prospect of commencing relations with a new orchestra and in a strange environment. We need not have felt so preoccupied by these considerations for in selecting the orchestra of the Paris Conservatoire we found an instrument of fine possibilities. In the first place, the average age of its members must have been at least fifteen years less than that of the members of the Vienna Philharmonic, and besides they were very sensitive in their response to Walter and displayed a youthful and cheerful enthusiasm which deeply impressed him.

The recording took place in the very modern Salle de la Chimie. At first only slow progress was made and after the session Bruno Walter apologized, saying, "You know, it is like a honeymoon, oftentimes things do not go so well. Anyhow, the material is good. We'll make up for it tomorrow."

During the pause we recalled our last recording in Vienna when in January 1938, in the old hall of the Musikverein, during an actual performance, we recorded the entire Ninth Symphony of Mahler. By a rare piece of good fortune these records, twenty in all, turned out extraordinarily successful.

This was Gustav Mahler's own orchestra. Bruno Walter, as a young man, was his first *Kapellmeister* at the Vienna Opera from

1901 to 1907, when Mahler resigned and left Walter co-director with Franz Schalk. Thus he worked at the feet of his master, studied all his compositions, and discussed with him his aims and ambitions. Indeed, the Ninth Symphony is dedicated to Walter, who with the Vienna Philharmonic gave its première a year after Mahler's death.

Bruno Walter is a tireless worker. His day in Vienna often consisted of a rehearsal in the morning, recording in the afternoon, coaching or taking a vocal rehearsal at 6 P.M., and a performance at the Opera in the evening. He actually fitted in a recording after the Opera on one occasion when it was pointed out to him that that was the only time when the Konzerthaus was free. It seems that he is only happy when every spare moment of his time is occupied. Just before the Anchluss became an accomplished fact he told me how thoroughly contented he was. He had just signed a contract for a long term with the Vienna Opera and was beginning to do fine work. This last season all the performances were on a much higher level of excellence, due to his meticulous preparation of the operas. He prided himself on presenting a new *Aïda, Dalibor, Orpheus* and *Carmen*. He was proud, too, of a new Roumanian dramatic tenor he had discovered and had signed up for seven years. There is no doubt of his great capacity in the organization and arrangement of an opera season, as shown by the results obtained at Covent Garden, at the State Opera in Berlin, and at Salzburg, Vienna, and elsewhere.

In the recording room Bruno Walter impresses one with his practical and easy approach to his job. This belies somewhat the romantic emotion he puts into his conducting in his renderings of Mahler and Bruckner. He has said that he always tries to approach even the oldest and most hackneyed work as though it were a new composition being played for the first time.

The freedom of his relations with members of the Vienna Philharmonic met with its reward in the unstinted support they gave him, which undoubtedly was very largely due to the fact that it is his habit to treat the members of an orchestra as colleagues and not merely as workers. When coaching an orchestra, he deprecates any appearance of teaching symphonic musicians how to count the beats, knowing that this would not only bore them but would offend the artist in them. Such perfect recording as that of Mozart's D Minor Piano Concerto, in which Bruno Walter plays the solo piano part and also conducts, could hardly be obtained without this instinctive cooperation of all the executants. These records, by the way, gave Bruno Walter great satisfaction and are among his greatest treasures.

He is very definite as to the value of recorded music and says: "What would we not give for records of Mozart, Chopin, or Beethoven—even of Liszt or Brahms? We listen hungrily to verbal descriptions of their playing given to us by people alive today who only know from hearsay how they played. It must be confessed that 'canned music' tastes a little of the metal that preserves it. It is not fresh fruit but, even so, it is a great blessing, and the engineers have a great responsibility to make it more and more real, as has the company to see that the recording of the performance of great musical geniuses is not neglected."

It was one of Walter's regrets, he told me, that he never knew Bruckner personally. All his knowledge of that great composer was gained from Mahler, who was intimately acquainted with him. For many years Walter tried to get closer to Bruckner but was never successful in doing so and says that only in the last ten years has he understood him, and now—he could not live without him. Bruno Walter has great faith in the enduring qualities of the music of both Bruckner and Mahler, since, to use his own words, "It is music that goes to the depths of a man's soul."

One cannot forget his success in reestablishing the Covent Garden opera after the war. From 1924 to 1931, first of all under Harry Higgins and then under Colonel Eustace Blois, he assembled a dazzling company of artists. German opera reached its highest peak of popularity in London during this brilliant post-war period. It was at this time that Bruno Walter began his serious association with talking-machine companies. The few experiments with acoustic recording can hardly be reckoned as important.

Whilst on the subject of Bruno Walter's career, I must not omit to mention the eleven years, from 1925 to 1938, of the most glorious period at Salzburg, where nobody was so active as he in restoring Mozart-worship at that shrine of classical music.

And now the slate must be wiped clean and a new career commenced in America, but Bruno Walter is a man with the vitality and the courage for it. As in the Derby race, ability to stay the course is the determining factor in a conductor's career. The life is a

[157

strenuous one in which accumulated experience flowers in the later years, provided a conductor has retained his health and vitality. Toscanini's achievements in the last ten years demonstrate that, as do also the careers of Sir Henry Wood, Koussevitzky, Weingartner and Schalk.

When Schalk was over seventy, with his hair and beard completely white, he arrived in London a few months before his death and begged me to obtain for him an invitation as guest-conductor because London had not heard him since the war and his international prestige was suffering in consequence. There are comparatively few men who have the stamina to survive in the race when they have passed their half-century.

Sir Thomas Beecham has been in and out of the recording studios and has conducted and heard more records than any other conductor, alive or dead. His own recording programmes are prepared with scrupulous care, and in vetting and re-vetting his own titles for issue he is extra vigilant. Once, I recollect, he had passed the records of Wagner's "Faust Overture" when he chanced to hear another interpretation by a rival conductor. At once he withdrew his records and started to record the work all over again. And yet some people have the face to dub him an irresponsible dilettante. John McCormack once declared that he learned more about singing from listening to Caruso on the disc than he was ever taught by a *maestro*. Of Sir Thomas it may fairly be said that orchestral records were his University of Music. All his distinguished confrères follow the monthly issues of new titles like a hawk. With the assistance of the Columbia Graphophone Company, he was able to establish the London Philharmonic Orchestra and keep it going for its first ten years (1930-1940). It has become a great institution and was the instrument he used for his finest records.

I suppose he is one of the few successful conductors whose relations with his orchestra are free and easy. And yet he manages to get the best out of them. When he is in charge there is a noticeable absence of tension. He is systematically late for rehearsals, but if by any mischance he arrives on time he is greeted with a rousing cheer. He never misses an opportunity to interpose witty remarks which are always rewarded with a chorus of laughter from his men. He has rarely been known to praise his helpers although, or because, they are his willing slaves. His favorite victims are well-meaning provincial dignitaries, chairmen of music committees and suchlike, and Lord help anyone who gets into a scrap with him!

He will address you with a studied politeness that is sometimes disarming, particularly when you discover that a seemingly innocent remark conceals a barb. To attain his musical ends this subtle and sensitive man will go the limit, defying all conventions to achieve his ideals. His memory is prodigious. With the flick of an eyelash he will glance at a complicated score and, thank you, the photograph is taken. At the first rehearsal of a new opera I have seen him conduct from the score without a stop or pause. At the second and third rehearsals the score was there, but was scarcely consulted. After that the score was entirely abandoned. On the fourth morning Sir Thomas came to rehearsal with only a scrap of paper, a memorandum noting a change of beat in the third act which, so far, had baffled him. However, before the third act was reached the memorandum had long since disappeared! But the change of beat was not overlooked.

In a concerto he has discovered that the practice of conducting without a score may distress the soloist. That unfortunate contretemps which occurred when he was directing Cortot in a Beethoven Concerto has led him to abandon this habit. Half way through the finale something went wrong; there was a lapse of memory somewhere. Relating the incident, Beecham said both manoeuvred to recover position. Each tried all the concertos he knew, but they were unable to hit it off. "We started with the Beethoven, and I kept up with Cortot through the Grieg, Schumann, Bach, and Tschaikovsky, and then he hit on one I didn't know, so I stopped dead. After this we began the movement all over again." Actually, between them, they managed to "cover up."

How well I remember his Russian Opera Season at The Lyceum! As usual, Sir Thomas was conducting from memory, but half way through the first scene of *Prince Igor* he and the chorus became hopelessly entangled. There was nothing to do but stop and make a fresh start from the beginning. As we all know, Beecham was the man who put Delius on the map and kept him there. The music of Sibelius, too, greatly appeals to him. He conducted the Delius Festival during the twenties and, more recently, a Sibelius festival of six concerts, both including many unfamiliar choral and orchestral works, without a breakdown, never once consulting the score—an uncanny exhibition of his peculiar genius. With the possible exception of Sir Henry Wood, I suppose there is no one who has done more for British composers than this great little man. Certainly no conductor has done more to improve the standard of British orchestral playing.

Being introduced recently at a dinner party to a well known and successful New York publisher of jazz music, Sir Thomas was curious about America's young composers. The publisher told him, "Yes, we have quite a lot of bright young men. They can't write a note of music, but what does that matter? If they can't pick their tune out on the piano with one finger, they whistle it! Some other guy writes the tune as they whistle. We plug these tunes and make lots of money out of them."

"I wish I could whistle," said Sir Thomas.

It was at the première of *Hugh the Drover* by Vaughan Williams that Malcolm Sargent, that unacademic young Doctor of Music, was conducting grand opera for the first time. Staged by the British National Opera Company during their short season, in 1924 at His Majesty's Theatre, London, this racy folk opera was cheered to the echo. There must have been a dozen curtain calls. Malcolm certainly made a grand start. After the show Albert Coates buttonholed him in the greenroom and praised him without stint, hailing him as a born conductor with a natural beat. His previous experience in Gilbert and Sullivan had given him that confidence and showmanship which has never deserted him. However, I think he will be the first to own that he shines more brilliantly as a director of massed choruses. In fact it is as conductor of the Royal Choral Society that he has made a memorable name for himself with the British public.

His association with Artur Schnabel in the Courtauld-Sargent Concert Series was of many years standing and it was during this period that Malcolm learned how to handle his man. His quick wit often turned the tables on the pianist, but he was so tactful in his exchanges that he would often leave his opponent in doubt. At a recording session when they were collaborating in the Beethoven Third Concerto, Schnabel bewailed his fate in classical idiom. We always expected it and were seldom disappointed. On the "Get

Ready" signal he sighed and groaned, "I feel like Prometheus in chains." And then, wringing his hands, he exclaimed, "Oh, why do I make myself a slave and play down to this machine?" After more of this Sargent answered: "You do it for the same reason that I and the orchestra do it." "And what is that?" said Schnabel suspiciously. "*MONEY*," smiled Sargent.

In this chapter I have only touched on a few of the many eminent conductors whom I have recorded and with whom I have had a more personal contact. They all have in common great musicianship, an ideal of perfection, and a personal magnetism or power of command which extracts every ounce of sustained effort and cooperation that the players possess. The records they leave behind are the only documents that will remain to attest their strenuous lives. I am proud of my responsibility for these documents.

Opera Recording—

Home and Abroad

CHAPTER X

Opera Recording—Home and Abroad

Compared with other countries the recording of complete operas was an ambition easily attained in Italy where opera is the popular musical diet and the record-buying public eagerly supports the enterprise. The resultant sales are large enough to cover the heavy expense involved in such an undertaking. As long ago as 1903, I recorded in Milan *Pagliacci*, Leoncavallo himself conducting. At that early date this was no small achievement, but Leoncavallo was always hard pressed for money and could not afford to be standoffish. He was a great, good-natured hulk of a man and a lot of his money went in entertaining friends in his attractive villa on Lake Maggiore.

Mascagni, who followed a few years later as conductor of his *Cavalleria*, was not so accessible and had a better business manager who made more favorable bargains for him. He also had in tow many friends and henchmen. It is always easy in Italy to recruit an entertaining escort of followers, mostly artists and singers without engagements or else passé. They are usually a personable and amusing lot, and of course in the entourage will always be found relatives, unto the third generation, who make any successful musician their willing dupe. As one might expect, in negotiating a contract they all have something to say and have to be seriously reckoned with.

Both composers accepted under protest the compromises in the orchestra made necessary by the acoustic process. Mascagni recently completed an electric recording of *Cavalleria* in connection with a celebration throughout Italy to commemorate the fiftieth year of that opera's first performance in Rome. This was the third time the Gramophone Company alone has recorded the opera in its entirety.

The appointment of Carlo Sabajno as our house conductor led to a fine series of the most popular Italian operas being recorded complete. The casts were made up of young singers chosen with a fine discrimination of their eventual position in the opera world. In fact, many achieved star rank in later life, thus vindicating Sabajno's shrewd judgment. Among them were Pinza, the *basso-cantante*, later to become Toscanini's favorite for *Don Giovanni*, Pagliughi, who sang Gilda for us and is now one of the greatest coloraturas and acclaimed by Tetrazzini as her successor, Baccaloni, the buffo, whose Leporello and Doctor Bartolo made Glyndebourne rock with laughter for several years, the tenor Pertile, who for ten years during Toscanini's reign at La Scala between 1920-30 was to be his favourite protagonist for the great rôle of Nero in Boïto's opera of that name. At the height of his career, he sang Rhadames in the complete *Aïda* which was our first attempt at an all-star cast. The other artists were Dusolina Giannini (Aïda), Minghini Cattaneo (Amneris), Masini (the King), and Giovanni Inghilleri (Amonasro). This opera was electrically recorded and can be considered the highest achievement of the conductor, Carlo Sabajno. As a set, it still holds its own among big recorded works for fine singing and a high standard of results.

Maestro Sabajno was a man of varied gifts. Son of generations of Piedmont landed proprietors, he was a born cultivator. In matters pertaining to the soil, especially fruit and vine growing, he could work magic. Throughout the winter the cool cellar of his villa supplied the most luscious pears, apples, tangerines, and grapes. Moreover he had an innate knowledge of the ancient laws of proprietors' and peasants' rights. As a musician he turned out masses of manuscripts, few of which were ever published. In his early youth he was *maestro sustituto* (deputy conductor) for Toscanini while he directed the Turin Opera, and thereafter made him his hero and lifelong friend.

Later on he was content to devote himself completely to the gramophone, and was responsible for many fine records of artists and complete operas recorded in Italy which found their way all over the world. Like most young Italian conductors, he adopted the tactics of every now and again disciplining the orchestra when he thought they were becoming careless or did not take him seriously. Any excuse was valid to open up an offensive. In his home town the musicians would stand for this treatment but once he tried it in Barcelona, notorious as a hotbed of anarchy. There was let loose a sharp volley of recriminations that grew louder and louder. Skelson, our technician, with a dry sense of humor, opened the small window between the recording-room and the studio and held out an axe. The storm subsided, and finally the disputants burst into laughter that ended in a truce.

Throughout this period I was his collaborator and once we made a memorable trip to Russia together. Here he found himself out of his element. The musicians would not submit to his discipline and frequent outbursts of passion made our sessions the joke of St. Petersburg. He made a great pal of Chaliapin, however, who spoke excellent Italian, and they larked and joked like boys until one of the jokes was turned on Chaliapin who was notoriously touchy. He spied over Sabajno's shoulder while the conductor unsuspectingly sketched a comic caricature entitled *Boris on the Battlefield;* then the fur flew.

After serving the Company twenty-eight years, Carlo retired and received a bonus as called for by the Italian law, one month's salary for every year of employment. He had a keen intelligence and it was as well to know that in dealing with him every move had a motive. One of his business axioms was that every man could be reached through some woman.

In our business many tragicomedies result from the contact of the artistic with the prosaic business worlds. Many times our promising young managers have been swept off their feet by the glamor of a prima donna or a *café chantant* singer. In this connection I remember a young Scottish director bursting into my office carolling, "Congratulate me, Fred—I have just signed up Anita di Landra." "Who is she?" I asked. "She's that blonde cantatrice at the Olympia." "My God!" I replied. My pessimism was soon justified. Two months later this harridan was running our office, and the climax was reached when she saw the gradual cooling of his affections. She haunted the place every day, raising hell while the distracted man beat a hasty retreat through the back door followed by a volley of insults.

In another instance a suicide was barely averted. A brilliant young

director while negotiating a contract with the prima donna G——
fell deeply in love with her. She was a really fine singer and at the
same time a sensible and good-natured creature, who realized that
for the advancement of her career she needed stronger protection
than he could provide. In order to put a greater distance between
herself and her lover she accepted an engagement at the Khedivial
Opera in Cairo and disappeared. At this point, our mutual friend
Sabajno was to interrupt the drama. Tracking the young man as
far as Brindisi, the jumping-off place for Egypt, he found him in
black despair and ready to take his life. Later the youth became one
of the most successful men of Italy and she the wife of a Pasha.

There was a continuous friendly rivalry between Carlo and the
Italian managing director of the Gramophone Company in Milan.
One morning a bright but dowdy young woman presented a letter
of introduction to Sabajno from a well-known singing teacher of
Bologna. It asked him to do what he could to further the career of
this young pupil of his who showed promise. Sabajno gave her an
audition which showed him that her voice was merely promising,
just that and nothing more. He told her she must work and practice
and make a point of hearing great singers. She replied: "But, *maestro*,
how can I do that? I have no money." A bright idea then struck
Carlo. He gave her a letter of introduction to his friend and rival,
telling him she was poor and asking him to be so kind as to let her
hear the records of Tetrazzini, Melba, Patti, and so on and thus do
a good deed. The *signorina*, the following day, visited the imposing
offices of the Gramophone Company and was gallantly received by
the managing director who, upon reading the letter of introduction,
fell easily for the worthy scheme of furthering the young singer's
education. She must have been a quick worker because he married
her within a few weeks—not a bad catch for a dowerless girl in Italy.

My visits to Milan were generally for long periods so it was more
jolly to live in a pension than a hotel. I and my English friends usually
put up at Rieger's Pension in the Via Boccaccio. Another well-
known pension was Bonini's in the Piazza del Duomo. Bonini was a
huge woman, a former mezzo-soprano, and attracted many artists to
her home. There was a lot of roulette and the pace was too hot for
me, so I preferred the quieter Pension Rieger, run by a disillusioned
Munich baritone and his wife. It was an excellently managed place,

and because it was quiet appealed to the more ladylike sopranos and their ambitious mothers or their protective aunts. There were always young American or English girls and boys there, sent over to be coached in opera. These foreigners cast an exotic glamor over the romantic youths of Milan for whom the blonde Anglo-Saxon was the ideal of feminine beauty.

Besides these guests there were some great singers who loved the homeliness of Rieger's, amongst them Maria Galvany and Elvira de Hidalgo, both great Spanish coloraturas. Hidalgo was the greatest Rosina of our day and in that rôle alone amassed a fortune. She was too busily occupied in Spain, Russia, and South America ever to sing in London and she sang seldom in New York. Like most unmarried sopranos, she was chaperoned by her mother. There was also a large rosy-cheeked Canadian who seemed principally engaged in strolling in the Galleria dressed in bohemian garb and telling people what a great Otello he was. I discovered that an elderly American lady was supporting him and was continually urging him to seek an opera début. He had the biggest room in the pension at one end of which was installed a platform. On this he would strut, emitting high C's fiercely and frequently. But his protectress wanted results and threatened to withdraw her allowance. So he secured from a small impresario, by the payment of 15,000 lire, a chance to sing *Otello* in the provincial opera-house of Brescia. Half-way through the opera his voice wobbled and he sang so flat that the gallery whistled, hooted and threatened a riot. The *carabinieri*, always ready for disturbances of this kind, stopped the show and insisted that the understudy should finish the opera.

The Galleria is an institution of Milan life. The spacious glass-covered arcade shaped like a cross is lined with bright shops and cafés with tables and seats set out in the open air. Under its central dome is to be found the gossip-center of the city and the singer's market for the opera world. Here the reigning tenors with their escorts of friends show off and receive the congratulations of their admirers. Here one can engage a bass for Spain, a prima donna for South America or a claque to punctuate one's high notes at a La Scala début. The claque is still a necessity to an Italian singer and the strength and size of it are only limited by the artist's pocketbook. I do not frown at this institution like some purists, because I feel that for the

Italian artist it is a sheer necessity that spurs him to excel himself, and at the same time acts as a cue to the public who need leadership for applause at the appropriate places.

There is always in Italy the standing scandal of paid débuts of American singers. For the singer studying abroad an opera début before returning to the home town is the badge of achievement and a small impresario is always to be found ready to risk a *stagione* in one of the hundred small opera houses with a shoestring backing. A really promising young vocalist does not need this because in Italy there are always scouts on the alert for good operatic material to exploit. Most pathetic were a blind American singer and his wife. I shall never forget what an uninspiring affair was a recital of his which I attended out of pity.

There never was such a jolly pension as Rieger's, with none of those frowsy old fossils found in Bloomsbury boarding houses. The mixed Bavarian, Italian, and French cooking would have done credit to the Savoy Grill and the carafe of red chianti thrown in with the fixed lunch tasted to me in those days like the nectar of the gods. There is no Rieger now. Swept away by the war I heard that, in 1917, demonstrators threw the furniture and pianos from the windows and set fire to them.

At that time the doyen of the Italian music critics was Carugatti of the *Corriere della Sera*. One met him in the crush-room of La Scala and in the Galleria, regal in his untidiness, with long, matted hair and beard, sombrero, and shuffling walk—he was a character of Milan. He was just but often devastating in his criticisms, feared yet respected by all artists. His honesty was quite incomprehensible to most Italians, yet one glance at his threadbare apparel was convincing testimony of his incorruptibility. I once traced him to the den in which he lived, and the dozens of cats and parrots in complete possession accounted for that musty halo which always hovered over him.

The wish to record complete Mozart operas was the last to be realized. Traditions set up in various places, each claiming its authenticity, made it difficult to satisfy all factions. One might argue that the Salzburg Festival would fill the bill and I tried many times to come to some understanding with the direction, but there were too many interests involved ever to hope for a solution. The chief obstacle was that the stage and artists there were occupied all the time without a break.

When I read of John Christie's project to found a Mozart Festival theatre at Glyndebourne I thought it a pipe dream, but when I learned that Fritz Busch and Carl Ebert were to have full artistic control I decided it was a serious effort. Their standing and names were a guarantee that it would not be tarred with the brush of the amateur. Although Mozart needs adequate solo voices it also requires a fine chorus and orchestral ensemble to do it full justice. Certain London cliques thought they had a vested interest in grand opera and were ridiculing John Christie's scheme. They simply declined to believe in him. They did not know the man, his business acumen, his tenacity of purpose, and his altruistic idealism. I saw enough of his careful groundwork and personal attention to detail to convince me that his success would be beyond dispute. From the opening of his first season in 1934, the festival went on from strength to strength. It had as background an English landscape garden, which gave it unique grace and distinction. The atmosphere was as nearly Arcadian as can be imagined.

Christie was sagacious in delegating the artistic administration to two men of great talent, while giving his own undoubted genius for business free play. I suppose no opera house in the world has been planned and laid out with such economy of material and such perfect taste. It was a happy thought, too, to provide a restaurant that gave one really good food and vintage wine. Christie himself is a connoisseur of both. It was not long before it became a rendezvous for the great and grateful. Here one could see famous musicians taking a busman's holiday and sometimes this led to embarrassing situations.

Since the advent of the Nazi régime in 1932 bitter feuds had sprung up between rival conductors. Most people in the world of music knew that the two celebrated conductors, Toscanini and Furtwängler, were not on nodding terms. They also knew why Toscanini reluctantly refused to conduct the 1933 Bayreuth Festival. Five years later, Furtwängler was lunching with me in London and told me he was going down to Glyndebourne that night as the guest of Karl Ebert for a performance of Verdi's *Macbeth*. Now it so happened that Toscanini was also to be at the Glyndebourne performance of *Macbeth* as the guest of John Christie. "Do you think I ought to go up and shake hands with him?" asked Furtwängler. "Not unless you're dead sure he won't give you the cold shoulder," I replied. From Christie I afterwards heard that the situation promised to be awkward, but by placing Toscanini in charge of Maestro Erede, Glyndebourne's second conductor, and Furtwängler in the care of Ebert, with instructions to keep them apart, no meeting took place. So Furtwängler's naïve hope of a reconciliation never materialized, and to-day this looks further away than ever.

With enthusiasm I signed with Christie an agreement for the exclusive right of making discs. We did our recording with the mobile van at the end of the season, when the company were well soaked in their parts and their teamwork perfect. The acoustics of the theatre were specially pleasing and, during the five seasons, the complete operas of *Figaro, Cosi fan Tutte* and *Don Giovanni* were recorded. These are unique and would otherwise never have been available in record form.

Before her marriage, Mrs. John Christie, under her maiden name of Audrey Mildmay, was one of the principal coloratura sopranos in the Carl Rosa Opera Company. It has been an ideal partnership in every way. Audrey's Susanna was a perfect part for her and some of the important opera directors of Central Europe invited her to appear in it as a guest-artist. John had a great desire that she should have the *cachet* such an appearance would give her, but when in 1938 and 1939 the authorities at Salzburg pressed her to star at their famous festival, he sent a negative reply for political reasons. This was the opportunity both had wanted and it had to be turned down.

It rarely happens that the actual recording of a complete opera is altogether plain sailing. Even with the greatest care and foresight in planning, accidents will happen which necessitate speedy action. In July 1938 it was decided to record *Tosca*. Beniamino Gigli was chosen for the role of Cavaradossi. He was then appearing at the Terme di Caracalla in Rome in a festival of open-air opera on the site of the ancient Roman baths, which in the time of the Caesars were a great public rendezvous and one of the glories of the ancient imperial city. We resolved that to suit our convenience and that of Gigli it would be better, if possible, to carry out the recording at the Teatro Reale, the official opera house of Rome, where we hoped also to utilize the chorus and orchestra of the theatre.

OPERA RECORDING—HOME AND ABROAD

We considered that the importance of the project justified us in approaching the Mayor of Rome in order to obtain his official sanction for the use of the theatre and the engagement of the chorus and orchestra for our work. The Mayor very courteously gave his assent but imposed on us a time limit which had to be strictly adhered to.

We set to work, but the recording was barely half-completed when our soprano, Iva Pacetti, suddenly collapsed. The doctor attached to the theatre was hastily called in and prescribed three days' rest. This was a disaster for us, as it meant that the orchestra and the chorus, about 150 persons in all, would have to be kept waiting, and furthermore the time limit left us only three days to complete our task.

In this emergency Gigli was really magnificent. "Come on, Fred," he said to me, "we'll go around and see Maria Caniglia and ask her to help us." We quickly covered the short distance to her hotel and enquired of the porter. Yes, by good fortune, she was at home.

After a few minutes the soprano appeared. "Is the house on fire?" she asked. "I was just sleeping, dreaming of something pleasant."

"Well," said Gigli, "this is your dream. Gaisberg here is in trouble and wants you to help him out. We are in the middle of recording *Tosca* and Pacetti has collapsed. The orchestra and chorus are waiting, and I want you to come right now and sing the rôle."

"What, right now? I'm still half asleep and haven't sung it for months!" By that time we had her in a taxi, though, and before she could protest she was in front of the microphone. Exactly one hour from the collapse of Pacetti the recorders gave the signal to start the love duet from the first act.

Gigli showed his magnanimity, since owing to the change of sopranos he would have to remake a number of titles already sung with the other Tosca, and this when he was singing trying rôles at the open-air festival at the Terme di Caracalla. During that season he was at the height of his form, for in spite of the summer heat and the heavy calls on him he sang so easily and with such purity and volume as to amaze everyone. His vocal resources and stamina seemed inexhaustible. During the pauses in recording he would joke with the men and the *comprimari*, who exchanged stories with him. His good nature and patience communicated themselves to all and helped to

[173

ease the many awkward moments that inevitably occur during a recording session.

I marvel sometimes that we ever obtained a perfect master-record On one occasion we made ten attempts at one title in the first act of *Tosca* and then gave it up and tried again the following day, when ten more attempts were made before we obtained a master. No wonder our recorder, not to be outdone by Maestro de Fabritiis, who threw the score on the floor, smashed a wax and swore that no one gave him a chance to make a mistake. Yet eventually a perfect set of master-recordings was obtained. When we listened to them we forgot their cost and that at one point the maestro had let out a terrific yell and broken his baton, or that at another the soprano had forgotten her entrance, or that the solo 'cellist had played flat in the eleventh position of his obbligato.

Once, somewhere in that vast theatre, an artisan, perhaps a little tinsmith, was hammering merrily on the roof like the cobbler Hans Sachs interrupting Beckmesser's serenade. In the middle of the *Te Deum* he would suddenly begin. Precious moments were wasted and two hundred people suspended their animation until the little "Hans" could be tracked down and stopped. In the great Teatro Reale it was like finding a needle in a haystack.

Our Scarpia was the good-looking baritone Armando Borgioli, whose young wife was in close attendance on him and, as is usual with the long-suffering wives of artists, had to listen carefully to every tone he produced to advise and encourage him. There is no business where a wife plays so important a rôle. The job really takes two to run it properly—the singer to produce the sound and the listener to criticize. Such marriages are nearly always successful.

De Fabritiis was one of the many efficient conductors one so frequently meets nowadays in Italy. They are steeped in the operatic traditions and know by heart all the words, music, phrasing, and breathing-places, how Toscanini does it and how Mugnone did it in a hundred operas. As we worked away the other Reale conductors would look in on us. Serafin and Bellezza were perhaps a bit envious of their colleague. But in this instance I doubt if they would have had the energy and enterprise to secure for us the Mayor's consent to employ all the resources of the Reale Theatre, and what a difference that made!

OPERA RECORDING—HOME AND ABROAD

Caniglia, one of the busiest sopranos in Italy, was able to give us the two days required for *Tosca* by going by air instead of by train to Palermo where she was the prima donna of their open-air performances. She was accompanied by her venerable, white-haired father, a retired doctor. This sensible girl, now only thirty and piling up a nice little fortune, informed me that when the right man came along she would marry even if it meant the sacrifice of her career.

Gigli spoke at this time of the luck of Lawrence Tibbett, who made his début at the Metropolitan Opera House in New York as Ford in Verdi's *Falstaff*. Scotti, the great Italian baritone, played the title rôle and after their scene together the public applauded and called for Tibbett, but Scotti would not let him take a curtain call, and persisted in going out with him. The public, however, insisted on Tibbett's appearing alone. The applause was kept up for twenty minutes until in the end the older baritone had to give way. The next day the papers printed bold headlines: "Great American Baritone Makes Good." The cry was taken up all over America and placed Tibbett among the stars. His salary jumped from $150 to $1,500, and more, a night.

An early goal of all recording companies was the Gilbert and Sullivan operas long idolized in all English speaking countries. For years gramophonists were begging for complete recordings of *The Mikado, The Gondoliers, The Pirates of Penzance* and so on, but until agreement could be reached with the owners who jealously guarded their valuable copyrights, this could not be done with the original Sullivan orchestral parts.

In 1917, after lengthy negotiations through the valuable help of Landon Ronald, terms were arranged with Mr. Rupert D'Oyly Carte, the proprietor, and *The Mikado* made its appearance in our catalogue early in 1918.

The other operas followed one each year, until the entire series was completed. Since most Gilbert and Sullivan artists were selected for stage as well as vocal qualities, we had to assemble a troupe chosen solely for recording gifts. The result was a company of what I think was the cream of vocalists of that vintage. For beauty of voice, they have never been excelled. Some, like Edna Thornton and Robert Radford, were headliners in the opera and oratorio worlds. Others like Violet Essex and Derek Oldham became famous in musical comedy. Ernest Pike, Peter Dawson, George Baker in gramophone records and on the radio were pioneers of both industries. The sisters Bessie and Sarah Jones were lively Welsh girls with crystal clear soprano voices, which they used as effortlessly as birds. Three others were professional members of Westminster Abbey choir, Walter Glynne, Harold Wilde, and Edward Halland.

George Byng, who directed, was our house conductor, whom we took from the old Alhambra Theatre, where for many years he conducted and arranged those elaborate ballets for which that house was famous in the nineties. Dear old George Byng was steeped in Gilbert and Sullivan tradition, and was a serious, meticulous drill-master who rarely smiled. This did not prevent our high spirited company from exacting as a sideline every ounce of fun and frolic they could invent during the sessions. This exuberance of singers when gathered together is, I have noticed, characteristic of them. The photograph of our troupe taken in 1921 during a session of *The Pirates of Penzance* speaks for itself of the momentary suspension of mirth just to oblige the cameraman.

Over a long space of years, Gilbert and Sullivan records formed the bulwark of the gramophone catalogues and cheered the hearts of England's sons in India, Australia, and New Zealand, besides the home circle of the vast middle classes of the mother country, to whom every word and note was known by memory and for whom Gilbert and Sullivan were an institution on a par with the Church and the Houses of Parliament.

One of the first innovations to follow electric recording was a mobile van, with which we could realize the dream of recording actual performances. We used it with all the gusto of a new toy. The Royal Choral Society choir of 800 strong was recorded during a *Messiah* performance in the Albert Hall, *Gerontius* at Worcester Cathedral during a Three Choir Festival, and massed bands of 1,000 players at the Crystal Palace. The Covent Garden Opera, Staatsoper in Berlin, La Scala in Milan, and the Paris Opéra were all recorded later during actual performances. Many of these records were issued to the public and had a great success. For instance, the sale of the "Hallelujah Chorus" and "Lift Up Your Heads" afforded the Royal Choral Society a revenue for several years that made up the loss on many a concert.

Yet often apologies had to be tendered for coughs, sneezes and snorts from the conductor. In Toscanini's case, for instance, he always sings along with the 'cello part and grinds his teeth. In the actual performances of opera the prompter, spitting out the cues and singing the entrance notes for the singers, disturbed the enjoyment of these records. Once at the Three Choir performance of *Gerontius*, during a sudden silent pause after a *forte* climax, a lady's voice talking about "a lovely camisole for 11/6d" was clearly exposed when the record was played back, and so ruined a fine set.

Before any of this "on the spot" recording could be projected commercially, complicated negotiations had to be undertaken with each individual unit concerned—choir, orchestra, soloists, conductor, Dean of the Cathedral and even the sexton, and their signed permission obtained before recording could legally be undertaken.

At first the public bought these records because of their novelty, but afterwards the sales dropped off and the heavy costs made the venture unattractive for the gramophone companies. Today the principle of actual-performance records has been generally abandoned except in special instances of an historic nature. I remember a magnificent set of a performance of the Mozart Requiem lasting one-and-a-half hours with a star cast, perfect in every way except for the unpleasant splutters of the horns in an exposed passage in one record, which Bruno Walter refused to pass. The Military Tournament at Aldershot is one of the exceptions where recordings of actual performances have been a continued success.

At the first Music Festival at Queen's Hall, a fine recording conducted by Toscanini, of the Brahms Second Symphony, was ruined by so much coughing, an unmistakable sign of an influenza epidemic, that the records had to be destroyed.

The Temple Church Choir, thanks to the masterly training of Sir Walford Davies, came into great prominence, but it was their gramophone recording of "Hear My Prayer," one of the early commissions of the mobile van, that brought it international fame and caused the dusty old "church of the lawyers" to be so overwhelmed by visitors from the Dominions and the U.S.A. that tickets of admission had to be issued. The recording took place in 1926 at a special private session in the Temple Church. Thalben Ball was the choirmaster and organist, and Ernest Lough, then between 14 and 15,

[177

was the solo boy. A happy combination of chance helped to make this lovely record: the soft, acoustic resonance of the church, a boys' choir with a fine discipline, a choirmaster who was a first-rate trainer, and a gifted boy with a musical sensibility and a silver voice just then at its prime. A year later the moment would have passed, for the voice had changed.

The fame of record C–1329 spread like wildfire and in a few years close on one million copies were sold. The royalties payable to the Temple Church really embarrassed the lawyers, so unexpected was their sum total. After bonuses to each member of the choir there was sufficient left over for a fine holiday. With the balance they founded a scholarship.

This event did a lot of good generally as it set a high standard for boy singers and brought promising recruits to church choirs. Mothers and fathers positively besieged us with requests for auditions for their hopefuls. Youngsters from the playing-fields both of Mayfair and Whitechapel were urged to challenge young Lough. Rival companies hunted high and low to duplicate our success; even a duchess saw in her pale-faced son the chance of paying off her overdraft at the bank. Well, it only happened once and then because the moment was ripe.

Master Lough achieved momentary fame and glory. As an adult he developed an adequate baritone voice of which he made skilful use because of his training and musicianship, but how could that voice ever satisfy the expectations of the possessors of record C–1329? Here, as a former chorister, I can testify that there is no finer pastime for a boy than choir work. The music, training, discipline in deportment under a wise choirmaster, that keen competition to be chosen as soloist—all these advantages provide a firm foundation on which to construct an enjoyable career, be it musical or otherwise. A member of a good boys' choir will always turn out to be an appreciative adult, and if he has a voice can always be counted on to make the best of it.

Masters of

The Keyboard

CHAPTER XI

Masters of the Keyboard

PADEREWSKI, from the first, diffidently consented to record and never completely reconciled himself to the ordeal. He always doubted whether a machine could capture his art. Today, knowing better what Paderewski was and the limitations of the gramophone, I am inclined to agree with him. His art involved such broad and unrestrained dynamics—the faintest *pianissimo* crashing into a great mass of tone. In other words, he painted on a vast canvas, and the gramophone could only reproduce a miniature of his mighty masterwork.

In the realm of music Paderewski stood apart. There was nothing niggardly about his tips, which often amounted to a small fortune. From his entourage he demanded and received loyalty for which he rewarded them well. Among those who served him his generosity and thoughtfulness were bywords. You could always count on him to do the right thing by you. I remember the late Lionel Powell, the impresario, with tears in his eyes telling me an instance.

Powell's last venture before his death was a tour with Paderewski which resulted in a substantial loss, owing to the prevailing depression. After the last concert Paderewski, as was his custom, gave a supper to all concerned. After teasing the deeply dejected Powell, he forced him to declare his losses and then promptly wrote out and handed him a cheque for £4,000, the full deficit. This is one of the many similar examples I could cite.

Whenever he was in London, no matter how busy, he always

managed to give me an audience and usually invited me to lunch. This was no mean privilege. The invitees would generally include his great friend, Alfred Clark, as guest of honor, and there would also be Lionel Powell and L. G. Sharpe who, from his previous career as a mate in the old sailing ship days, had changed his occupation to that of Paderewski's London representative and concert agent. We three would have the great man to ourselves, and one was always certain that the food, wine, and service would be nonpareil. In the world of hotels and restaurants a protest from Paderewski would be a stain on the manager's escutcheon.

During the hot summer of 1936 he was occupied with making the film *Rhapsody*, travelling every day to Denham where he collaborated with Marie Tempest. They became great friends. That these two highly temperamental people managed to keep their self-control was surprising in the atmosphere in which they worked. I was deeply impressed by Paderewski's acting, or rather, ability to be himself, devoid of all artificial pose. In ten "shots" he alone of the entire cast was consistent throughout. And Paderewski was a personality. On completion of the filming, he came to our Abbey Road Studios to record the ten or more piano pieces introduced in the film.

In February of the next year I paid my last visit to his Swiss estate, "Riond Bosson," to play over the samples and arrange terms for their issue in record form. The household assembled at noon in the large hall to await his appearance. There was his sister, a lady of eighty, very alert and carrying her years well, his secretary and nephew Mr. Strakacz, with his wife, besides six or more friends from the neighborhood invited for luncheon and to hear the records. At one o'clock the Master descended the staircase smiling, and greeted each person present with a few apt enquiries about their health and activities. It resembled a small court. He then led the way to the dining room where, seated at the head of the table, he saw that everyone was cared for. Recalling that the day was Washington's Birthday, he courteously toasted America in my honor. The records I brought with me were heard in the music room later and proved a great success, as they were exceptionally fine and provided a fitting climax to a delightful occasion.

It was in the same room, in 1911, that I first recorded him. On the piano were large photographs of Queen Victoria and Queen Alexan-

Paderewski making his first gramophone records at his home, "Riond Bosson," in Switzerland in the year 1911. The author is shown listening.

dra, both autographed and with cordial dedications. There were also many portraits of other royalties and of the American President. Conspicuously absent were members of the house of Hohenzollern. Paderewski never gave concerts in Germany nor tarried long in that country. The salon was fragrant with the atmosphere of a past age and made one feel a bit sad. I missed the warm welcome of Madame Paderewski, who had not long since passed away and whose genius in entertaining rivalled that of her husband. Gone was the parrot which accompanied them on all their travels and whose elaborate cage always distinguished the Paderewski luggage. This was the bird that always hovered on his master's shoulders or perched on his foot while he practised, and seemed to enjoy the music. It was thoroughly spoiled, but they regarded it as a mascot and so tolerated its impertinences. I missed, too, the all-pervading presence of Paderewski's faithful Marcel, now dead, who accompanied him for forty years as valet and baggage man wherever he went. If one saw the thirty or forty pieces of luggage that the Paderewskis carried, one could realize the magnitude of Marcel's task. On the long and arduous tours in America, when a private car became their home for months on end, Marcel would be called upon to act as a fourth at bridge.

Once more I look back on the week I spent at "Riond Bosson" and that tall, vigorous man with the world at his feet. What an opportunity to study him at close quarters! A billiard table offered him relaxation from practising (as it did Mozart) and I knew him for a first-class player. Unlike most of his brother pianists, he avoided poker, the great American game, but for bridge he had a passion. He always kept two or three impoverished students at "Riond Bosson" living and studying with him free of cost. Some of these were plainly mediocre but he was too kind to turn them away. One such was a Brazilian lad who had been living there for some years and could make no progress. One morning I found consternation, approaching hysteria, reigning in the household. Ashamed of his own backwardness, the hypersensitive boy had thrown himself on the railway track in front of an approaching train. Luckily my recordings were just finished, so I packed up and took my leave, knowing it would be some days before calm could be sufficiently restored for me to continue my work.

I shall never forget the great revels held on Paderewski's Saint's Day, the Feast of St. Ignatius, when, in addition to his neighbors, friends assembled from all over Europe to join in the celebrations. The grounds were hung with festoons and flags. There was great feasting and music, and in the evening we had fireworks. These fêtes were carried out in a truly regal way, as befitted his wealth and position. At that time Paderewski owned a large estate in Poland where he kept the finest herds of prize cattle in the country. He was sole proprietor of the only first-class hotel in Warsaw. In his fight for Polish freedom he dissipated the greater part of his fortune, a sacrifice that has not received the sustained recognition which his conduct merited. But still he remains one of Poland's greatest figures.

Of the greatness of Paderewski and Chaliapin neither gramophone nor film can give anything but a faint suggestion. It is only when I hear a record of either that I realize the futility of trying to reflect their genius by mechanical means. It is notorious that, apart from Ernest Schelling, the finely cultured American pianist and conductor, Paderewski had few intimates among professional musicians. I doubt if he could have found their company sympathetic. Certainly he moved in a sphere quite unattainable by them, which naturally made them envious. He was too great for them.

Recognizing him for his prowess as a master pianist, one is prone to forget that Paderewski was a gifted composer. His light and graceful "Minuet" shows no signs of diminishing popularity. A versatile genius of catholic tastes, he even wrote an opera, *Manru*, with a Polish setting. This reminds me that I once asked him which, in his opinion, was the greatest opera of all time. His answer was typical of the man: "Suppose there were a huge conflagration and only one operatic score could be saved, and that the last copy in existence, without doubt it should be *Die Meistersinger*."

In fulfillment of a promise to complete some titles begun in the previous year, Paderewski paid his last visit to our studios on November 16, 1938, arriving punctually at four despite a thick fog. He played seven sides, his titles including "Moment Musical No. 2" (Schubert), his own "Chant Voyageur" and a Chopin Mazurka, Nocturne, and Valse. I thought he was beginning to show his seventy-eight years. As I helped him up the steps he remarked that his sister was over eighty and in more robust health, though two years his senior. I noticed occasional lapses of memory, yet now and again there was a glimpse of that magnetic charm and thoughtfulness, as when he grasped my hand on his arrival and in tones of deepest sincerity said, "Mr. Gaisberg, how are you and how is your dear sister?"

In his playing I found a lack of virility. To help compensate there were fine flashes of poetry, and in the cadenzas he showed all his old-time bravura. For his last concert tour in England in the autumn of 1937, he visited some of the provincial cities and everywhere he had a good "house" and a wonderful reception. No London concert was given and I have often wondered why.

In direct contrast to Paderewski is that illustrious Russian, Serge Rachmaninoff, who builds around his family life a wall that few have been able to penetrate. He shuns society and public functions; he speaks rarely and then with slow deliberation in deep chest notes, but he is ever eager to spot a joke which sends him into a laugh that shakes his whole frame. But where does he get that ability to adjust his affairs, in this world of shifting political and economic values, with a skill that has made him one of the richest artists of our day? From the first days of his arrival in 1917 in New York, already famous through his ubiquitous "Prelude," he began recording for our associates, the Victor Company, and has continued with them ever since. The fact that he and I, with Caruso, Titta Ruffo, Maxim Gorky and Chaliapin, were all born in the same year has helped to endear him to me.

He is proud of his Tartar blood which gives him his dry wit and aloofness. I have often had the rare privilege of sitting with him and watching him take from his case a cigarette, carefully dividing it into three parts and leisurely smoking one after the other through a holder as he recalled his early days in Russia and told stories about his giant friend, Feodor Chaliapin, an endless source of amusement to him.

Once my friend relaxed and attended a semi-public function. In London he actually consented to oblige his good comrade, Benno Moiseiwitsch, by accepting a special invitation from the Savage Club and turning up for a Saturday evening supper in his honor. That night the Savages did themselves proud, providing a tip-top entertainment. Everyone expected him to join in the spirit and play a few pieces in return for their hospitality. After supper George Baker, the Secretary, rose to propose Rachmaninoff as an honorary member. This was seconded amidst deafening applause. There was a dead silence as Rachmaninoff slowly lifted his long body out of his chair and, with barely a trace of a smile, said in his hollow voice just five words, "Fellow-Savages, I thank you," and then sat down again. Not one note did he play the whole evening.

In the case of Rachmaninoff, the podium's loss became the keyboard's gain. In 1908, he was appointed second conductor at the Bolshoi Opera House in Moscow at a salary of £600 per annum. He conducted at the opening night for the first subscription, the opera being *Pique Dame*. After the second act he received an ovation that lasted several minutes, during which the manager rushed up and shook him warmly by the hand, congratulating him on his success. Rachmaninoff drily replied, "Now you will have to raise my salary: if the first subscribers, who are the most discerning audience in the world, receive me so warmly I ought to receive an increase." This remark might have been made in fun but for the fact that it was Rachmaninoff who made it. Shortly after, the manager sought him out and showed him a contract, renewing his engagement for a further two years. "Of course it includes the increase?" asked the conductor.

"Why, certainly," said the manager.

"Well, what's the salary?"

"Twenty thousand roubles a year." Even Rachmaninoff was taken aback and answered that it deserved serious consideration. It was a high figure for a youngster—$10,000. However, he took the long view and to everyone's surprise rejected the offer on the plea that he had made up his mind to concentrate on composition and solo piano playing. It was a courageous decision and I feel sure he has had no cause to regret it. As a pianist he has a large and enthusiastic following, and if they do ask for the "Prelude" the responsibility is his for having perpetrated it. In 1917, when he migrated to America, he had to recoup his losses. He did more than this, for through his piano recitals he converted them into colossal gains. Later on, the Boston Symphony and many other orchestras tried to induce him to become their conductor, but he always refused on the plea that it was impossible to combine solo work with conducting.

Soon after the introduction of the electrical process, he produced a magnificent set of records of his Second Concerto, with Leopold Stokowski and the Philadelphia Orchestra. They found their way into the homes and hearts of thousands of gramophone-lovers to whom the "Prelude" alone was familiar. This started them on bigger and better music. After a long stagnant period, when he could not be tempted to preserve his own work in disc form notwithstanding attractive offers, he has resumed recording and there have recently been issued records of his other two concertos interpreted *par excellence* by the Master himself. Like most, if not all great executants who write music, he has a soft spot for his own compositions. One Sunday evening in March 1937, I spent a few moments with him and Madame Rachmaninoff, discussing a proposal to record his new Third Symphony which, the previous November, was first performed in public by the Philadelphia Orchestra under Stokowski's bâton. He felt so touchy over its cool reception that he even offered to pay for rehearsals for recording it.

In appraising him one must not overlook the great part played by his wife. Over long periods he has been a sufferer from neuralgia. Her care and attention and her soothing company are just the sedative he requires. The Rachmaninoffs have two daughters and are one of the happiest and most devoted families I have ever met.

Ever since 1908 Wilhelm Backhaus has been one of the solid pillars of recorded music. He was still in his 'teens when he began and is a case of your child-prodigy withheld from the public to the benefit of his later career. One of the most prevalent derangements, brought about by post-war conditions and the unholy mess and tangle of international relations, affected the income-tax claims made by various countries where celebrity records were sold. Every artist arriving in London sought me out to advise and help him. Some, allowing the claims to run on, decided to give England a miss. However, when he did come over after the war, Wilhelm Backhaus, like Kubelik, Chaliapin and others, was agreeably surprised to find a nice little accumulation of royalties amounting to several thousand pounds. But, unlike them, he was rated an enemy alien and had to present his claim to the German courts. Made during the inflation period of the German Mark, his £5,000, reduced to shillings, was only enough to buy a box of cigars.

Nevertheless, he had built up a goodwill in concert and gramophone circles that quickly brought him rewards. By great good luck he made a bestseller in the 12" record of the "Naila Valse" by Délibes, later coupled with the Liszt "Liebestraum," in the early days of the first decade. From time to time they were re-recorded and finally by the electrical process in their present form. So persistent have been the sales of these two titles that their total sales amount to a quarter of a million records. But then Backhaus is a great pianist and musician with few equals among his contemporaries. There was a large quantity of fine piano music by Brahms which, but for him, would have remained unrecorded. Brahms' writing for the piano needs prodigious dexterity to produce a clear, clean performance. For the average virtuoso its preparation would require too much effort for mere recording. To Backhaus' eternal credit he stopped at nothing to make that rich programme of Brahms an outstanding achievement.

Arthur Rubinstein was born in a musical household at Lodz, Poland, in 1887. At the age of four he revealed a devotion to music that astonished his family. So much so that his sister, who was going to Berlin to be married, took him along with her in order to bring him to the notice of the great Joachim. The Master put the child through some searching tests. For instance, he would hum a melody and the infant would play it immediately afterwards on the piano, transpose it into any key asked for, and even improvise on it. The boy also played him some Haydn and Mozart sonatas. He says it is on record that when he was only two and a half years old, while his sister was having a piano lesson the teacher played some false notes. The child immediately pulled at the lady's skirts and made a face, indicating his displeasure.

His father wanted him to be a violinist, but the temperamental child was set on learning the piano and broke three fiddles before he was given his way. Later, as we shall see, he broke some records in quite another sense. The result of Arthur's visit to Berlin was that three sponsors guaranteed his musical training for seven years: Joachim, the Mendelssohn family, and Herr Wachover, a Berlin banker. After his sixteenth year he gave up all masters, Barth, Joachim, and the rest, and taught himself.

Rubinstein insists that the Mazurkas more than any of Chopin's other music express the Polish nationality. His own love for them dates from his boyhood, when he soaked into his system the village life, as portrayed by the dances at weddings and harvest festivals. In recording these dances, he would often get up and illustrate the steps of various types of mazurka, all in different tempi. Outstanding was his interpretation of Nijinsky in the famous C–Major. This melody could fairly be called Nijinsky's theme-song. Just a few bars conjured up the graceful and poetic figure of that unfortunate genius.

It was not until 1912 that the young Rubinstein first came to London where he created a sensation through his superb teamwork with Casals in a sonata recital at Queen's Hall, their programme being drawn from Brahms, Grieg, and Beethoven. Later that season he collaborated in another sonata recital, this time with Jacques Thibaud, the famous French violinist. As one might expect, he is widely travelled, having toured Soviet Russia on many occasions. There he often received payment in kind and his trophies include rare snuffboxes, beautiful and costly fur coats and fine miniatures. In practically every country in South America he has made a phenomenal success. Nothing can keep him down. During his last tour there he crossed the Andes nine times, each time flying at 15,000 feet.

At first Rubinstein more or less neglected England where, except for a few socialites who faithfully patronized his Wigmore Hall recitals, he had no real following in the popular sense. However, since 1938 he has made amends and, thanks to his large and interesting repertory of gramophone records, he is now a big draw. Perhaps of all his titles the Scherzi, Nocturnes, Polonaises and last, but not least, the Mazurkas of Chopin are chiefly responsible for his popularity in British and American concert-halls. In 1938, his extended tour of the United States created a furor and must have added thousands of dollars to his growing income.

Just prior to the outbreak of the present war, Rubinstein settled in Paris, hoping to make his permanent residence there. So popular had he become that a concert announced by him at the Salle Pleyel, holding 3,000 people, would always attract a capacity audience.

And now I come to a feat of his which must surely have broken all records. During December 1938 he recorded in our studios the 52 Chopin Mazurkas complete. When we first approached him he was none too enthusiastic. Although he had always played many of the most popular ones, he was not intimately acquainted with the bulk of the series and was inclined to think that, recorded as a whole, they would prove monotonous. However, he got to work and soon found that in every one there was some beauty hitherto unrealized. In the flush of his enthusiasm, Rubinstein wrote to the Gramophone Company:

"I have always considered that the Mazurkas are the most original, if not the most beautiful, of Chopin's works. In the days of Russian dominance we were not allowed to read Polish history or study Polish art, and we found our outlet for our emotions in Chopin.

I was therefore particularly happy when my dear friend, Fred Gaisberg, asked me to act as perpetuator of this most beautiful work.

It is very difficult to get into the mood of 52 different Mazurkas, and I viewed the job with apprehension, thinking it would be difficult to cast myself into just the right expression of so many works, every one of which has a distinct characteristic. To my great joy I found that both Mr. Gaisberg and myself became more and more enthusiastic with every new Mazurka. I only hope that in the few notes of the gramophone record, the listeners will hear at least some of the love I have felt whilst recording this work.

I do not know if I have succeeded in what I tried to do, but I hope that my records of these Mazurkas will help to convey to the vast audience of the gramophone, all the world over, a little of what Chopin's music means to the Poles."

No doubt because of their strong regional characteristics, Rubinstein has made a special study of Spanish and Catalonian music. He was for many years on intimate terms with those great composers Albéniz and de Falla, and also with Arbós, the conductor of the Madrid Philharmonic Orchestra.

Musicians, like men of letters, are keenly sensitive to political injustice. Some notoriety was given to the stand Rubinstein took against certain anti-Semitic measures passed by the Italian Government in the spring of 1938. It was then that he wrote a personal letter to Mussolini returning his decorations. He told me that when the latest of these decrees was promulgated he happened to be in the South of France, and went straight to a telegraph office where he wrote out a strongly worded telegram to the Duce. When asked to send it, the clerk was panicstricken and begged the pianist to wait. Meantime he would consult his superior officer, and in a couple of hours would be able to obtain a ruling as to whether such a message

Arthur Rubinstein exchanging anecdotes with Jascha Heifetz during a luncheon interval at the Abbey Road Studios. From a photograph by the author.

could be transmitted to a foreign country. Three hours later, Rubinstein returned and was told it had been passed for dispatch. As he left the office, after paying the fee, newsboys were already running down the street with an extra featuring the story. Although it was the French who had double-crossed him by their unauthorized disclosure of a private message prior to its actual dispatch, this only made him angrier than ever with the Italians.

I first met Arthur Rubinstein in 1913 when, as a Gay Lothario of 28, he visited Chaliapin in his Jermyn Street flat. I was struck by his precocity and satiric wit. He seemed a young edition of my good friend, Landon Ronald, whom he greatly resembled. He was to become a pet in court circles at Rome and Madrid, where he received many decorations, and was altogether too much of a playboy to bother about recording. Indeed, it was only after his marriage that he buckled down seriously to work. Once started, his capacity for study and work of the highest order knew no bounds.

In July 1933, in London, he married the daughter of the conductor, Emil Mlynarski. She soon presented him with a little girl. To the amazement of his friends, this confirmed bachelor, who must have been nearly forty when he married, became the idolizing father. He must have wasted many precious practice hours dandling the child on his lap. He even brought her to our studio, where she would sit on his knee and pound the piano, his eyes meanwhile popping out of his head with admiration. On one occasion we took a photograph of this performance.

Arthur Rubinstein, so brilliant himself, has little regard for his fellow pianists. An exception is Horowitz, whose gradations of tone and perfect scale-passages are a source of continual wonderment to him. Rubinstein asserts that D'Albert had exquisite scale-runs and tonal perfection, whereas Busoni had both the poetry and technical equipment in an equal degree. It is noteworthy how universally Busoni was appreciated by his fellow pianists. To my lasting regret I lost him to a rival recording-company, and unfortunately for history, the masters of the titles he made have been destroyed. Credit for his own training Rubinstein gives to one man only, Heinrich Barth of the Berlin Academy, to whom he went as a boy of eight. Strangely enough, although he trained in Germany, Rubinstein has played there seldom. The Germans, he maintains in the face of their opposition, are not a musical people. They accept the heavy, pedantic music of Pfitzner, Reger, and Bruckner with their long-winded "development," just as they enjoy a stodgy meal of sauerkraut and sausages. The French he praises for their quick appreciation of the modern school, and he sees in their rejection of Brahms an intuitive discovery of his artificial structure. The English he calls a musical nation who lack self-confidence in spite of their Elgars, Waltons, and Baxs.

When Vladimir de Pachmann came to us to record all seriousness was laid aside and we settled down to an hour's variety show. I would like to know how those old fellows continue to put up with the fatigue of giving recitals. Moritz Rosenthal at the age of 77, Emil Sauer at 80, and Lamond at 78 were still active. At 85 Pachmann departed this life. There was one pianist, Planté, who was close on 100 when he gave his last recital in France. There is no denying that pianists go on long past their prime and live on the glamor of their previous reputations. Most of them have to use a special shallow depth piano and only give a shadow of their quondam masterful performances.

During his regular visits to London over the last thirty-five years of his career, Pachmann collected a loyal coterie of ladies who attended all his concerts and sat as near his piano as he would permit. Some of them were genuine survivors from the Victorian Age. When the concert was over these elderly adherents stormed the platform and even invaded the artist's dressing-room. I suspect that more than one of them imagined that he cherished a secret regard for them.

Pachmann was a great *raconteur*, but I feel quite sure that many of his best stories were of purely imaginary incidents. One such must have been that about a Chopin Recital he gave at the Beethovensaal in Berlin to the usual crowded audience. When he walked on the platform he paused, pulled a pair of woollen socks out of his pocket, and reverently laid them on the top of the piano. His admirers gathered round him after the concert and asked for an explanation of this strange ceremony. Pachmann solemnly replied that the socks had belonged to Chopin and that to have them in front of him gave inspiration to his playing. Of course there was a scramble by the audience to see and touch these sacred relics. "Ha, ha!" laughed the old man, as he told me the story. "They were my own socks."

It was always a problem to get him to Hayes, our old recording studios, for he objected to motor cars—a well founded aversion since travelling in one invariably made him seasick. This aversion dated from a motor accident he sustained in America a few years ago. One rainy evening, after a recital in Cincinnati, a car was carrying him and his secretary to a supper party to be given in his honor, when it overturned. As the little pianist was extricated from the wreckage more dead than alive, he is said to have remarked pettishly: "Now we shall be late for supper and they will have eaten all the food."

On his last visit he complained bitterly of feeling ill during the short half-hour run in a luxurious and well-sprung Daimler. Of all artists Pachmann had the greatest need of an audience to inspire him. Realizing this, when we got to Hayes we marshalled into the studio a score of our prettiest typists, who were thrilled with this unexpected treat. They created the right atmosphere and Pachmann played superbly. He was even allowed to make his little asides on certain passages which he can never play without some comment on their beauty and significance. There was one dramatic nocturne (B—major, Op. 32 No. 1) in which he described as an episode in Chopin's early life when, as a boy, in a cabin in the snowclad forests of Poland, he heard the howling of the wolves at the door and was terror-stricken. This, no doubt, was all Pachmann's imagination, but most descriptive of the piece in question. When his efforts were played back to him from the record he was so delighted that he clapped his hands in praise of his own performance.

After the session was over he invited me to dinner at his hotel. While we were waiting he gave me a lavish recital, carefully explaining the secret of his rippling scales, which were the envy of every pianist and the like of which may never be heard again. He had invented a mythical godmother whom he called "Madame Kapushkin." Any difficult question was referred to her and from her he sought advice on all his knotty problems. At the dinner table there was always a place reserved for her and the evening was begun by ceremoniously drinking her health. Pachmann, abstemious in all his other habits, loved Havana cigars. After dinner he would lounge in an easy chair, smoking one after another and recalling tale after tale of his extraordinary career.

Pachmann was the "Peter Pan of the Piano," and that satirical wit, Godowsky, had many stories about him. Four celebrities: Godowsky, Arbós, Kreisler, and Pachmann met in New York at a luncheon which developed into a Festival of Self-Praise. Warmed with good-fellowship and wine, the little rogue began: "Well, friends, there are four great musical geniuses, myself, Godowsky,"— he paused while his friends waited to hear the conclusion of the whole matter—"and Bach and Beethoven."

Another profound musician to whom I have contentedly listened for hours on end, while he was building up that fine series of records of Bach's 48 Preludes and Fugues, was Edwin Fischer. Naive and simple, a big, blue-eyed, tousle-headed baby of a man, the type that seems to cry out for a mother's care, at four years of age he could play Mozart and Haydn sonatas. However, his general education being then of paramount importance, he postponed all study of the piano until after he had finished high school at sixteen. Then he returned to it in earnest, making his début at the age of twenty-one. His chief hobbies are oil-painting, at which he is an adept, and his chamber orchestra with which he regularly gave concerts in Switzerland, Paris, Brussels, and all over Germany and Italy. They were greatly esteemed for the choice of their programmes and received fine support from the public. They have also made many celebrity records of outstanding merit. Of these I could single out for special mention some of the Mozart concerti which he played and conducted from the piano. As a pianist, Fischer is exact and even meticulous, and for his tone-color unexcelled.

Envy and dismay filled every violinist who went to hear the seventeen-year-old Heifetz when he arrived fresh from St. Petersburg for his first recital in New York. Pianists were similarly affected when the young Russian piano virtuoso Vladimir Horowitz made his London début at the Aeolian Hall ten years later. Both Heifetz and Horowitz had an uncanny technique that left one dumbfounded. Though apparently Heifetz never suffered from nerves, the intensive concentration seemed to leave Horowitz all on edge. Both were alike in their schoolboy exuberance the moment their work was over.

I was present at Horowitz's debut and immediately laid plans with my old friend Harold Holt to secure this amazing young man before others could snap him up. It was a wise move, as he leaped into fame so rapidly that he was soon overwhelmed with engagements, and to extract records from him was always a tough proposition. And then intervened a period of several years of almost complete retirement following his marriage to Toscanini's daughter, Wanda.

At this time I met Horowitz's father, an electrical engineer of sixty-four from Moscow. He sprung a surprise on his son Vladimir and his famous father-in-law by arriving in Paris on his honeymoon with his young bride. In an interesting talk he told me he was a power engineer and held an important post under the Soviet Government, which had given him four months' leave for a holiday with his young wife, Sonia. He had attended a recital at Queen's Hall and was deeply impressed with his boy's triumph. It was ten years since he had last seen the lad, who was only twenty when he left Russia and had not been back all that time. As I am always curious to learn all I can about the background of my artists, I encouraged him to talk about Vladimir.

The pianist's mother was his first teacher. Later he studied with the celebrated Blumenfeld, a pupil of the one and only Anton Rubinstein. Horowitz's father played the 'cello and his eldest brother taught the violin at the Moscow Conservatory, while a younger sister of Vladimir was then giving piano recitals throughout Russia. Hence young Vladimir was brought up in the appropriate surroundings. He can trace his musical lineage even farther back, for his great-grandmother actually had the honor of giving Anton Rubinstein piano lessons. (I treasure a photograph he gave me of teacher and pupil taken together.) The Horowitz home in Moscow was a great music center where family and friends would assemble to play chamber music and pianoforte duets. Vladimir's father was for a time attached to a power station at Kieff, and it was in that city the pianist was born. When he was only ten he played the Tschaikovsky Piano Concerto with Arthur Nikisch in Berlin. During his ten years' absence from Russia his father's sole consolation was found in the gramophone records I was able to send him

[195

to Moscow. On the arrival of each consignment, they were eagerly unpacked, tried over, and pronounced unique.

Memorable was the début that Brailowsky made as an H. M. V. artist at our Abbey Road Studios. His achievement as a recorder is unique in that, among the thirty-odd sides which he made, not one had to be repeated because of a smudged or false note on the part of the player. We all agreed that never had we seen such uncanny exactness and security of technique. Our curiosity was aroused as to how he attained this perfection—and satisfied when he told us that his teacher was Leschetizky. He boasts of being the last pupil of that great Polish professor, long resident in Vienna, who leaped into fame through the success of his first pupil, Paderewski.

While Brailowsky was talking to me, I reminded him that Paderewski had played on the studio piano just a month before, at the close of a short English tour, when he came to us to record a Chopin Nocturne and Valse. When asked whether he had given concerts in Russia, Brailowsky explained that although his father was a Cossack and his mother a Muscovite, he had never played in that country. He went to Vienna to study two years before the first World War and never returned to his native land. His visits to England entailed a great sacrifice because he had to dispense with the customary companionship of his pet dogs, who travel with him to every country but England, where strict quarantine regulations are in force.

His greatest achievement, and one of which he is modestly proud, is that series of six concerts which he has now given in three or four capitals of the world, with programmes embracing the entire 170 works of Chopin. One can only marvel at his memory, but Brailowsky explains that he forgets to remember and thereby his memory rarely fails him.

Which reminds me of the historic jest of Hans von Bülow which, let me say, has no personal application whatever to Brailowsky. Said a companion at a colleague's recital: "Did you hear X improvising what he could not remember?" "Yes," said von Bülow, "it wasn't as bad as what he *did* remember."

One of the wisest and most remarkable artistic enterprises of the thirties was the engagement of Artur Schnabel in England as the executant of Beethoven's piano works complete. When in 1930

Malcolm Sargent, on Bruno Walter's recommendation, placed him under contract for the famous Courtauld-Sargent concerts outside of Germany he was only known as a professor at the Berlin Hochschule. His success in London was immediate, and gradually he collected a big following of enthusiasts who regarded him as the greatest living exponent of Beethoven. I was agreeably surprised at the serious-minded crowds that filled Queen's Hall to capacity and would follow his playing with weighty tomes of the sonatas propped on their knees.

It was given out that Schnabel would never stoop to recording, as he considered it impossible for a mere machine to reproduce the dynamics of his playing faithfully. Therefore when I interviewed him he was coy but, all the same, prepared to put his theory to the test though he would need a lot of convincing. At long last I was able to overcome all his prejudices. Tempted by a nice fat guarantee he eventually agreed that it was possible to reconcile his ideals with machinery.

I can still see the dubious looks on the faces of our directors when I joyfully told them that we would get him, on the sole condition that we must record all the Piano Sonatas and the five Concertos of Beethoven complete.

His recording of the Brahms First Piano Concerto gave us a very severe problem to tackle later on. The work is really heroic and made great demands on our technical staff. Georg Széll was the conductor engaged, and he made a special trip from Glasgow, where he was the permanent conductor of the Scottish Orchestra, to direct. The collaboration of these two great musicians was ideal, as the records will prove.

Schnabel is both a trial and a joy to his recorders. He strews their path with obstacles, but in the process rewards them with many refreshing stories. I think Mr. Purser, in charge of technical recording for the Abbey Road studios, described Schnabel and his conduct in the recording room to perfection when, at the Gramophone Convention at Hoddesdon, he recounted a typical Schnabel session. He said the day was fixed for him to record a piano concerto with orchestra in our large studio. After a good deal of thought and experiment, the engineers had arranged the piano and the position of the orchestral players as their experience dictated. With the men assembled and their conductor waiting on the rostrum, Schnabel arrived, and slowly and deliberately planted himself in the middle of the room, observed in silence by us all. He stood his ground firmly for some moments, and then to our dismay announced: "I play *here*."

I supervised every one of our twenty sessions per annum during the next ten years, and rate the experience of hearing his performances and listening to his inevitable impromptu lectures as a most liberal allowance of instruction combined with entertainment. His records are proof positive that his study of the Beethoven Sonatas was truly profound. However, during the intervals, he would furnish light relief by regaling me with a constant flow of opinions on every conceivable subject in a spate of witty stories. On conductors he had a good deal to say, both pertinent and the reverse. With Artur Nikisch he exchanged no conversation although he knew him well. According to him, Nikisch was a *bon vivant* and liked having a good time. Cards were his chief weakness. Conducting was his job, but all work and no play would have made this Artur a dull boy. Like Richard Strauss, Nikisch was essentially human, as human as Tonio claims the players in *Pagliacci* to be. He never overworked himself or his orchestra. Schnabel placed Karl Muck among the greatest conductors of that period. Some conductors he thought too easygoing, and he complained that their men rarely troubled to criticize them. Furtwängler he admitted to be another of the finest living conductors. Having many interests outside his profession, Schnabel felt he was well worth listening to, especially as he possessed a great intellectual curiosity. In this respect Furtwängler differed from Toscanini and Koussevitzky, both of whom were completely wrapped up in their art.

Schnabel also used to declare that since conductors had entered the film world they had been aping the prima donna and waving their hands like any nautch girl. But why shouldn't they? After all, cinema audiences expect an "acting" conductor to be a bit of a showman. He told amusingly of a visit he paid to a famous conductor after a fine rendering of a Mahler Symphony. They were great friends and, as a leg-pull, Schnabel told him he should go on the films. The conductor looked round suspiciously, not sure whether to take this as a compliment or a joke. (This was at the time when most star conductors were expecting to be summoned to Hollywood at any moment.) And then Paul Althouse, the tenor, chipped in with "How about his hands?" As in a dream, the great man stretched out his arms like a fan-dancer and regarding them intently, murmured: "Mine are better than Stokowski's."

'These great celebrities are none too charitable towards each other, but once Schnabel may have surprised even himself when, in one of his rare moods, he called Emil Sauer "A cavalier." Over Moritz Rosenthal he was less gracious. Discussing the rivalry between these two pianists, he expressed grave doubts as to whether Rosenthal could eclipse Sauer's domestic record. At 75 he married one of his pupils, a young Mexican girl who had been studying with Brailowsky in New York. When her teacher had to suspend lessons because of a recital tour, Brailowsky passed her on to Sauer in Vienna, as both teachers followed the same method. Sauer fell in love with her, married her, and became the proud father of a child.

Schnabel disapproves of all prodigies and calls them "Five-legged artists," just like those five-legged cows seen on exhibition in a circus. When they mature, he says, they generally lose one leg and cease to draw the crowds.

Like Toscanini, Schnabel is blessed with a prodigious memory. In his current repertoire he generally has at his fingertips when he starts out on his winter concert tour all the 32 Beethoven Sonatas and the 5 Concertos, besides 6 other concertos, the Diabelli Variations, most of the Schubert, Mozart, and Brahms sonatas as well as some 30 miscellaneous pieces. A few years ago Koussevitzky decided to give a historic survey of the great piano concertos, during an eight-week season, consisting of some 21 examples. On looking around for a protagonist he came to the conclusion that there was only one artist who had so vast a répertoire—Artur Schnabel.

He glories in what he calls his "Back to Bach Movement" and says that most pianists start their career with Bach and progress up to Brahms. He, on the contrary, began with Brahms and was hailed far and wide as a Brahms player. Now, in his maturity, he turns to Bach and claims that it is this background of previous experience that enables him to appreciate Bach at his true worth.

Schnabel's relaxation used to consist in holding Master Classes in his beautiful home overlooking Bellagio on Lake Como. Tremezzo would be alive with sounds of diligent piano-practising, coming from the open window apartments of his piano pupils, scattered over the village. When May began you would see a procession of some twenty pianos being moved along the roads from Milan to Tremezzo. Schnabel brought prosperity to this charming village, and the inhabitants regarded him with respect and goodwill. His classes and lectures started at 8 A.M. and would continue without interruption until 1. After lunch Schnabel used to ride and walk, making friends with the neighbors and indulging in what he called his secret vice—meaning composition. In his efforts to be excessively clever he has produced some of the most unpalatable music I have ever listened to. You can tell him so to his face, and he will only give you a smile of self-satisfaction and reply that perhaps posterity will appreciate him.

As I have already mentioned, before he came to London Schnabel was only known as a Professor of Music at the Berlin Hochschule. There is a familiar proverb, "Once the student, always the student." For "student" substitute "teacher," and you have his character in a nutshell. He is a born pedagogue and never so happy as when seated at the piano, with his legs crossed, his left hand caressing the keyboard and his right gripping a choice cigar, surrounded by a bevy of students, chiefly girls, who hang on his every word.

Kreisler—

And Others

CHAPTER XII

Kreisler—and Others

THE absolutely unknown Fritz Kreisler made his recording début at our Berlin studios in 1903, and since then has contributed to our catalogues hundreds of intriguing bits of music. As the demand continued and fragments from the great composers became scarcer he himself composed dozens of *morceaux* in the vein which he knew the public enjoyed. Our associates, the Victor Company of America, had signed him up on a five years' contract at the height of the record boom in 1925. His fees were the highest ever paid to any instrumentalist and no doubt it was for this reason that they played for safety by confining their issues to selections of the broadest popular appeal. With the collapse of the record market they lost the incentive to give to the world the violin works of the Old Masters played by the greatest exponent of our day. For stunt purposes they did issue two or three of the classic sonatas played by Rachmaninoff and Kreisler. These were sharply criticized. As a cynic said, "With a Rachmaninoff at the piano and a Kreisler at the violin, poor Beethoven was bound to fall between the two."

It was only when I reproached him some years later for not having recorded the great concertos and sonatas that Kreisler consented to do so. We laid out a comprehensive programme and planned a working timetable. This gave me an exceptional opportunity to study the artist and enjoy his engaging personality at close quarters.

During my visits to Berlin to supervise this job I was a frequent guest at his comfortable villa in the Grünewald. It was a small replica of "Sans Souci" with a large music room overlooking a well-kept park. The many paintings, Chinese porcelains, rare manuscripts, and tapestries indicated the home of a keen collector. I have been told he rarely made a mistake in his art purchases. They perhaps explain, too, why he persisted in clinging to Berlin as his home when every colleague who could do so had long since decamped. His home and his collections were the work of a lifetime and he was going to hang on to them until the bitter end.

Charles Foley, his American manager, was present at one luncheon party when some good yarns were exchanged about their travels. Foley probably owed his success as an impresario to the fact that for many years he limited his clientèle to three artists only: Kreisler, Rachmaninoff, and Geraldine Farrar. Also, he confined his activities to the United States. He was friend and manager rolled into one.

Harriet Kreisler, who is always with her husband on his tours, had a few funny stories to tell about the discomforts of a recent Far Eastern trip. On their way to Peking at midnight when they were fast asleep, the train was held up by a bunch of Chinese Communist generals who bundled them out of the only sleeping-car on the whole of the Peking-Mukden system. Later, when crossing Manchuria, they were molested by bandits. For several weeks they stayed in Tokio's principal hotel. This edifice stood on reclaimed marshland and was guaranteed earthquake-proof. Harriet told me how, while they were sitting in the lounge admiring the illuminated Corinthian pillars, a small whiskered head would pop out and grin at them. Huge water-rats from the marsh had taken possession of the hotel. They were enthusiastic over the success of the twenty sold-out recitals Kreisler gave in Tokio alone. Even the rickshaw men would stop him and, carefully unwrapping a Red Label record, invite him to autograph it.

We asked him then about the press controversy, started in 1935, when he confessed to being the composer of a list of violin pieces which he had published as adaptations of various classical composers. They included:

        Boccherini — *Allegretto*
        Cartier — *La Chasse*
        Couperin — *Aubade Provençale*

Fox Photos, Ltd., London

Kreisler recording in Berlin. In the group the author is seen turning pages for Franz Rupp, the pianist.

Couperin	—	*La Précieuse*
Dittersdorf	—	*Scherzo*
Francoeur	—	*Sicilienne and Rigaudon*
Martini	—	*Andantino*
Martini	—	*Preghiera*
Porpora	—	*Minuet*
Pugnani	—	*Praeludium and Allegro*
Tartini	—	*Variations on a Theme by Corelli*
Vivaldi	—	*Violin Concerto in C*

Critics took this deception as a personal affront and not one voice was raised in Kreisler's defence. Fritz explained to me how he fell into the habit when, as a youngster, he felt the need of a bigger repertoire of encore pieces for his popular recitals. It was the time when he spent lean years in London, glad of a £5 engagement. The trifles in question were not modern enough to appear under his own name, yet, as has been since proven, they were so desperately needed by violinists that they were soon found on almost every violin-recital programme the world over. I thought the case he made out in his reply to Ernest Newman was excellently phrased, and even if it did not vindicate him, it at least showed a fine discrimination in his choice of words. Adrian Boult and even Artur Schnabel congratulated him on his article. He told me he had no moral reason to be ashamed of these deceptions and enjoyed the publicity he was getting out of them. Harriet told how in their rooms in St. James, surrounded with noisy colleagues, including Thibaud, Fritz would write these compositions quite openly and as openly discuss and play them over. "What are you doing, Fritz?" they would ask him. "Oh, I am composing a Pugnani piece for the violin," he would reply laughingly. None of his cronies took him seriously enough to worry over his compositions.

Kreisler recalled his first concert in London at the old St. James' Hall when he played the Beethoven Concerto with Hans Richter conducting. It was three weeks before Mafeking Day, and so marked was his success that Richter then and there engaged him for a second concert, the date falling (as it happened) on Mafeking Night. So great were the crowds in the street that neither artists nor audience were able to reach the hall.

Kreisler, superb as a yarnspinner in the Viennese and Yiddish dialects, gave us one about Godowsky. The great virtuoso was once importuned by a doting father to pronounce on his daughter's ability as a pianist. Godowsky heard her and wrote: "Your daughter is not without a lack of talent, and she manages to play the simplest pieces with the greatest of difficulty."

We spoke of a lucrative offer to broadcast in America, just turned down by Kreisler, and I asked him why he alone of the great violinists refused to play for the radio. His attitude was that to broadcast was a questionable advantage to an artist, because the date set might find him out of form, and then millions of listeners would judge him on his defects.

He also told us of his visit to Toscanini at his hotel in New York in 1933. The *maestro* had just received a long cable from Winifred Wagner urging him to accept the conductorship of the forthcoming Bayreuth Festival. Seated before a Richard Wagner manuscript, a precious gift to him from the composer's family, with tears in his eyes he pondered on the wording of his refusal. The artist in him was tempted to help his dear friend Winifred, but the man could not go against his own moral convictions. In the end, of course, he severed connections with both Germany and Italy, and elected to remain in America.

One can easily see the great part Harriet plays in the Kreisler household and how she sets the pace and keeps things moving. She has wit, energy and charm, and knows full well the many talents her Fritz possesses and how to bring them out. His friends know how true it is when she says, "I *made* you, Fritz. You would only have been a fiddler like dozens of others, but I made you *Kreisler*." After dinner, in the music room she is the centre and at her feet he sits, regarding her with affectionate pride, leading her on and now and again supplying an idea or reminding her of an incident.

Harriet and Fritz arrived in London in 1935 to record the Mendelssohn Concerto and his own Quartet in A–Major. Harriet attended the rehearsals and acted as floor-manager. When she could not come she would ring up from her hotel every half hour, and Fritz would have to report on the progress of each record. The quartet in question was only long enough to cover seven sides, or three and a half discs. The gap would have fazed most musicians, but not Kreisler. Remembering his "Dittersdorf Scherzo," he then and there started adapting it for the quartet, completing his task during intervals between recordings. When they came to play the fourth record not a single note of it had to be altered. He dedicated this impromptu work to me and presented me with the manuscript.

After the recording we adjourned to the home of Sir Louis and Lady Sterling, whose Sunday suppers had become a regular feature of bohemian London. People like the Sterlings, who keep open house on Sundays, have helped to dispel that Sabbath gloom which, I have found, is the bugbear of continental artists visiting England. At the Sterlings one always met agreeable colleagues in the theatrical, film, and musical worlds. On this occasion Schnabel and Kreisler were soon deeply engrossed in discussing the political situation in Germany and were joined by ex-Mayor Jimmy Walker and Lauritz Melchior, greatly to the discomfort of a bridge party in the next room, which included Chaliapin and Gigli.

Kreisler is the most accessible of men and enjoys talking to the orchestra after a recording session, examining their fiddles and trying them out. One day in February 1938, he lunched with the Prime Minister and, the next day, with myself and our recorder, Davidson, who had just returned from Japan, where I had travelled in the same capacity forty years ago and where Kreisler had lately been on tour. We had a good time swapping experiences. To so many musicians the microphone is an ordeal. I have seen other violinists who stand in front of the orchestra and tire them out by their fretfulness and nerves, but never Kreisler. When he has finished his cadenzas and the red light goes out they all applaud him wholeheartedly. Then they go up to him, one after the other, and recall those pre-war days when he was not the great Kreisler but just a colleague who often visited their homes where they would play quartets until the early hours of the morning. They all readily admit that he is a good comrade. What they cannot understand is that he, of all the violin virtuosi, rarely touches his instrument from one concert to the next. In other words, he does not put in the five hours' daily grind of exercises which most violinists regard as a necessity to keep up to form. It is his boast that he does not practise because he declines to be a slave to his instrument. In this respect he is the envy of his friends Casals and Rachmaninoff. I remember the Russian once drily remarking to me that Kreisler gave so many concerts that he never needed to practise or prepare himself beforehand.

I have known Kreisler to leave his expensive instrument in our studio from one session to the next, whereas most other violinists would not let their precious Strads out of their sight. Bronislaw Hubermann at the Hyde Park Hotel, London, had been flourishing a cheque he received from Lloyd's for £8,000, insurance he collected for the loss of his Strad in New York. He told me that while he was on the platform with the New York Philharmonic playing a concerto his reserve fiddle was stolen from the artists' room. He immediately notified Lloyd's by cable and hurried over to collect. Kreisler merely laughed at the incident and said: "It doesn't matter how casual I am, my two violins are so well known to every collector I don't see how they could fail to come back."

With the introduction of the electrical recording process arose the difficulty of finding halls with suitable acoustics for recording. It became necessary to centralize our recording activities in premises specially constructed for the purpose. In 1929 one of the most lovable men I have ever met, Trevor Osmond Williams, in charge of our Artists' Department, was working tirelessly on a plan to build a group of studios adapted for recording orchestras, large and small, and solo players and singers. His efforts bore fruit when the St. John's Wood Studios in Abbey Road, London, were inaugurated in 1931. These soon became the mecca of musical London and of international celebrities on a visit or passing through.

Numberless are the famous musicians who lived almost in the shadow of our Abbey Road studios. At 27 Abbey Road lived the great soprano, Trebelli, and at Compayne Gardens not far away was Ben Davies, the eighty-year-old tenor. Sir Charles Santley lived on Marlborough Hill; Scalchi in the Finchley Road. Nearby also had lived Nordica, Ada Crossley, Antoinette Sterling, Ella Russell, Marie Tempest, dainty Florence St. John of the Gaiety Theatre, and lovely Edna May of the *Belle of New York*. There more than once had passed the great philosopher, Herbert Spencer, or Thomas Huxley, when strolling towards Regent's Park. Tosti, the composer of "Good-Bye" and "Beauty's Eyes," lived in the vicinity, as did also the great Irish *basso cantante*, Signor Foli. Near neighbors were the soprano Malibran, and her celebrated brother,

KREISLER—AND OTHERS

Manuel Garcia, the teacher and inventor of the laryngoscope, who was over 100 years of age when he died.

In Loudon Road lived the soprano Grisi. "Ivy Cottage" at 20 Grove End Road was the home of Teresa Caroline Titiens. Joachim, the famous violinist and friend of Brahms, stayed in Grove End Road. Richard Wagner resided with his friend Ferdinand Praeger in Wellington Road when he visited London in 1877 to conduct his own compositions at the Albert Hall. St. John's Wood is still the haunt of well-known musicians, painters, and stage folk.

The simple façade of the early Regency residence we purchased hardly prepares one for those commodious halls in the rear of the premises. The large hall is reserved for the biggest symphony orchestras and contains a fine full-size Compton three-manual organ; the middle one is used by theatre and dance orchestras and small combinations; the small hall is designed for chamber music and solo work. There are ample artists' retiring rooms with a canteen and cloakroom for the bandsmen. All the halls are acoustically treated on scientific lines, air conditioned, and soundproof. Their modern equipment allows for every kind and degree of sound recording by light film or the wax process. For many years the establishment was unique of its kind. It houses an interesting exhibit of the various steps in record manufacturing, from a polished wax disc to the copper negatives from which the black copies or complete records are pressed. Another feature is a long wide corridor hung with photographic enlargements of famous artists. The employees vulgarly call it the Rogues Gallery.

In February 1939, for example, the recording programme there contained the names of Fritz Kreisler, Adolf Busch and the Busch Quartet, Artur Schnabel, Alexander Brailowsky, and Andrés Segovia.

The Kreisler recording was interesting because it called for the collaboration of the London Philharmonic Orchestra, Malcolm Sargent, and Fritz Kreisler for the first time, and a great success was secured. After the recording of the D major Mozart Violin Concerto the event was properly celebrated by a luncheon at the Garrick Club with Kreisler, during which he told us how he played for Brahms that composer's concerto, and afterwards listened to the fifteen-year-old Hubermann give an astonishing performance of

[209

the same work for Brahms. He is proud of the compliments that the great composer showered on them. He met the illustrious Brahms on many other occasions in Vienna, frequently played to him and took part in the hero worship of the master that pervaded the Viennese society of that day—the Vienna of the brilliant court of Franz Joseph, the city of bohemian café life where Mahler, Brahms, Bruckner, and Hugo Wolf might casually meet in the course of a day. Through his exceptional position as the son of Dr. Kreisler, the celebrated physician, the young violinist had been able to mingle freely with the élite of what seemed to us a dream world.

I read with regret of the death of Jan Kubelik, the Czech, at Prague at the early age of sixty. He was born at Michle near Prague and was five years younger than Kreisler. But unlike the Viennese violinist, he started right off as a musical prodigy. Kubelik's dazzling but meteoric career suffered a grave handicap when he developed ear trouble, which interfered with his intonation. In recent years his public appearances were few and far between. At the age of eight he made his début at Prague in a Vieuxtemps concerto, and then commenced his studies with the master-teacher, Sevčik. At twenty-two, when Kreisler, though twenty-seven, had barely begun his career he had reached the highest pinnacle of popularity and on an American tour was then earning unprecedented fees. A year later he married, and I well remember him bringing his bride (née Countess Czakyszell) to the H.M.V. studios in City Road. It seems that as a young man he bought an estate of Prince Hohenlohe's in Silesia for £160,000 out of the fortune which he earned from his engagements.

He was a shy, demure man whose demeanor seemed to express an apology for his existence. However, in congenial company he would expand and lament his enforced absences from his family. Later, my brother visited the Kubelik estate in Bohemia and gave me a graphic description of our friend lining up his six daughters, all violinists, in a row and conducting them in a concerted piece of music. What a sight it must have been! The last arrow in his quiverful was his son Raphael, who in 1937-38 visited London as conductor of the Czech Philharmonic Orchestra and made a brilliant success, staying long enough to record selections from Smetana's "My Fatherland" Suite.

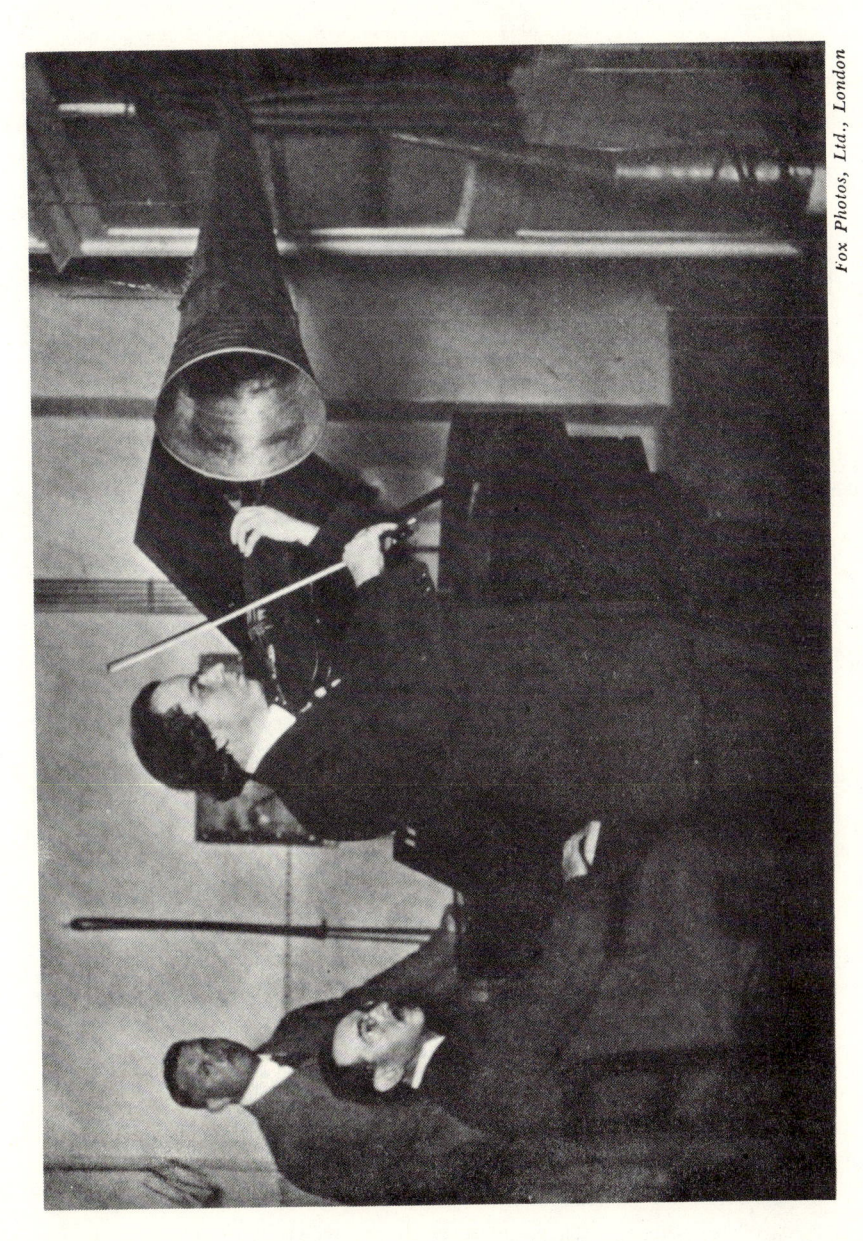

Kubelik, in his prime, making a record by the old acoustic process. The others are Seidler-Winkler at the piano and Max Hampe.

Fox Photos, Ltd., London

KREISLER—AND OTHERS

That sturdy boy, Mischa Elman, followed Jan Kubelik as a London favorite, representing the rival school of Leopold Auer at St. Petersburg. He was chaperoned by his short, stout father who became almost equally famous through his bargaining ability and as a confirmed son-worshipper. Mischa made his début in velvet Fauntleroy shorts at the age of twelve, and through that broad, velvety tone of his made the Tschaikovsky Concerto his very own. For many years he was second only to Kreisler as a gramophone bestseller. What a lot of cash and *kudos* the great fiddlers of that period used to gain, thanks to Berliner's gramophone invention! On royalties from records alone their average earnings would net them from £5,000 to £20,000 per annum, and their income from recitals and concerts would often be many times greater. Elman became the butt of some of the wittiest wags in the musical profession because of his naive and challenging attitude towards his brother violinists. But he took it all in his stride.

There is a yarn about a persistent autograph fiend who got Elman to sign his name at least five times for him, on five separate occasions. At his sixth interview Mischa, flattered by this persistent devotion, asked the youth: "Well, my boy, you seem to like me, but why all these autographs?" Cornered, the kid blurted out: "Oh, I'm trading my pal five Elmans for one Kreisler."

Elman is another of those proud fathers. He was once boasting to an acquaintance about the talent of his youngster of seven, who had taken up the fiddle. "That's fine," said the gentleman. "Maybe he will become a second Menuhin." He loves these jokes on himself and tells them with tremendous gusto.

Adolf Busch and his Quartet widened their gramophone repertoire by recording some marvellous Beethoven and Schubert quartets. Perhaps the records made by this very earnest and sincere quartet were exceptionally inspired because of the very successful four recitals they had just completed in the Wigmore Hall. Kreisler took a busman's holiday and went to hear them. He told me afterwards what a joy it was to listen to the Busch Quartet with their solid string tone. He spoke of Adolf Busch as one of the great idealists in present day music. How much work goes into these concerts, and how small the material reward! Kreisler agrees that,

[211

even after discounting all the snobbery of Berlin enthusiasts, one must recognize Busch as the real successor of Joachim.

Recording the guitarist Andrés Segovia is really a holiday. He brings his own instrument and we need only provide a chair in front of the microphone. It all looks very simple, but we and the recorders are fascinated by these magic fingers delicately intoning the music of Spain, and our minds picture the sufferings of that unhappy land. We know that Segovia himself has lost all and is now an exile travelling with his wife from land to land, looking to the day when they can return to their home in Barcelona.

Sometimes centralized studios would prove too central when two artistic or political rivals would indiscreetly be booked for the same afternoon, and when they would meet by accident in the corridor or retiring room an awkward situation might arise. After two or three amusing incidents of this sort we learned that big as the studios were there was room for only one "king" at a time, and thereafter we revised our schedules accordingly.

Even our air-conditioned halls rarely gave satisfaction to the strings, so sensitive to humidity and temperature were the instruments. More than all others Hubermann used to fidget with the strings and bridge adjustment. This great musician and designer of a plan for the Federated States of Europe would fret and worry over a false string or faulty intonation until everyone was exhausted before recording began. Szigeti, another intellectual, was equally nervous when recording. The most phlegmatic and casual of recorders was Casals who, I am sure, could extract golden tones even from a cigar box strung in a monsoon. I have seen his only D-string break in the middle of recording a Brahms sonata. Nothing daunted, he would tie it up with a sailor's knot, relight his pipe and continue recording. The results can be judged on his records.

Compared with the violin, 'cello records have not such a universal appeal and to submit terms that would approximate those of Kreisler, Heifetz, or Menuhin was not easy. I take a particular pride in his records of the Dvořák 'Cello Concerto. I had heard that Casals was to visit Prague for a concert with the Prague Philharmonic Orchestra, Georg Széll conducting. Both were old friends of mine, and this seemed just the opportunity I was waiting for to record the Concerto on its native heath. An exchange of telegrams with all

The Gramophone Co., Ltd.

Casals recording Dvořák's violoncello concerto in Prague. Photograph by Professor Prykner.

parties concerned quickly fixed the day after the concert as the recording date. Flying to Prague, I engaged the famous Deutsche Haus, celebrated for its fine acoustics, and set up the equipment. The news spread quickly and the project assumed national importance. Casals flew from Barcelona, arriving more dead than alive but full of hope for a Republican victory in Spain, where at that time he was Minister of Fine Arts in the Catalan Government.

The dress rehearsals and concert before packed houses were a huge success. Casals' élan and stamina kept him going for the whole of the next day when over twelve unsurpassed records were made, and then the little man collapsed, every ounce of his strength exhausted. He first heard the records two months afterwards when he came to London for a Queen's Hall concert with the B.B.C. He pronounced them magnificent and was extremely satisfied and grateful for the marvellous results. Later on these records were played over to Jan Masaryk, then Czech Minister in London and himself a fine musician, who was so carried away by their beauty that he secured a set for himself on the spot.

The difficulty of holding a team of celebrities together was brought home to me after my first flush of success with the Cortot, Thibaud, and Casals trio. Beginning as youthful colleagues in 1905, all of them famous soloists, all of approximately the same age, temperament, and sympathy, they would consistently meet once a year for a holiday and trio practise. It was even possible for them to give one or two recitals in Paris and London every autumn. In October 1926 I succeeded in coming to terms with them and signed them up for a long term contract. Before the end of the year the great Schubert B–flat Major Trio was recorded and on sale. So well did it go that I hastened to add four more important works before the split came and, for some reason never clearly ascertained, the three refused to record again as a trio, although each of them had cashed in thousands of pounds from the sale of trio records at the cost of a few days' work. I did hear a rumor that they all thought that being ranked as trio players might injure their status as soloists. So, as a combination, they faded out.

The Cortot-Thibaud-Casals trio having disappointed me, I tried to form a similar combination, to consist of Huberman, Schnabel and Feuermann, and sketched out a schedule of recording dates in

London for the month of December 1939. For this purpose I would have had to bring Feuermann over from America and Huberman from Zürich, paying all their expenses. Schnabel, however, was making London his port of call en route, for an autumn tour in the United States. This was my third attempt, and this time Hitler intervened.

If I were asked to select the closest parallel with Cervantes' Don Quixote from all my living acquaintances I would choose Casals without hesitation. I never thought such chivalry could exist in real life. I already knew he supported twenty-one relatives. I also knew him as a staunch upholder of the Catalan Socialist Government, although his support involved the confiscation of his beautiful home and museum in Barcelona and his farm at San Jorge in return for a mere subsistence wage. To cap all, the government of the day organized a rival orchestra that displaced the People's Orchestra he had created and financed out of his own purse for many years. Again, he devoted two years' study to Donald Tovey's ponderous Concerto and loyally championed it at great personal sacrifice. I have known Casals to travel hundreds of miles to play to assist friends without any thought of a fee.

Typical of him was his refusal, purely for domestic reasons, to visit America, although it offered him the surest means to recoup his finances, depleted by the Spanish Revolution in which, at the age of 64, he lost the savings of a lifetime. His visits to London were the signal for all sorts of picturesque and ragged Catalan refugees to rally to his hotel, where he would sympathize with them and would never let them depart empty handed. I remember his pride as he took me to the Olympia in Barcelona of a Sunday morning and showed me five thousand workers in blue jeans assembled to hear his orchestra in a Bach and Beethoven programme. Once he arranged an all-Brahms programme there, when he and Thibaud played the Brahms Double Concerto, with Cortot conducting. Next day I recorded it and the results remain today a unique and historic collaboration between the three principals and the Pau Casals Barcelona Symphony Orchestra. Casals' greatest achievement was his creation of a musical life in Barcelona. Only those who know that city will appreciate what this meant. His Musical Society contained over 10,000 names, mostly of working men who paid only a nominal fee for membership. I know the complex character of those workers and I marvel at Casals' achievement. Even London's East End is a more fertile pasture than Barcelona's stony ground.

Casals' greatness I have never doubted. Today Toscanini alone is his equal as an interpretative executant. His genius is the type that only the gramophone can hand down to posterity. I persistently worried him into recording complete the unaccompanied Bach Suites for the 'cello. The war has merely postponed the issue of these records, which are in safekeeping. In connection with this recording Casals told an interesting story of how he first became acquainted with these masterworks. At the age of thirteen, after seven months' study in Barcelona, he began to earn his living in a café on the outskirts of the city, playing in a trio the regular café répertoire of light music, valses, fantasies, and the like. He was soon promoted to solo work and the small café became popular for its good music. He suggested to the proprietors that one evening per week should be devoted to chamber music. Thursday was set aside for better class music, the city's intellectuals began to come in, and the fame of the restaurant spread. As Casals had to enlarge his répertoire, he asked his father to accompany him to a music store and have a look round. There, lying on the counter, was a volume of the Bach Suites. The music was absolutely unknown to him and, as far as he knew, to any other 'cellist in Spain. Thus, at the age of thirteen he began to study these suites and for fifteen years he worked continually at them.

He became the first of all instrumentalists to play an entire Bach Suite at a public concert. Later on, the day came, one of the happiest of his life, when he played the E Flat Suite at the Albert Hall before 8,000 people. It can fairly be said that he rediscovered these works, since after being regarded as of academic interest only, he again set these works in their true perspective as living music. Of the fine 'cello programme of gramophone records I can feel justly proud, and my satisfaction is all the greater at knowing that his principal income today is derived out of the royalties from their sales.

Appreciation from an Adolf Busch, a Donald Tovey, or an Adrian Boult is worth that of a thousand critics, and Casals is one of those great men to whom the special homage is given which exalts the disciple as well as the prophet. Take, for example, Barbirolli. I have seen him regard Casals, while playing, with misty eyes eloquent of a lover who can never aspire to attain his love. Casals has always held out for the highest fee and for that reason has appeared less often than his colleagues. This is not because he is mercenary but purely as a matter of prestige, so dear to the heart of a Catalan.

London, notoriously a difficult terrain for an artist to secure a foothold in without years of preliminary spadework, relaxed for once in favor of three artists whose chief advance publicity lay in records made in America during the war and issued in England by my company. For their Albert Hall débuts, Heifetz in 1920 and Galli-Curci in 1924 each had a sold-out house before the day of their concert. With the more modest Queen's Hall Alfred Cortot was similarly favored. Prior to these events the Gramophone Company had issued a record of each that earned amazing popularity: Heifetz made Schubert's "Ave Maria," Galli-Curci "Lo, Here the Gentle Lark" of Bishop, and Cortot Weber's "Invitation to the Dance." Thousands of these were bought and treasured by enthusiasts. Coming as they did immediately after the post-war music famine, the visits of these stars were eagerly welcomed by the public, who remained their constant supporters. Once committed to giving concerts in the Albert Hall, seating from 8,000 to 10,000, Galli-Curci and Heifetz had to continue there, if only to retain their prestige, even when conditions became less favorable for celebrity artists. What Tetrazzini and Kreisler could easily do year after year these rising stars had to copy. Cortot, as great a musician if less glamorous, chose the smaller hall for his first appearance and for this reason more firmly consolidated his position with genuine music lovers in London.

My choice fell on him to assist the company in building our record library of Chopin's piano music, because of his profound study and poetic performance of Chopin's works and also because he happened to have been trained by that great composer's last pupil and disciple, Decombes. Equally important are Cortot's records of Debussy, whose elusive moods he captured so cleverly and whose music he has done so much to popularize. I often marvel at the ease with which he worked and the amount he accomplished. His restless mind was always inventing new activities; in the course of one season alone these would range from orchestral conducting to lecture-recitals, from opera production to students' courses at his wonderful École Normale where he boasted of having an advanced class of 800. Spare moments were filled in by the writing of profound essays on Chopin and Debussy, or the editing of piano classics for publishers. To these one must add the eighty recitals each year, which brought him in returns rich enough to permit him to indulge in that expensive hobby, the collection of rare manuscripts. It was this pastime, he told me, that prevented him from specializing as an orchestral conductor. Of all the musicians of my acquaintance he is the only one comparable with Paderewski in his all-round balance of accomplishments as man, artist, writer, and musician. Unlike the great Pole, he shrinks from society and has no ambition to play a leading rôle in world affairs apart from the arts.

Jascha Heifetz I found an extraordinary blend of artist and playboy. To the despair of all his fellows he would easily electrify an Albert Hall audience and then go straight off to a cocktail party where he could hold his own with the best of them, reporting the next morning for a record session, immaculate and with his nerves intact. I found his company stimulating and his prowess as a cocktail-shaker great. He liked to keep a party noisy and moving and, boylike, was always reluctant to go to bed. People seeing him on the concert platform thought him cold and impassive, but I found out that actually he was frozen with stage-fright. He confessed to me that he had never been able to overcome this fear. In his wife, Florence Vidor, a film star of "silent" days, he found an ideal partner who knew how to handle him.

Since his sensational début in London, when he was only twenty, he has been a constant visitor to England and the Continent. I take some credit for his collaboration, which I arranged, with Arthur Rubinstein, a man of equal genius, in a superb recording of the César Franck Sonata. I shall always remember the luncheon which followed that session, for the exchange of steely repartee between these two brilliant young musicians.

The furor created by Heifetz on his first appearance in New York produced a classic story. Godowsky, the great pianist, was standing with Mischa Elman listening to the concert. Half way through,

Elman is said to have turned to his companion, and, wiping his forehead, said: "Let's get out of here, it's terribly hot tonight." "Not for pianists," said Godowsky.

Heifetz later told me the story of his European tour in the spring of 1939, and how he was caught in the maelstrom when the Nazis suddenly descended on Austria. He had given a concert in Prague and was travelling to Budapest on the day Hitler was marching into Linz. Playing the following evening he sensed that the audience was restless and that something was wrong during the first part of the programme because he could not rivet their attention. The second part went better and he managed to hold them all right. It was only after it was all over that he learned the news of the invasion. He was grateful that he had not heard it earlier, or he would have been too upset to carry on.

The next day there was a great rush to get out of Hungary but it was impossible to obtain places on the Arlberg Express for Paris. By luck two sleepers were returned a short time before the train started. As they went through Vienna, except for the Swastika flag on every house, they saw little of the Anschluss movement. On the frontier they had no difficulty at all. At the Gare d'Est next morning a large crowd of anxious friends had assembled, and when the train pulled in and Jascha and Florence put their heads out of the window a cheer went up. Such experiences were the lot of many artists on tour in the disturbed Europe of the past decade.

The lot of a musical prodigy is usually an unhappy one. Papa Menuhin has often explained to me his justification for presenting Yehudi in public at the early age of eight. His object was to save his children the hardship he had shared with his wife. As young Palestine Jews they had met and married. Her parents were teachers; Moshe Menuhin himself taught mathematics. They emigrated to the United States, where in New York at first they suffered great privations. With Yehudi, Hephzibah and Yaltah still infants, their mother, besides teaching in a school, had to do her own shopping, run the house, and amuse the children. Twice Yehudi was gravely ill with pneumonia.

Yehudi's great start in life was due to the patronage of Mrs. Erman of the Wells-Fargo Company, for whom the child of five played at a private charity affair. He was raised on a soapbox and presented with a dollar bill, his first fee. Later on Mr. Erman advanced Moshe money to finance a European trip to further Yehudi's musical education under Adolf Busch and, later, Enesco.

One must always regard Papa's publicity acumen as on a level with Yehudi's violin playing. He was a tireless correspondent and besides attending to all the business details of the boy's tours, he replied personally to hundreds of letters received every day. By slow and steady progress Yehudi came to assume the post of arbiter of all family disputes. His decision was usually deferred to since his family recognized his level-headed commonsense. Even as a boy he possessed the qualities of wisdom and sagacity, though it seemed to us incongruous to see them revealed in a lad with such a winning, irresistible smile.

Early in life the parents accepted the fact that their three children were exceptionally brilliant. With wise foresight, they laid plans which they rigidly adhered to for educating and at the same time shielding them from a curious public. I and the members of my family were fortunate to be accepted in the inner circle of their home life, and in spite of my first inclination to condemn Moshe's intense urge for publicity, I must confess myself a convinced admirer of this broadminded, democratic, lovable couple and their three unspoilt children. Contact with them has restored my faith in humanity. Who cannot but praise the parents' firm stand against the blandishments of society leaders to use them to decorate "At Homes"? Nor were they carried away by the fanatical Orthodox Jewish movement of this decade, which they were pressed to support. Moshe told me that he detested fanaticism and regarded it as the greatest curse of the Jews and the reason of their isolation from the national life of many countries. His motive in emigrating to America was to escape this blight and he warmly welcomed the marriage of Yehudi and Hephzibah into a Scottish Methodist family as a practical step towards solving their racial problem.

Moshe's resolve not to be submerged in Jewish racial prejudices was brought on by his early experiences when he lived with his grandfather, a holy man in Jerusalem, by whom he was thoroughly grounded in Hebrew and the tenets of the Jewish faith. The holy man was intensely devout and unnecessarily strict with his young grandson. Moshe has taught his children Hebrew; Yehudi both reads and writes it perfectly, but the family are now far from being strictly Orthodox.

The seclusion of the family from society tended to make the children curiously unworldly. Out shopping with Yehudi in a large New York store, he purchased a comb for 75 cents. On receiving change from a dollar bill, he asked me if he should tip the salesclerk. Yaltah, out with my niece in London, paid a taxi with a 10/-note and asked if it was enough, though the meter registered only 1/6d.

It was after a concert in Holland with Mengelberg that Yehudi courageously called up Nola Nicholas in London on the telephone, popped the question, and was accepted. The next morning at breakfast the young man told his mother of Nola's acceptance. Whereupon Hephzibah capped him with the announcement of her engagement to Lindsay, Nola's brother.

The father welcomed visits to our recording rooms as a distraction for Yehudi from the common round of his studies and concerts. It was a safe contact with the outside world and the boy thoroughly enjoyed himself. Sometimes all three children would come along and then, although normally well behaved, the two younger were curious and listened gravely to their brother and plied him with excited questions as he proudly lectured to them on the process of recording sound. Every year since his tenth birthday I have had charge of this gramophone recording and have observed the steady progress from child to man that each successive visit to our studios unfolded.

I shall never forget the first visit of the fair Hephzibah to collaborate with her big brother in a Mozart Sonata. The delight of hearing the music of these fair, fresh children moved me profoundly. He, the veteran recorder, very seriously explained to the prim young recruit just what to do and what not to do to make a perfect record. Days like these were high-spots in my gramophone career. Lunch with the family usually followed, when they would enthusiastically relate to Mamma and Yaltah every detail of their day's experience.

As an important milestone in Yehudi's boyhood I engineered a meeting with Sir Edward Elgar, whose Violin Concerto I thought had been scandalously neglected. The sequel I relate in my chapter on that great composer.

In the bad old days it was customary to exploit the genius of an infant prodigy prematurely and without any kind of settled plan. Moshe Menuhin was too farsighted for such extravagances. To begin with he rationed his son's public appearances to five concerts a year, all given within the compass of a few months, leaving the rest of the time vacant for his study and development. Perhaps this led him to intensify his advance publicity campaigns. Very soon he became more than a match for enterprising journalists out for a scoop.

However, about the time he signed Yehudi and Hephzibah up to appear for the Ford Motor Company in a half-hour N.B.C. radio recital at which Yehudi reserved the right to play chamber music, a New York reporter called him up to ask if it was true that Yehudi had given Henry Ford his first lesson in chamber music. "Certainly not," replied Moshe, "we had no personal contact whatsoever with Mr. Ford, as the business was done through an agency." Less than three hours later he was handed an early edition of an evening paper and was reading headlines:

YEHUDI MENUHIN GIVES HENRY FORD HIS FIRST LESSON
IN CHAMBER MUSIC

This was proof enough that the story must have been already written up while the reporter was still on the telephone. Moshe made a strong protest as this announcement placed his powerful patrons, the Ford Motor Company, in an embarrassing position with their chief. Being an honorable man he offered to cancel the agreement—an offer which was not accepted. As a sequel the reporter had the nerve to threaten Moshe with a libel suit!

The old delusion that artists have no sense of business is dispelled by such men as Gigli, Chaliapin—and Moshe Menuhin. When it comes to driving a hard bargain I take my hat off to Moshe.

Feodor Chaliapin

CHAPTER XIII

Feodor Chaliapin

DURING the last war and the revolutionary period in Russia concerts and opera were carried on under difficult conditions. Chaliapin, used to the lavish productions sponsored by the Romanoff family, complained frequently about the restrictions on expenditure caused by the war, but he still gave concerts and made occasional opera appearances in both Moscow and Petrograd.

After 1917 things got increasingly difficult, and he had many conflicts with the Soviet government who were jealous of the fees and goods that he was able to extract from his appearances. I have heard him describe how instead of roubles, which by that time everybody scorned, he demanded his payment in flour, potatoes, bacon, and butter.

His greatest preoccupation was his family and how to accomplish their security. At last he was given full permission to go abroad on the strength of a scheme he put forward for a tour of Europe and America, to further the interests of Communism and to raise funds for a relief fund, since the whole of Russia was at that time in the throes of a widespread famine. On account of the universal fear of the contagion of Communism, obtaining visas to enter England and America was a long and difficult matter. Eventually these were secured, principally through the good offices of the Gramophone Company, but only on condition that he limit his activities solely to giving concerts for the Famine Relief Fund.

My post-war association with Chaliapin started in this way. H. G.

Wells, invited to Russia to observe the success of the revolution in 1919, had been a guest at the home of Chaliapin in Petrograd. When he returned, Chaliapin gave him a letter addressed to me, which is now in the archives of the Gramophone Company. This letter asked my help and begged me to watch for a further communication from him, in which he would inform me of his plans to leave Russia. It suggested that our place of meeting should be Riga; he would be entirely without funds, which I was to provide, and he also asked me to plan a programme so that he could resume his concert and operatic activities in Europe and make further gramophone records. I was not surprised, therefore, when I finally received a further request to meet him in Riga at a certain time and place. Through the courtesy of the Gramophone Company I was able to keep the appointment.

This was in 1921, when there was a famine raging in Russia so great that the Americans had organized an extensive Relief Fund with Herbert Hoover at the head. In Germany the mark was falling to the billion point. To get across the Polish Corridor meant being challenged and often held up indefinitely; in fact, the passengers in my train had to descend and a number were detained. Conditions in Riga were chaotic. In that magnificent city where my company had a £100,000 factory, Chaliapin and I were offered modern apartment houses of ten suites for a few hundred pounds.

We met in the early days of September. The Communists in Riga more or less took charge of Chaliapin, looking on him as one of their partisans. His wardrobe was in rags and tatters and he looked most forlorn in his threadbare clothes. The money which I was able to hand over to him, representing the royalties earned on his records during the war period, comprised his entire capital on which to start life over again.

While waiting for passport visas permitting him to enter England, he gave two concerts in Riga and one in Libau, which were sold out. The audience were very enthusiastic and this gave him great satisfaction, as it seemed to augur well for his reception abroad. His favorite pastime was to visit the various food and delicatessen shops and gaze at the quantities of sausages and hams on exhibition. Gazing into food-shops continued until the end of his life a fascinating pastime for him. The well stocked shops of Paris, London, and New York gave him endless pleasure.

On arriving in London he fulfilled the conditions of his visa and gave five Famine Relief concerts, retaining for himself a certain proportion for expenses. His opening concert at the Albert Hall was filled to the last seat by an enthusiastic and fashionable audience and he was fêted and lionized by a host of the friends he had made in 1913 and 1914. The staunchest of these and one who remained a close friend until her dying day was Violet, Duchess of Rutland, with her daughter Lady Diana Manners, now Lady Duff-Cooper. The Duchess of Rutland died in December 1937, and when I passed through Paris in February of the next year and visited Chaliapin for the last time he showed me a beautiful letter that he had received from the Duchess shortly before her death. Both Feodor Ivanovitch and Maria, his wife, recalled the many kindnesses they had received from her hands. During post-war days, her friendship was an invaluable aid in securing visas for passports when there was such universal dread of the growth of Russian Communism. She never failed to attend a concert or opera performance and front seats were always reserved for her and her family.

When these Albert Hall concerts were given in 1921, it was the first time London had heard Chaliapin in a recital programme; hitherto his appearances had always been in opera. He had created quite an original concert technique that immediately found favor with his audience. His programme featured dramatic songs and lieder, which he dramatized, each a rare cameo portraying love, sorrow, or joy in lyrical and dramatic tones. He provided libretti with the translation of the words and after announcing the number of the title selected, he would pause for a few moments to enable the audience to scan the lines. I assisted him in preparing his libretti and was in attendance both at rehearsals and on the concert platform in the early days, to give him the English pronunciation of the titles and numbers. I also acted as interpreter in all his newspaper interviews and I am certain that his favorite accompanists in England, Gerald Moore and Ivor Newton, were grateful for my presence and assistance during the concerts.

After the war his voice seemed to be more sensitive to colds, due to the hardships of the revolution, and his abnormal desire always to sing up to his highest standards sometimes inclined him to postpone concerts that should have taken place. In Russia and in fact all over Europe, it appears a simple matter to cancel a fixture on the morning of the actual day by merely pasting the words *Concert Cancelled* across the poster in front of the opera house or concert hall. By some magic this news spreads and within a few hours reaches the ears of practically everyone. This, however, cannot be done in the big cities of England and America and the concert managers always suffered agonizing moments until Chaliapin actually made his appearance on the platform.

I was in Chaliapin's bedroom at the Waldorf-Astoria Hotel on a Sunday evening, half an hour before he was due to make his postwar début in New York in 1922. He was surrounded by the impresarios Solomon Hurok and Frederick Coppicus, his accompanist Rabinovitch, and myself. The air was charged with anxiety. Chaliapin with his laryngoscope, seated in his underwear before a mirror, was inviting us to look down the instrument to convince ourselves that those inflamed spots on his vocal chords made it impossible for him to sing. The concert had already been postponed twice on account of his laryngitis. The two American impresarios were wringing their hands, saying they would be ruined by another cancellation and begging him to go to the concert if only to apologize to the audience. Chaliapin in despair threw himself on the bed and moaned "Bozhe, Bozhe, what have I done to deserve this?" He paced the room, knocking his head on the wall and again cried to God "Why should I be so punished?" Then suddenly Nicolai, his little valet, said in Russian: "Feodor Ivanovitch, go to the concert; God will give you back your voice when the moment comes." Chaliapin stopped short, and with a look of scorn at the valet said "What has God got to do with my voice?"

It was already past the hour for the commencement of the concert when we made a combined effort and started to dress him, in spite of his continued resistance. I put on his socks and fastened up his boots, Hurok tied his tie and we dragged the protesting giant downstairs, thrust him into a taxi, and started for the Manhattan Opera House. Driving up to the stage door, we could see by the commotion that the house was sold out and that the restless audience had worked itself up into a fever of impatience. No sooner did we enter the artists' room than the ballerina Anna Pavlova, who was waiting there for him, threw herself on his neck. They both cried together, she in greatest sympathy for his plight.

Chaliapin tried to persuade the doctor in attendance to go on to the platform and announce to the waiting audience that Chaliapin was going to appear, in spite of his warning that his septic throat made it impossible for him to sing and that if he attempted to do so he would probably lose his voice for ever. This the doctor was too shy to do. Then we tried to induce Solomon Hurok to make the announcement, but his English was still so imperfect that he lacked the courage to face the howling audience. The task was eventually imposed on me and in my innocence I accepted.

I was placed in the middle of the stage with the curtain down, alone in that vast space. I could hear the yells of the audience from the other side, like those of hungry lions in a den. In a moment the curtain quickly rose and I looked out on a sea of faces. There was a hushed silence. Closing my eyes I cried out the apologies of Chaliapin and asked the indulgence of the audience. There was a great roar as I retreated to the wings. Then Chaliapin strode forth, followed by his accompanist, and for the next five minutes the cheering was continuous. Through his superb acting he made it plain that he was suffering; he even produced tears to win the sympathy of the public. Then he literally barked out, in a sick voice, five songs. It was indeed a pitiful performance, but the audience had to be satisfied as there certainly would be no money returned.

By a back door he and I fled from the theatre to a quiet Harlem speakeasy where I did my best, through a long evening, to console him. Early next morning I hustled him down to a secluded farm in the heart of New Jersey before reporters could get at him, and kept him there until his throat was well.

After his bitter experiences in Russia Chaliapin's first post-war visit to London must have come as balm to his despairing heart, since everywhere he met with the warmest reception and sold out houses. I shall never forget the simple pleasure he took in studying the types and characters of the down-and-outs that we encountered in our midnight strolls on the Embankment, or his delight in the homely food at the coffee stalls and the shelters of the taxi-drivers. He had a theory that where the taxi-drivers ate, there one would get the tastiest food—sometimes he was right. He spent a great deal of time, with evident delight, in the Savile Row tailors' shops where he replenished his wardrobe, spending close on £400 on his first shopping tour. He insisted on fraternizing with the cutters and fitters and toasted them with champagne on the last day of fitting, telling them how he honored all artisans who took pride in their work.

When the time came for him to leave for America, he begged me to accompany him and this I was fortunately able to do. In November 1921, we embarked on the S. S. *Adriatic* and our voyage across the Atlantic started under good auspices, for the ship carried perhaps the most distinguished contingent of passengers it had ever held. Not many hours after the boat sailed from Southampton, H. G. Wells, who, as mentioned before, had met Chaliapin in Russia, sought him out and renewed his acquaintance. They were shortly joined by Colonel Repington, war correspondent of the *Daily Telegraph*, and Dr. Richard Strauss. On this quartet was centred the greater interest of the rest of the passengers. Mr. Wells was most active in the sports on deck and challenged Chaliapin to deck-quoits and cricket. The evenings were given over to poker for schoolboy stakes. At this game Mr. Wells was an amused spectator, watching Chaliapin and Dr. Strauss trying to bluff each other. These games were usually participated in by Chaliapin, Strauss, Lucrezia Bori, and Elisabeth Schumann, and caused great amusement to the onlookers. One of the highlights of shipboard gossip was the famous Follies girl, Peggy Hopkins Joyce, then Mrs. Stillman, who was returning to America. She proved an alluring distraction to Chaliapin and an endless source of prattle for the rest of the ladies.

The usual concert was organized, in which all the artists took part and it is doubtful whether such a coterie of celebrities ever appeared at one concert in happier fellowship. When Chaliapin sang "How the King Went Forth to War" the deckbeams fairly shook. He was in his most happy and boyish mood and for the sheer pleasure of the thing, sang song after song to Dr. Strauss' accompaniment. Wells and Chaliapin had drawn some twenty caricatures of the various passengers and these were put up for auction at the close of the concert, bringing prices that Old Masters might have fetched. There was particularly spirited bidding for a caricature by Wells of Chaliapin arriving in the Land of Liberty, which brought £15.

Upon arrival at Ellis Island, the *Adriatic* was besieged by an army of reporters, journalists, and cameramen who cornered first one and then the other of the celebrities, and did their utmost to draw out of Chaliapin his opinions on the political situation in Russia, a topic which he insisted on avoiding. Among those who came to meet us was Solomon Hurok, the well-known impresario. Although he was Russian-born and raised in America, both his Russian and English were of the sketchiest kind at this time. However, he installed himself as interpreter for Chaliapin. Surrounded by the reporters hungrily waiting for copy, Chaliapin in beautifully intoned Russian held forth at some length on his opinion of Russian art and dramatic art in general, gesticulating with those eloquent arms and fingers of his. It was one of his best performances. He stopped, and with one voice the reporters cried out to Hurok: "What did he say?" Hurok tersely summed up the whole thing by replying: "He says he thinks America's fine!"

Chaliapin's foreboding of misfortunes awaiting him in America was partly realized. He had no sooner arrived in New York than he was attacked by severe laryngitis which as stated made him postpone his first concert three times. After these disasters, in order to obtain perfect repose and to escape the pursuit of compatriots, reporters, and society leaders, he discovered a quiet village in New Jersey fifty miles from New York, where in a simple farmhouse on the outskirts of Jamesburg, he took a milk cure. It was not long before the villagers' curiosity was aroused by this blonde giant who took his daily walks through the village streets. The enterprising proprietor of the local movie house soon discovered that this stranger was a singer, and one morning stopped Chaliapin in the street, suggesting that as he was doing nothing else, he might earn a little money if he would sing a few songs on Saturday night at his theatre. For this he boldly offered three dollars! Chaliapin suggested that he could pay four, but the proprietor replied that his house only held twenty when it was full, and that was the end of their negotiations. Chaliapin had that very day refused an offer for twenty performances in South America at $2,500 a performance.

The extravagant praise of the critics and the enthusiasm of the audience over his appearance at the Metropolitan Opera House in *Boris Godunoff* was certainly in marked contrast to his chilly reception in 1908. He was hailed as the greatest artist in the world, both lyric and dramatic, and it would seem that the resources of language had been exhausted by the critics in their search for words to praise his work. The consequence was that Gatti-Casazza, the manager of the Metropolitan Opera House, induced him to make four further appearances and to sign an agreement for twenty performances the next season, should his government permit him to come abroad again so soon.

I attended with him many rehearsals at the Metropolitan, where they gave him a free hand in the stage direction. He would act each part and I can recall now the various perfect cameos of portrayal. He was never satisfied with the casts they gave him or the productions, and it can be said with safety that New York never saw the glory of Russian opera under the same favorable conditions as London did, particularly in the seasons of 1913 and 1914 under the direction of Sir Thomas Beecham. Undoubtedly these London productions were, outside of Russia, the highest point of Russian opera.

Chaliapin loved fine clothes. I remember the day during these seasons when he acquired a tall grey top hat. We walked from the hatters to Drury Lane, he watching his reflection in shop windows as we passed and getting great satisfaction out of it. We arrived somewhat late at the theatre and had to hurry over dressing. This was in 1914, and the Russian chorus struck just before the Coronation Scene in *Boris Godunoff*. It was a command performance and the Royal Family were in the house. The scene took place without the chorus, who were obdurate. After the scene, Chaliapin rushed to the back of the stage and remonstrated with the ringleader, who argued back. I saw Chaliapin strike him one blow which completely knocked him out. With that the choristers threw themselves on Chaliapin and bore him to the ground. They would have mauled

Chaliapin in his famous grey topper, on a visit to the recording studios at Hayes, Middlesex. At the extreme left are the author and his brother Will.

him badly if the mezzo-soprano, Patrenka, had not covered him with her body. Finally I and the stagehands were able to draw him into his dressing room and lock the door. How it all ended after this serious interruption I am not quite sure, but I remember Sir Thomas Beecham's treasurers arriving with a sack of gold and passing out a golden sovereign to each chorister, after which the show continued. Those Russian choristers were an unruly crowd, rather spoilt by success and steeped in revolution even then. They and Chaliapin had many tilts. They were certainly a wonderful chorus and made history, in that they received encores for their acting and singing, like any prima donna, and afterwards took their curtains.

During an appearance in *Mefistofele* an incident occurred at Covent Garden when the conductor failed to follow Chaliapin. He walked off the stage and the curtain was dropped. Commenting on the affair afterwards, he said that although at the rehearsal the conductor had followed him to his entire satisfaction he had betrayed him at the performance. In other words, he attempted to take matters in his own hands and make Chaliapin follow him. Chaliapin insisted that the conductor should be an accompanist, like a pianist, responding to the moods of the singer. According to the day, he might feel depressed, relaxed, or perhaps exhilarated and the music must move in sympathy; it could not be taken in a fixed and inflexible tempo. For this reason he never sang in Wagner operas, where chessboard moves are imposed on the characters. He would add that if it was just to secure an approved musical performance, there was no need for the management to pay him £400; a first-class bass singer could be obtained for £40 who would obediently follow the beat. Likewise, he protested violently at the obscure lighting in the *Barbiere di Siviglia* at Covent Garden. He interrupted the scene, striding across to the wings and crying out, "Luce, luce!" The public, having paid to see him, should not be deprived of light, he felt.

A whole article could be written on the heroism of his accompanists. His demands on these gentlemen were exacting and only the most experienced and talented could hope to survive. They had to sense his every mood and his liberties with the music. This gave them little time to bother about the technique of piano-playing.

If they were at all sensitive they were bound to be confused before the public when they missed his cue. When he was not in particularly good voice he would be in a highly-charged, nervous state and the poor pianist was then bound to have embarrassing moments when Chaliapin would beat on the piano for the pianist to increase or decrease his pace.

He was very fond of talented Max Rabinovitch as an accompanist. Also he made it possible for the Russian composer, Koenemann, then Director of the Moscow Conservatory of Music, to enjoy a trip abroad by acting as his accompanist in a tour of the British Isles and America. I remember when that modest and simple man arrived in London direct by boat from Petrograd. He was a dilapidated and humble sight in his greasy and ragged clothes. Madame Chaliapin and I took him to Harrods, where we rigged him out, to his intense joy, in a lounge suit and evening dress. The poor fellow was so bent that it was difficult to fit him, and in his dress suit and Russian beard he made a comic sight on the concert platform, in contrast to the immaculately groomed Feodor Ivanovitch. This excellent composer was pathetic in his joy and gratitude for the treatment he received at the hands of his patron. Chaliapin's rendering of his song "How the King Went Forth to War" made it possible for him to enjoy a very handsome income from copyright royalties when these sums were translated into Russian roubles in Moscow.

Chaliapin returned to Russia after his 1921 trip abroad and then set to work to bring out his entire family, with the intention of never returning. This entailed long negotiations and much wirepulling, but eventually 1923 brought him again to London with his complete family. They had travelled by boat from Petrograd to Stettin and for some months they settled in London. Later on, he took up permanent residence in Paris.

Chaliapin and his family were always most generous and considerate to their servants and helpers and were in turn worshipped by them all. I remember the number of quiet old people who haunted the servants' quarters of the Chaliapin home, seemingly with very little to do and yet living on his bounty. At their own table there were always two or three elderly governesses or nurses whom they would call "Naniushka" or by some other affectionate diminutive. Chaliapin's cuisine was run on regal lines, since invariably there would be besides the family half-a-dozen guests or retainers. Their chef was a Russian of great culinary attainments and the meals were not so much dinners as feasts. Whole sides of lamb, sucking pigs, large salmon, great soup tureens of borsch, and *shchee* abounded. Round about Easter and Christmas there were days of solid feasting when the visits of the clergy and choir, with their incense and blessings, were an important element, since the Chaliapins were devout members of the Russian Orthodox Church. On these occasions Chaliapin would radiate geniality and good humor on his family and guests. There would be the grandmother, 97, the three daughters Martha, Marina, and Dacia, the sons Feodor and Boris, the children of the first marriage, and a few ex-governesses, nurses, and guests. Perhaps Serge and Madame Koussevitzky, or Kusnetzova or Hidalgo, the soprano, and her husband, would be there, or there might be some high official of the French government. Invariably there would be some of his old Russian cronies and the impresario, Michel Kachouk, and his brother, who were always a spellbound audience for his stories and jokes. Sometimes one would find Maxim Gorky or Serge Rachmaninoff and his wife. It was an experience to see Rachmaninoff's face light up as he listened to Chaliapin's amusing stories. These were the only occasions on which I have seen this great musician, with his monkish face, really relax.

Best of all was Chaliapin in the summertime, on vacation, when he would be surrounded by the children and would consecrate his time to romping with them on the seashore or in the fields. I remember particularly happy summers passed with him in La Baule, St. Jean de Luz, and Kitzbühel.

Certainly the achievement of this poor boy of Kazan, who in his early life suffered the pangs of hunger and misery which are the common experience of the Russian poor, reads like a fairytale. In speaking of the famine in Russia he told the reporters how, as a lad of seventeen, he found himself in the town of Kazan without a penny in his pocket. Day after day he would walk through the streets and hungrily gaze in the windows of the bakers' shops with a hopeless longing. Once he said: "Hunger is the most debasing of all suffering; it makes a man like a beast, it humiliates him." He also told them of the time when he and Maxim Gorky were working on the boats on the Volga and had to improvise trousers out of two pairs of old wheat-sacks which they tied round their waists. Who could see Chaliapin impersonating the rôle of Boris and imagine that he had ever been anything but a great Tsar all his life?

Chaliapin was Russian to the core and it was a cruel fate that sent him to live and die in exile. Transplanted so late in life, he could never adjust himself wholly. He always lived in the hope that a political change would enable him to go back to Russia. One cannot blame him for refusing Maxim Gorky's offer on behalf of the Soviet Government to return there. I was present in the Kaiserhof, Berlin, when after dinner Gorky pleaded with him for two hours, setting forth the honors, position, and rights the Soviets were prepared to guarantee him if he would return. Gorky urged him as a Russian to go back and put his shoulder to the wheel, no matter what he felt. Chaliapin replied that he was not young or adaptable enough to risk the change.

Gorky and Chaliapin were both from Kazan and of the same age. They were staunch and lifelong friends. Often the long conference was interrupted by painful coughing from Gorky who was already ill. This was the last time the friends met. The next day, Gorky and his wife continued their journey to Moscow where he died, true to his political creed.

The thousands of Russian emigrés the world over learned of Chaliapin's death with grief and dismay. He was the symbol of their glorious Russia of the good old days. In the eyes of all Russians he even ranked with Stenka Razin of legendary fame. His every action was news to them and a welcome topic of conversation. He could and did go to the most remote spots, tack up a poster in the morning, and in the evening his concert would be crowded with every Russian who could beg, borrow, or steal the price of admission. While they hung breathlessly on his every tone, he would pull aside the curtain and give them a glimpse of the glorious, glamorous Russia of bygone days. I have watched him, with a lump in my throat, soothe and caress these poor homesick aliens in Riga, New York, Budapest, Shanghai, Adelaide, San Francisco.

FEODOR CHALIAPIN

To Paris I journeyed in April 1938 to pay my last respects to the great artist, and there mingled with the thousands of Russians of every degree who filled the small Russian Cathedral in Rue Daru and overflowed into the streets. I saw real, unabashed grief. For six days Chaliapin lay in state in his home in the Avenue d'Eylau while a constant stream of friends and fellow countrymen as well as fellow artists looked their last on him. On the day when he was buried the funeral cortège stopped at the cathedral where a Mass for the Dead was read, with an unaccompanied chorus consisting of the famous Afonsky Choir and the Aristoff Russian Opera Chorus. The service, mostly choral, lasted two-and-a-half hours, during which the Twofold Litany by Gretchaninoff, an old favorite of Chaliapin's, was sung. The Metropolitan Eugole officiated and the Liturgy for the Dead was rendered. Many of his old colleagues sang as choristers, among them Pozemkovsky, Alexander Mozjoukin, Kaidanoff, Zaporozhets, Borovsky, Madame Davidoff, Smirnova and others. It was the most wonderful choral singing I have ever heard, and everyone was profoundly moved. After the custom in France, about midday the long funeral cortège, with many vehicles of floral tributes, began its journey to the cemetery. Members of the Paris Opéra, headed by Serge Lifar, had arranged to honor their colleague. The procession paused in the courtyard of the Opéra where, in the open air, amidst the hum of the Paris traffic, a prayer for the dead was read and the choir intoned a chorale. I had not expected such a display of emotion by these choristers and former colleagues, and turned to my neighbor Prince Zeretelli for an explanation. "Chaliapin dead," he said, "all is forgiven. They realize now that there will be no other like him. Whatever his faults, for them he was Russia."

[237

Elgarian

CHAPTER XIV

Elgarian

MANY English composers have passed through our studios, assisting in the recording of their works. The names that come foremost to my mind are those of Edward German, Vaughan Williams and Edward Elgar. The first two were shy, retiring men of so few words that one had few points of contact and could retain only first impressions of them. German in particular was so grave and solemn a man that one marvels how he could have written the gay and spirited *Nell Gwyn* and *Henry the Eighth* dances. He was very methodical and businesslike and knew precisely the commercial value of his music. In like manner he was tidy in his appearance without being modish. His movements were quick and energetic, and he was an excellent conductor, especially of his own compositions.

In complete contrast was dear, lovable Vaughan Williams who always reminded me of Bruckner in his complete disregard of dress or food and his detachment from all worldly affairs other than music. When recently he recorded for us his Fourth Symphony I noticed how gently and unobtrusively he indicated his wishes to the men. His movements were rather awkward and he employed a minimum of gesticulation. Though obviously enjoying the performance, he rarely offered a suggestion. By nature self-effacing and silent to a degree, he has not the equipment for a good conductor and rarely essays that rôle. The greater part of his music as well as that of an equally eminent composer, Arnold Bax, remains still unavailable on records to the shame of the record-makers of our generation, who should be broadminded enough to set aside a fund, deducted from their more profitable popular record business, for the purpose of archive recording of the best contemporary music. This is the principle Italy adopted for subsidizing grand opera on a high level.

Meeting Elgar for the first time, one would hardly take him for a composer and I have a sneaking idea that he relished this deception. When he first came to our studio I thought I had never seen anyone who looked less like a musician. The Elgars seemed a prim and comfortable family of the county class, very provincial and sheltered—a product of some cathedral town of England where afternoon tea is the chief ceremony of the day. With this quiet background in mind, his unexpected weakness for telling yarns, backing horses, and enjoying his pint with a crony at the local pub seemed particularly amusing.

He was proud of his membership at Whites in St. James, where no one dreamed that a musician had invaded them. He certainly knew horses and kept up to date on form as his usually successful punting proved. Yet sometimes he played a "hunch" or a tip from the newsboys of Worcester, who all knew him and volunteered their advice. He had a number of good stories and took an artist's delight in telling them.

In all of these pastimes he found an escape and gave one the impression of a schoolboy playing truant. He did not seek out the company of his musical contemporaries, with whom he did not seem at ease. He was a friend and admirer of Richard Strauss, the only living composer with whom he could bear comparison. He boasted that Strauss had to have recourse to a piano while composing and scoring, whereas he himself worked at a desk without that assistance. Like Strauss he also had a certain reputation as a conductor and was turning out fresh works even in his seventieth year. Even in his seventy-fifth, he invaded the operatic field, Strauss' field, and played for me excerpts from an unnamed opera he had under way, including a fine love-duet set for soprano and tenor. During that same year he proudly played parts of a piano concerto and a beautiful slow movement and an intriguing scherzo of a Third Symphony. His brain was intensely alert and at the end of his life seemed suddenly to have acquired a creative urge that would not let him rest.

Elgar's association with my company before 1925 was chiefly decorative, his name carrying the prestige of England's greatest composer. After that date the introduction of the electrical process made it possible to record with satisfaction his great symphonic works under his own bâton, one after the other, until the year of his death. Thus the greatest English composer has, for the first time in history, left to posterity his own interpretations of his works. I took personal charge of the many sessions required to accomplish this task. Lady Elgar and their daughter Carice, who afterwards became Mrs. Blake, always accompanied him until his wife's death. Then Carice came with him alone, assisted by old Richard, his chauffeur and valet, a countryman of Worcester. On February 24, 1920, in the old acoustic recording days, Lady Elgar paid the last of her many visits to Hayes, remarking that it was her first trip out of doors for seven months. We were naturally flattered that the occasion should have been a visit to the works. I observed how especially tender and solicitous Sir Edward was towards his wife and he seemed intensely happy to have her out with him after her long illness.

My brother, Will, had instructed me to make these recording visits a ceremony and to "build up" the event. I usually had interesting people to meet Elgar and often he himself liked to invite to a gramophone session his friends Bernard Shaw, Barry Jackson, and Algernon Blackwood. Invariably Alfred Clark, the Managing Director, would welcome him and during the break for tea enjoy some of Elgar's tales.

A high spot was the recording of the "Nursery Suite" which he composed for Princess Elizabeth and Princess Margaret Rose and dedicated to them. On that occasion the guests of honor were the Duke and Duchess of York, who then heard that lovely work for the first time and warmly expressed to me their pleasure and gratitude on behalf of their children for the great composer's efforts. An interested spectator was the late Sir Landon Ronald, one of Elgar's ablest interpreters. The orchestra gave a fine performance and the affair was, generally, a huge success. Sir Edward was never in finer form and fairly glowed with contentment and delight.

Shaw was also present on this occasion and likewise when our Abbey Road Studios in St. John's Wood were first opened. He had just returned from a holiday, and hearing that Elgar was to conduct his "Falstaff" Suite, dashed from Euston to the studio. The longstanding friendship between the dramatist and the composer derives from the time when G. B. S. was writing his musical criticisms for *The Star* under the pseudonym of "Corno di Bassetto." Indeed, Elgar stoutly refused to be misled by some musicians who declared that Shaw hid his ignorance of music under a cloak of trenchant humor.

On his way to the studio for the "Falstaff" recording in the company's most imposing Daimler, Elgar remarked: "This is a fine car, it is well sprung and rides splendidly. I appreciate your gift. It is most nice of you to present me with it." This playful mood persisted when he entered the large concert hall and saw the paraphernalia set up for a film, and a great orchestra awaiting him. He turned to me and said with emphasis, "This, Gaisberg, is going to cost you a lot of money. I shall want at least £500 for all this." The affair was Sir Edward's début in the talkies and took place in 1931.

During the war Elgar wrote many fine *pièces d'occasion* and I doubt if ever a composer so ably acquitted himself in that particular type of pomp and pageantry. His noble melodies and brilliant orchestrations gave that spiritual uplift which those four years of grey existence demanded. Who can forget the thrill of his *Carillon* with the dramatic Henry Ainley declaiming to the music? This record is in the H.M.V. catalogue (Historic Section), a vivid reminder of those awful days.

During the war period I also took records of his musical play, a fairytale of Algernon Blackwood called *The Starlight Express*, with that fine operatic soprano, Rosina Buckman, and a great but tragic baritone, Charles Mott. *The Starlight Express* was full of lovely melodies and he spent many happy days at the Kingsway Theatre assisting in its production. One of the tragedies of the war was the death on the Somme of Charles Mott who, already a favorite gramophone record-maker, showed every indication of becoming a baritone of international possibilities. His death produced a profound sorrow amongst us of the musical world and was especially regretted by Sir Edward.

In 1932, Elgar was commissioned to write a suite for brass band to be the main contest piece in the annual brass bands competition at Crystal Palace. It was his last completed work on a biggish scale. He gave it the title of "Malvern Suite" and dedicated it to his lifelong friend and admirer, George Bernard Shaw. We promptly recorded it in the presence of a distinguished group of friends and the following correspondence passed between us:

>   Marl Bank
>   Worcester
>   1st July 1932.

My dear Frederick (Barbarossa)

Many thanks for sending the copies of the (excellent) "Voice"; by this post I return the desired six duly (and joyfully) autographed.

I wish you would cause to be sent to Bernard Shaw the "proofs" of The Severn Suite, it is dedicated to him and he ought to have it now; do not *destroy* the enclosed postcard which gives the correct address for the records. Perhaps H.M.V. would like to commission (say £5,000) for such a symphony as G.B.S. suggests; the postcard is worth more than my music!

My love to you,

>   Yours ever,
>   Edward Elgar

Here is Shaw's postcard, which was enclosed:

>   Ayot St. Lawrence,
>   Welwyn
>   Herts.
>   29th June 1932.

The above address is right for the Suite. Send it to Charlotte; suites to the suite.

I have only just had my gramophone fixed up to my wireless. My first try on it will be "Falstaff."

We go to Malvern on the 24th. I am neurotic with overwork.

Why not a Financial Symphony? Allegro: Impending Disaster, Lento maestoso: Stony Broke, Scherzo: Light Heart and Empty Pocket, Allegro con brio: Clouds Clearing.

>   G.B.S.

My answer:

4th July, 1932.

Dear Sir Edward,

I shall be only too pleased to send the proofs of the "Severn Suite" immediately to G.B.S. The postcard certainly deserves this tribute.

By the way, did you say you wanted that postcard back again, or are you going to let me have it? I shall hold it here until you instruct me what to do with it.

I hope you do not mind if I circulate it among some of our people who would enjoy the idea of commissioning a "Financial Symphony."

With kindest regards and hoping you are in the best of health,

Yours sincerely
Fred Gaisberg

To which he replied:

Marl Bank,
Worcester.

This is to certify that Frederick Barbarossa, as a reward for general good conduct, may hold as his own property in perpetuity the postcard in the writing *G.B.S.* addressed to the undersigned adumbrating the manufacture of a symphony.

(Signed)   Edward Elgar
(Witness)   Marco

This fifth day of July nineteen hundred and thirty-two.

Marco was his dog.

In spite of the existence of a magnificent recording of Elgar's Violin Concerto by Albert Sammons, whose authority and interpretation of this greatest English work for the violin will never be bettered, I had a great ambition to have Sir Edward himself conduct the work. As a youthful and pliant performer without prejudice, who would respond best to his instruction, I selected Yehudi Menuhin as the most promising soloist. I posted him the music with a letter asking him to prepare it for recording, and promised him that Sir Edward would coach him and conduct the records in person. Also I suggested he could include it in an Albert Hall Sunday concert programme with Sir Edward in charge of the orchestra. Yehudi was enthralled with the work and his father accepted the idea in its entirety, even planning an additional performance of it to follow in Paris at the great Salle Pleyel. The spring of 1932 brought the

Sir Edward Elgar with Yehudi Menuhin and the author (left) from a photograph taken outside the Abbey Road Recording Studios, St. John's Wood, London.

The Gramophone Co., Ltd.

Menuhin family to London, where frequent meetings between the great composer and his young admirer took place. Yehudi's fresh agile mind, so quick to grasp the instructions, drew from Sir Edward high praise and encouragement; in fact, he became very fond of the lad and his sisters.

The great day arrived for the concert. The Albert Hall was filled to the last seat. A brilliant and expectant audience such as only London could produce had come to hear the fifteen-year-old boy and the seventy-five-year-old composer collaborate in what was, all agreed, a thrilling and moving performance. I have never seen such spontaneous enthusiasm as that which recalled to the platform again and again the old man and the young boy, hand in hand. Ever thoughtful, Sir Edward wrote me this letter of appreciation:

>   Marl Bank
>   Worcester
>   22nd November, 1932.
> My dear Fred,
>   I hope you were at the concert on Sunday—I think you were.
>   Now I should be a very ungrateful person if I did not at once send hearty thanks to you, who are really the cause of it all, for bringing about the wonderful performance. Yehudi was marvellous and I am sure would never have heard of the Concerto if you had not set the thing in motion.
>   However, although this is the biggest thing you have done, it is only one of the many kindnesses you have done for me.
>   Kindest regards,
>   Yours sincerely,
>   Edward Elgar

Our recording, carried out a fortnight ahead of the concert, can be regarded as one of the milestones of recorded music, to be ranked with Rachmaninoff and his Second Concerto, Fritz Kreisler and Franz Rupp in the Beethoven sonatas, Bruno Walter and the Mahler Ninth and *Das Lied von der Erde*, Casals and the Dvořák 'Cello Concerto, and Artur Schnabel and the 32 Beethoven piano sonatas.

Now the climax, in the shape of the projected Paris concert, was to follow. Carice had made it a condition that I should act as escort, which I was delighted to do, and here is Elgar's characteristic response to this enterprise:

Marl Bank,
Worcester
24th April, 1933.

My dear Barbarossa,
Thank you for your letter; I am truly glad to hear you are mending. The best news is that you will go to Paris. Can we travel together? It would be a boon inestimable to me if we could, or rather if you could put up with me. I have not been to France for years and have forgotten all the French I ever knew and Paris must have changed since 1880 (!)—the first visit was made then: let me hear as soon as you can if you can endure me.

All good wishes for a speedy recovery,

Ever yours,
Edward Elgar

On the Sunday before Ascot a crowd saw us off at Croydon Airport, among whom was Carice, who gave me precise and careful instructions for looking after her father. It was a fine day and Elgar enjoyed it with just a tinge of anxiety when we struck some airpockets on this first flight of his. He seemed to feel like a hero and had a daring smile on his face like a pleased boy. I still possess a crossword puzzle he successfully completed on that journey. We put up at the Royal Monceau Hotel, Avenue Hoche, and celebrated our first night in Paris with a fine dinner in the bright company of Isabella Valli. Exhilarated by the journey and a good night's rest, we arrived fresh and bright next morning for a rehearsal. Yehudi and members of the Orchestre Symphonique de Paris gave him a warm welcome, and as they had previously studied the music with Enesco, they quickly comprehended the points he wished to make.

We were guests for lunch of the Menuhin family who sensibly saw that Sir Edward did not tire himself. In the sunny garden of their modest villa at St. Cloud overlooking the Seine we had a lunch prepared by Madame Menuhin herself. This al fresco event was a jolly affair and the amazing Elgar was as fresh and boyish as Yehudi himself. Madame Menuhin explained that she had pondered long what to serve that would appeal to the palate of an elderly English gentleman. She had finally recalled a favorite Palestine recipe, and obtaining seven different kinds of fish, she boned and hashed them, with appropriate seasoning. Then the fish was molded into a loaf and boiled for an hour. The dish was a great success with Elgar, who called for a second helping and gallantly complimented her on her cooking. Yaltah and Hephzibah, Yehudi's sisters, were there too, as grave and interested as grownups. After the meal Mamma wisely sent them off to play and Sir Edward to bed for forty winks, as we had yet to carry out a daring plan to motor to Fontainebleau for a visit to Delius which entailed a forty-mile cross-country trip to Grez-sur-Loing on the outskirts of Fontainebleau.

For this journey Menuhin had offered his new American Buick, but before we had proceeded very far ignition trouble developed and as we dared not fall behind in our schedule and keep poor Delius waiting, a Paris taxi was hailed and we proceeded in this speedy if ancient vehicle.

We arrived at the Delius' home in Grez well after five. It was a very simple two-storied whitewashed farmhouse with a sloping roof. The façade was of grey plaster covered with a trellis of red and white climbing rose-vines. The principal feature was an archway with a portcullis actually on the main street, wide enough to drive a farm wagon through into a courtyard. At one side of this was a barn, and the other opened straight into the living room which Delius used as his study, from which a staircase led to the floor above. It was a long room with a low ceiling and three old-fashioned windows looking out on a pretty rose garden. All the furnishings were dowdy and rather grimy with use, such as might be found in a Bayswater boarding house.

Delius was sitting in the middle of the room, facing the windows, very upright, with his hands resting on the arms of a big rolling chair. Illuminated by the afternoon sun, his face looked long and pale and rather immobile. His eyes were closed. Mrs. Delius was sitting beside him expectantly waiting for our arrival. Genial, resourceful Elgar quickly established a friendly, easy atmosphere and in a few minutes they led off into an animated duologue that somehow reminded me somewhat of a boasting contest between two boys. Delius waved his left arm freely; his speech, halting at first, became more fluent as he warmed up to his subject and we forgot his impediment of speech. He seemed mentally alert. From this conversation I gleaned that they were both non-keyboard composers and that both had important compositions under way. Both emphasized the importance of the gramophone to them and Delius also

[249

stressed the wireless. He spoke jestingly of the number of publicity-seeking youngsters who pursued him to his retreat and insisted on giving bad performances of his music. They talked of their Leipzig days as students of Reinecke and Max Reger, of their friends Percy Pitt and Granville Bantock. Delius, recalling his years in America, spoke of frost being the ruin of the Florida orange groves, and told us that the destruction of the forests had changed the climate and brought about the crash of his Florida venture.

Mrs. Delius showed us a photograph of the Royal Academy portrait of her husband, with the comment that to her it seemed expressionless and a libel on the real Delius. They passed on to authors, Elgar extolling Dickens and Montaigne, Delius Walt Whitman and Kipling. But Elgar's flight to Paris was the crowning achievement that Delius could not hope to match. Still, the idea fascinated him. It offered the sole possibility for a man in his condition to visit his beloved England once more. Finally, in a lordly way he waved his arm and instructed Mrs. Delius: "Dear, we must fly the next time we go to England." He then brought the afternoon to a climax by ordering a bottle of champagne opened, and a toast was drunk all round.

Before twelve months had gone by, both men were no more.

The concert next day was a brilliant repetition of the London performance and the presence of the French President and many Ministers of State made it an international event. The Concerto was received with enthusiasm but one felt that it had not made the impression that was its due. I fear Elgar's music will never receive solid appreciation from Frenchmen, at least in our generation.

Our flight back to London on Derby Day enabled Elgar to "play his fancy" for that exciting event. On landing safe and sound at Croydon, we were met by his daughter Carice who motored us to Willie Reed's home. There a bottle of wine was opened to drink to Elgar's seventy-sixth birthday and the bestowal upon him of the Order of Merit by the King. A happy photograph records this toast.

In August 1933 I left Paddington for a short visit to Elgar who met me at Malvern Station with his two dogs. At "Marl Bank" were his niece, Miss Grafton, and his secretary, Miss Clifford, both unpretentious and sympathetic and with a lively sense of humor. They must have been excellent managers as the house was run smoothly and it was very comfortable and tidy. They were deeply attached to Sir Edward and understood him in all his moods. My host showed me over his house and opened a portfolio by his bedside containing his Third Symphony upon which he was at work. He told me how much he missed his daughter, Carice, who was then married and living in Surrey. It was an exceptionally hot day so until teatime we sat talking in the drawing room where he used to compose. Here was a Keith Prowse baby-grand piano, always open, on which Sir Edward would illustrate when discussing music. Here, too, in an old desk or bookcase he kept his orders and decorations, of which he was tremendously proud. Another bookcase contained his original scores and he showed me such treasures as the manuscript of his "Introduction and Allegro for Strings," "Wand of Youth" and "The Kingdom."

After tea he took me for a drive in the Malvern Hills. We stopped at the pretty little Catholic Church of St. Wulstan where Lady Elgar is buried. Nothing could have been lovelier than the view from her grave on the hillside over the sunlit plains of Worcestershire. Sir Edward remarked that he had given instructions for his body to be cremated. However, this was not to be, and he is interred with his wife. We then drove to Sir Barry Jackson's modest house, lying in a nest of flowers which seemed to catch the last rays of the setting sun. On our way home my host pointed out the school where he taught music in his younger days and the house where he gave his first violin lesson, and what was more interesting still, many places associated with his various compositions.

In the main street of Worcester he indicated a small shop where his father once ran a music and piano store. On the day of our drive his newsboy had a wire tipping a certain horse which he backed. The horse won but much to his chagrin was afterwards disqualified. Half-a-crown each way was his limit. As usual, he stopped to watch a cricket match on the village green.

At dinner the dogs Marco and Mina each had a chair on either side of Elgar. They behaved very nicely and ate out of his hand. Later Miss Clifford played two Haydn symphonies, the "Clock," and the "Prague" as well as the finale of Mozart's "Jupiter," all of which Sir Edward followed with the scores. He counted 24 cadences in the *finale* of the "Prague" and observed that they still held your interest. Musically he was a devout classicist with a special affection for Haydn and Mozart, but Brahms he found dull and at times uninspiring, especially in the Rhapsody for Alto and the Requiem. He had an extraordinary musical memory from which he would often produce numerous illustrations, humming them over or playing them on the piano. In spite of his classical leanings Elgar spoke of Richard Strauss with evident admiration.

Next morning they gave me breakfast in bed and Sir Edward looked in to see how I was faring. He told me he had had his bath at seven and always got up at that early hour. At eleven he took me for a walk in the grounds, which included a fine kitchen-garden. There was a lovely 18th Century courtyard the walls of which supported rows of sturdy apple and pear trees. We were joined by Sir Barry Jackson and his producer, Scott Sunderland, and spent a pleasant hour exchanging experiences. As a lad, Elgar used to play in a theatre orchestra at Worcester. Elgar had one memorable contact with Beerbohm Tree who, to fill up a pause between the acts of a play he was producing, turned grandly to the conductor and said: "Play something from Beethoven to fill in—play the Ninth Symphony."

Some extracts from my diary concern my host's unfinished opera of which I never saw the libretto. To judge from the musical excerpts I was privileged to hear, it seems a pity he did not live to complete it.

Another entry describes my impressions of his Third Symphony:

> He then started on his Third, the opening a great broad burst animato, gradually resolving into a fine, broad Elgaresque melody for strings. Second Movement is slow and tender in true Elgar form. The third is an ingenious scherzo, well designed, a delicate, feathery short section of 32nds contrasted with a moderato sober section. Fourth Movement in a spirited tempo with full resources—developed at some length. The whole work strikes me as youthful and fresh—100% Elgar, without a trace of decay. He makes not the smallest attempt to bring in any modernity. It is built on true classic lines and in a purely Elgar mold, as the Fourth Brahms is purely Brahms. The work is complete as far as structure and design, and scoring is well advanced. In his own mind he is enthusiastically satisfied with it and says it is his best work. He pretends he does not want to complete it and surrender his baby. His secretary, Miss

Clifford, says he has not done much recently on the Symphony and seems to prefer to work on his opera. I think he misses the inspiration and driving-force of Lady Elgar. Some sympathetic person of strong character should take him in hand and drive him on. Some exciter is needed to inflame him. He complains of the drudgery of scoring.

I told him about having recently heard his Serenade for Strings. He said: "What grand music, what a wonderful melody, who else could have written it?" All this as though speaking of someone other than himself. This habit of rhapsodizing over his own creations as a mother over her own children was accentuated as he grew older. Especially did he love to compare himself with the younger man, Richard Strauss. In the field of composition he was pardonably vain and although some seven years older, he said he was turning out fresher and more inspired music than Richard. However, he would pay high tribute to Richard as a conductor and spoke of performances of Mozart that were a joy under the Strauss bâton.

Elgar first visited Germany in 1882 as a student. Ten years later, with his wife, he returned, going to Bavaria, to Garmisch and Partenkirchen. Thereafter for ten years they went back every year for their holidays for eight to ten weeks. He became very fond of the country and the Bavarians and loved their friendly, happy disposition. This was before Strauss made his home at Garmisch or it became a popular resort.

He begged me to take him to Bavaria; he longed to see it again. He even toyed with the idea of going to America, since Serge Koussevitzky had invited him, but he wanted a festival of his works and not just a concert.

During Elgar's last illness I conspired with Harriet Cohen and the Stratton Quartet to record the Piano Quintet, the String Quartet and the Violin and Piano Sonata. They supported my idea wholeheartedly and this enabled me on each of my many visits to the sickchamber always to bring new surprises to the stricken giant. He looked forward eagerly to these occasions and I took a delight in pampering him. Besides his own works, I would bring many other records as quickly as they were issued and would invent other diversions to assist his daughter to hold his interest and keep him cheerful. The gramophone played a great rôle in his life at this time and for five months was his chief consolation. Carice knew that he felt he was being left out of things, and grasped any suggestion that offered him distraction.

In January, Carice and I carried out the idea of holding a gramophone recording session by telephone circuit. With the energetic assistance of my friend, Rex Palmer, who interested the Post Office and obtained their sympathetic cooperation, the work was successfully accomplished. Ignorant, biased prudes tried to knock out the idea as being morbid and scandalous. I only know it gave Elgar two full weeks of diversion and anticipation.

On his own initiative, Sir Edward dedicated to me a small work entitled "Mina," the name of his favorite spaniel, and one day he called me to his bedside. He asked for a pen and producing the manuscript from under his pillow wrote across it a dedication to me. I could not restrain tears of emotion as I thanked him. A few days later, I rushed up a gramophone recording of it rather hastily done. Soon after I received this letter from Carice Blake, dated February 15th, 1934:

Dear Mr. Gaisberg,

I had the opportunity of playing the "Mina" record to father today. He wants me to tell you that he much enjoyed hearing it and thinks it so kind of you to have had it done. He hopes you will not mind his saying that it is too fast. He knows the time was not marked and it wants more stress on the first note in the opening part. The next tune should be much softer and quieter. Later on the part played by Billie Reed is twice as fast as it should be and the harp-part (the first note of the second tune) does not come out enough.

He is so sorry to make all these criticisms and hopes you may have an opportunity of making another record—he does not wish this one published as it stands.

Yours affectionately,
Carice S. Blake

P.S. This is the best I can make of what he said and hope you will understand. Unfortunately, I am no musician. He was wonderfully lucid over it, but we have had 36 hours of pain and we are all nearly crazy. C.S.B.

This manuscript is in my possession. Grove's *Dictionary of Music Supplement* mentions "Mina" as his last work. It also mentions, as a work without *opus* number, the scoring of the slow movement of Chopin's Sonata, Op. 35, popularly known as the "Funeral March" which I, on behalf of my Company, commissioned him to orchestrate. It was his last serious work and the very fine scoring indicates that he thoroughly enjoyed the task. His masterly arrangement was performed at the Elgar Memorial Concert, given by the London Philharmonic Orchestra conducted by Sir Thomas Beecham, on February 25, 1934, at Queen's Hall.

Slowly, as day after day my friend unconsciously faded out, I was in constant touch with Mrs. Blake and his great friend, Willie Reed. There seemed to be some indecision as to where his remains should rest, and finally the interment took place on a bleak, cold day at St. Wulstan's Church cemetery on the Malvern Hills, just where he took me that August day nine months previously. It was preceded by a Requiem Mass, celebrated at the Roman Catholic Church of St. George's, Worcester. Notwithstanding this, I feel that he would have expected the decision to be taken out of his or the family's hands and a Westminster Abbey burial insisted on by his colleagues and countrymen. If it is admitted that his music is the personification of the British soul and that he is the greatest musician since Purcell, which is George Bernard Shaw's opinion, then he should be where Purcell is.

And So,

Good Day!

CHAPTER XV

And So, Good Day!

The name of Alfred Clark has appeared several times in these pages. He is the fine thread running through the very fabric of H.M.V. history from those primitive workshop days to the pinnacle achievement of a complete opera performance, with Gigli and Maria Caniglia, recorded by the electrical process. And this miracle offers you two hours' exciting entertainment at your own fireside. It seems incredible that a man still in harness could have maintained his leadership of this great industry for over fifty years. But so it is. From the old Edison tinfoil dents in the famous phonograph that feebly wheezed "Hello, hello!" to the last word in radio Clark's influence has been at work the whole time.

That Alfred Clark always kept ahead of the game shows his exceptional faith in the destiny of the gramophone. Only recently I recalled to him the first time he heard the gramophone in Emile Berliner's studio in Washington in the summer of 1896. He admitted that although he was a friend of Edison's and devoted to the phonograph, he immediately fell in love with the natural tone of Berliner's disc and above all was impressed with the simplicity of stamping out endless copies of one record. Today he is chairman of the merger group known as Electric and Musical Industries, comprising H.M.V., Columbia, Parlophone, Regal, and Zonophone. He plays another rôle with equal distinction. At Hayes is that unique record library he founded and still keeps up to date. This comprehensive collection contains an example of every record, foreign and domestic, with its own matrix, issued by the Gramophone Company since 1908. Well over 250,000 titles are carefully indexed and housed in safe shelters. Another useful unit is a reference library of catalogues, foreign and domestic, since the year 1898. In this section will also be found all books, periodicals, and pamphlets relating to the industry, the artists, and the compositions recorded. Trade journals and publications dealing with the Law of Copyright are also included in the scheme.

Provision has, of course, been made for the scientist and the inventor. I allude to the museum of models and full size machines, showing the evolution of the gramophone. Among the exhibits are an old Edison tinfoil phonograph, and a Berliner toy hand-driven gramophone that played a 5-inch record on which a simple nursery rhyme was recited. How amusing to realize that lack of confidence in its clarity is shown by the printing of the words of the rhyme on the back of the disc! Here, too, is the phonograph used in 1878 by Sir William Preece (the radio pioneer) in his first lecture on Edison's revolutionary invention, before the Royal Society. I have touched on this event in a previous chapter. Another feature, a series of metal matrices and discs of plastic materials, shows the evolution of the sound record from the toy stage of 1896 to the full symphony orchestra of today. But for these vivid reminders of pioneer days, this blasé generation would take the modern gramophone record for granted, without realizing that it has taken fifty years of patient research and unquestioning faith to bring it to its present state of perfection.

There was a complete impasse in the further development of direct sound-recording when the electrical process came along. In 1896 I assisted Berliner to make a record by using a telephone microphone to which a stylus was attached. The result, I remember, was a thin metallic thread of sound. The experiment was years ahead of its time. Had not the electrical process arrived at the right time the gramophone might have followed the dodo or the player-piano into extinction. Berliner's wildest dreams could hardly have conjured up the Fleming valve that would amplify a thousand times and more the finest electrical current.

When the Western Electric achieved electrical recording as a sideline to their research in telephone communication, a mine was

Alfred Clark with the author (left), examining the first spring-driven gramophone motor.

AND SO, GOOD DAY!

sprung in my world. My colleagues, versed only in the simple acoustic methods of recording, had to begin all over again by studying electrical engineering. With dismay they saw young electricians usurping those important jobs of theirs, the reward of long apprenticeship. However, a few of my old associates were equal to the emergency and mastered what was to them a new science.

Berliner's dream of using the spoken record as a means of correspondence or as a document has failed. Perhaps this is because the average person is virtually dumb when asked to record. In the case of the Berliner family themselves when they assembled to speak New Year greetings to their old grandmother in Hanover, their eloquence was limited to such bald statements as "Hello, Grandma, this is Hannah," or "This is Joseph" from the children one after the other, and finally Emile would bring up the rear with similar trite wishes of good health and prosperity. Similarly, I remember once arranging a meeting between Sacha Guitry, Yvonne Printemps and Chaliapin, with the idea that as they were unprepared for a microphone, their conversation would result in a spontaneous recording of historical interest. But we were disappointed. After the first effusive and theatrical greeting between Sacha and Chaliapin and a peal of laughter from Yvonne when she noted their embarrassment, they froze up and long, awkward pauses intervened.

Berliner had no doubt whatever that in time to come the gramophone would be of great educational value. And here his faith has been amply justified. On November 17, 1919, this new activity, pioneered in England by H.M.V., was entrusted to a single man, the late Walter Yeomans, who was practically given carte blanche to set it in motion. In July, 1921, we commissioned the indefatigable Percy Scholes to write the first book of its kind. It was called *Learning to Listen*. A cordial notice in the London Times Educational Supplement attracted such wide publicity that it was the means of launching the movement successfully. Demands for lectures reached us from near and far, and Yeomans set to work and organized a staff of two, Alec Robertson and Mrs. Leigh Henry. By degrees they covered the whole of England and most of Scotland, Ireland, and Wales, giving talks and demonstrations in and out of schools, public libraries and the like. Owing to the innate conservatism of local education committees, it was a tough fight to get the gramophone accepted as a serious means of musical education. But it soon became apparent that the piano by itself was wholly insufficient, for example, to illustrate orchestral music.

Emile Berliner seemed to be particularly carried away with the idea of preserving the voices and historic utterances of the great statesmen and leaders of his generation. The gramophone has now covered two worldwide upheavals, but historical utterances have been preserved only by English and American recording companies. Theirs is an altruistic work since no immediate commercial gain accrues from the sale of such records. For the time being, the British Museum accepts the deposit in its vault of a metal matrix and one pressing of certain historical records selected by their custodian.

To the artist-performer the gramophone is what the canvas is to the painter or the pen to the author. The painter has the great galleries and the author the world's libraries in which his masterpieces may be preserved for all time. Perhaps one day we shall have endowed national selective libraries of the records of great singers and instrumentalists. I hope the start may not be too long delayed because records that seem plentiful today have a habit of disappearing without any trace tomorrow.

Great interpreters came and went before the record made its appearance, and the world has been left no richer for their studies and work. Today the name of Trebelli means nothing to us, but for tomorrow the records of a Patti, a Caruso, or a Tetrazzini set a permanent standard of achievement for future singers. So it is with instrumentalists. Said to have been the greatest pianist of his time, Busoni made records which have all been lost through lack of foresight. Thus we can never answer the question "How great was Busoni?"

In his forecast, Berliner overlooked the record's value as a means of self-expression to the music lover who is not himself a performer —the non-singer who collects *lieder* or the non-pianist who collects Beethoven's piano music. Then there is the sensitive amateur with an exclusive craving for 18th Century music, or who only cares for Bach and is always searching the catalogues of Europe and America for further examples of the Master. I know a purist whose catalogue of pre-Mozartean classical music surprised me, not only by its completeness but also by the fine discrimination shown in the choice

AND SO, GOOD DAY!

of titles and performance. This friend was no performer, and yet at heart he was a true artist who found an outlet in his zeal as a collector. A perusal of his catalogue revealed a wealth of 18th Century music already recorded, yet I am convinced that there is plenty more to come from that period, all of it material for which the gramophone is a perfect medium.

Into the frame of 4½-minute records another great branch of music fits admirably—German *lieder*. If the gramophone record serves no other purpose, its value as a perfect medium for the ideal interpretation of those lovely but difficult songs of Hugo Wolf, Brahms, Schumann, Schubert, and Richard Strauss, where the collaboration of two great artists is essential for a satisfactory performance, would be achievement enough. In this connection my colleague Walter Legge has earned full marks for his tireless promotion of the private subscription scheme. As special subscription records the pick of Hugo Wolf's 257 songs have been made available to hundreds of music lovers who find the music too difficult for any but highly-accomplished performers. The six Hugo Wolf albums already issued are a monument of successful endeavor, and I doubt if another generation will ever produce so fine a body of interpreters for these songs as Alexander Kipnis, Elisabeth Schumann, Alexandra Trianti, Elena Gerhardt, Gerhard Hüsch, John McCormack, Marta Fuchs, Herbert Janssen, Helge Roswaenge, Karl Erb, and Elisabeth Rethberg, together with such gifted accompanists as Coenraad van Bos, Gerald Moore, and Michael Raucheisen.

Elena Gerhardt, the greatest of these, is responsible for the entire first album of the series, issued in 1931. Happily, she chose to record when her art and her voice were still in full bloom. The result is a series of records worthy of inclusion in the choicest anthology of gramophone music. Fortunate indeed is the connoisseur who possesses the complete six Hugo Wolf Albums to provide him with hours of interest and delight. Unfortunately, some of them are already out of print.

Although a far-sighted man, Berliner did not forsee that new world which the gramophone was to open up for the blind. Apart from its appeal to them as a musical instrument, they have today their "Library of Talking Records," lasting twenty minutes each,

[263

suitable for those unable to master the Braille system of raised type which is none too easy except for the very young. Already a wide selection of the world's worthwhile literature, including the Bible, is available, free, on talking-records, and a special system of parcel-post delivers them, franked, at the door of the blind student.

The chief mission of the record will always be as an entertainer. I look to it to remain very much in its present convenient form of 10" and 12" discs of plastic material. Two questions have often been put to me: "Why is the industry so slow in adopting a film or tape roll record which could play a complete symphony?" and "Why do we stick to the present form of plastic disc that only plays 4½ minutes?" To both I reply that, with all its shortcomings, the disc is the most practical to handle and store, economic to manufacture and comparatively durable. The most expensive ingredient of a disc is shellac, forming roughly one third of its composition as well as of its cost.

One of the most practical uses to which gramophone records have been put is their adaptation as an adjunct to stage and screen productions. "Effects" have been recorded of airplane evolutions, horses cantering or galloping, street noises, trains, and trams in motion. Here, too, are bells of every description. Many churches have had their complete chimes recaptured by the disc. Most church towers built over 150 years ago are too fragile to sustain the continuous vibration of heavy bells. Therefore records, greatly amplified, are often used as substitutes. So realistic do they sound that the passer-by cannot tell the difference between the record and the original peal.

The gramophone is even used to teach parrots human speech. I myself have listened to one of these ambitious birds not only trying to follow the voice part in a song record but actually endeavoring to imitate the orchestral accompaniment. And here is the strange but true story of Karl Reich and his canaries, for the details of which I have to thank my old assistant, R. H. Beckett, who writes:

> Karl Reich of Bremen conceived the idea of training canaries to sing like nightingales. As soon as they were hatched, the canaries were separated from all other birds except the nightingale. This procedure was continued for several generations until the canaries acquired the true nightingale song.

AND SO, GOOD DAY!

For months prior to the recording session Reich played records (to be re-recorded later with the birds' song superimposed) to his canaries. The sessions were arranged during the spring, when his birds were in their best form, and always in the morning. Just before dawn Reich would feed them on their favorite titbits, ants' eggs constituting the biggest proportion of their meal. All windows were flung wide open, Reich moving about on tiptoe and making weird caressing noises with his mouth. Mealtime over, he retreated to a corner of the room behind a curtain, with a slit through which he would observe his feathered friends. He had many novel ways of enticing them to sing. Sometimes he would rustle a piece of paper or carefully pour water from one pail into another. He would keep this going until they burst into full song, when he would give the cue to start recording. These preliminaries sometimes lasted a few minutes, at other times an hour or more.

When the canaries had been enticed into full song a record was played through a loudspeaker, and the song of the birds superimposed on the dubbed record. At times a full orchestra was engaged for the accompaniment, but this did not prove as satisfactory as the record because the musicians were unable to remain sufficiently quiet over the long periods imposed by the preliminary preparations.

There were many disappointments, but through patience and perseverance many pleasing records were secured. During the week allocated each year for the recording session, it was unusual to obtain more than five double-sided records.

These records became universal "best-sellers."

It was a happy day when Compton Mackenzie, the novelist, who was a keen record collector, assumed the leadership of that large unvocal public by founding a magazine in which collectors could air their grievances against the commercialism of the recording companies. Ever since then systematic and successful efforts have been made in England to cater for the more sophisticated tastes. With the help of his wife and his brother-in-law, Christopher Stone, he gradually collected a staff of disinterested critics and technical experts. Thus, in 1923, the first number of *The Gramophone* was launched, and today it has a worldwide circulation.

Compton Mackenzie and Christopher Stone were the actual founders of the National Gramophonic Society, which arranged for non-commercial records to be specially made for their members. In the fourth number of *The Gramophone*, the Editor proposed the formation of "a sort of Medici Society of classical records to persuade the recording companies that there is an articulate body of potential buyers of records clamoring for the best and willing to pay for it." Subscribers were privileged to vote for the works to be recorded, and these were pressed in a limited edition.

It was for the N.G.S. that Ethel Bartlett and Rae Robertson made their first two-piano works. With this society John Barbirolli, then a violoncellist, made his début as conductor, on the wax.

Happy is the man who has congenial associates. His path is made easy and his work a pleasure. After the merger with the Columbia Company I made many trips for recording complete operas with Charlie Gregory, a colleague who had joined the Columbia Company as a boy in Washington, when I was with that company briefly in the early nineties. His unbroken service with them has already reached the amazing total of 45 years and still continues.

Gregory and I, in the autumn of our careers, recorded in association such widely diverse subjects as:

Act 1 *Walküre* complete, in Vienna with Lotte Lehmann and Melchior, and the Vienna Philharmonic Orchestra, Bruno Walter conducting.
Mahler's Ninth Symphony with the Vienna Philharmonic Orchestra and Bruno Walter, in Vienna.
Dvořák's 'Cello Concerto with Pablo Casals and the Czech Philharmonic Orchestra and Georg Széll, in Prague.
Tosca with Beniamino Gigli and Maria Caniglia, at the Reale, Rome.
Berlioz' "Symphonie Fantastique" with Bruno Walter and the Conservatoire Orchestra, in Paris.
Beethoven's Triple Concerto with Weingartner and the Vienna Philharmonic Orchestra, in Vienna.

All were solid achievements that Gregory and I skimmed off the top of those boiling cauldrons of unrest during the five years just preceding the outbreak of the present war.

The memory of his congenial companionship during our free time and long train rides, when we recalled our early phonograph days and the long treks each made over separate roads, is something to cherish for all time.

Every story must have a climax and this one may as well conclude with an account of the banquet organized by my colleagues to celebrate my fifty years in the gramophone world, on April 21, 1939.

In that company as my gaze rested on one face after the other, a kaleidoscope of associations flashed before me in rapid succession.

AND SO, GOOD DAY!

Ted Pearce and Arthur Clarke, my companions of many expeditions and assistants in some notable recordings; Albert Coates and Lawrence Collingwood, with whom I carried out hundreds of adventurous sessions when the amazing electrical process first came in. There was sunny Peter Dawson making his last appearance in England: he sailed for Australia the following day. There was honest Gracie Fields, everybody's darling, Richard Tauber, one of the best fellows ever born; the man, like his voice, is pure spun gold. Past history was present in the persons of two pioneers: Alfred Clark and Louis Sterling, both still powerful factors in the talking-machine world. The higher realms of music were present in the person of the unquenchable Felix Weingartner, a link with Liszt, Wagner and Brahms. Bruno Walter arrived that day from Paris on his way to America, flotsam cast up by the maelstrom in Europe. Harold Holt, pillar of the international concert stage, also graced the occasion. Achievement was represented by F. W. Ogilvie, the newly appointed Director-General of the B.B.C. and John Christie, founder and proprietor of the Glyndebourne Mozart Festival. To my intense pleasure I also noted the presence of two sympathetic and approachable gramophone enthusiasts, Christopher Stone and his celebrated brother-in-law, Compton Mackenzie, both jealous guardians of the destiny of the gramophone record.

Messages of remembrance from all parts of the globe poured in from those unable to attend: Paderewski, Schnabel, Elisabeth Schumann, Russell Hunting, and so on.

To have so many of my colleagues and business associates present gave me real satisfaction. It was good to see Charlie Gregory, a pioneer from my old Washington days. Here too must go the name of Isaac Schoenberg, the scientist, who among many other achievements helped to bring television to its successful issue.

While I wished to be modest in acknowledging this personal tribute to myself, I could not help feeling pleased that the occasion provided a neutral ground for all the elements composing this great industry to get together, and that it was eagerly awaited and taken advantage of. In a way the evening marked the close of an epoch. It was one of the last gatherings of musicians in London before the war set in. It almost seemed as though some premonition had brought about a rally of the clans before the storm burst.

[267

THE MUSIC GOES ROUND

I can only hope that in my fifty years with the gramophone I have deserved the tribute paid me by Compton Mackenzie when he proposed my health:

We can always speak to each other in terms of music, and in time of trouble we are always able to compose everything in our minds and do honor to him who, in the truest sense of the word, has been international.

Index

Acoustic records, favored human voice, 85; accompaniments inadequate, 85
Addis, Tom, 48
Ainley, Henry, 244
Allen, Gus, 39
American Graphophone Company, 10
Arbós, Enrique Fernandez, 194
Attlee, John York, 7

B.B.C. (British Broadcasting Company), 110, 125, 150, 153, 213, 267
Baccaloni, Salvatore, 166
Backhaus, Wilhelm, 187
Baker, George, 176
Bantock, Granville, 250
Barbirolli, John, 149, 154-155, 266
Barraud, Francis, "His Master's Voice," 25
Barrientos, Maria, 103
Barth, Heinrich, 188, 191
Bartlett, Ethel, 266
Battistini, Mattia, 93-98
Bax, Arnold, 241
Beckett, R. H., 264
Beecham, Sir Thomas, 98, 144, 158-159, 232, 255
Beethoven, all the Piano Sonatas and the five Concertos recorded by Schnabel, 197
Bell, Alexander Graham, 4
Bell Telephone Company, 4
Bergil, Victor, 131
Berliner, Emile, 4, 18, 260, 261, 263; record of the Lord's Prayer, 11, 14

Blackwood, Algernon, 243, 244
Blois, Colonel Eustace, 123, 157
Bodanzky, Artur, 133
Bonci, Alessandro, 45
Boninsegna, Celestina, 110
Borgatti, Giuseppe, 105
Borgioli, Armando, 174
Bori, Lucrezia, 124, 230
Bos, Coenraad van, 263
Boult, Adrian, 215
Brailowsky, Alexander, 196, 209
Brooks, Arthur, Columbia Graphophone Co., 137
Bruckner, Anton, 147
Buckman, Rosina, 244
Busch, Adolf, 209, 211, 215
Busoni, Ferruccio Benvenuto, 262
Byng, George, 176

Calvé, Emma, 150
Campanini, Cleofonte, 105
Caniglia, Maria, 173, 175, 259
Carugatti, 170
Caruso, Enrico, 16, 37, 45, 46, 48, 134
Casals, Pablo, 212, 213-216
Cattaneo, Minghini, 166
Chaliapin, Feodor, 30, 62, 75, 90, 124, 134, 154, 207, 225-237, 261; Volga Boat Song, 71; visit from Titto Ruffo at hotel, 99; disastrous cold at New York performance, 228
Chemet, Renée, 62
Chevalier, Albert, 39
Child, C. G., 16, 115

[269]

INDEX

China, experiences in recording, 63
Christie, John, 171, 172, 267. *See also* Glyndebourne
Christie, Mrs. John (Audrey Mildmay), 172
Claque, still a necessity to an Italian singer, 169
Clark, Alfred, 18, 243, 259, 267
Clarke, Arthur, 267
Coates, Albert, 148, 267
Coldstream Guards Band, 83
Collingwood, Lawrence, 267
Columbia Phonograph Company, 5, 6, 19, 44
Conductors, physical endurance and vitality, 141; conductors' antics, 144; diverse methods of controlling orchestra, 144; best English conductors excellent accompanists, 151; careful students of orchestral records, 158; great musicianship, ideal of perfection, and power of command, 161
Conried, Heinrich, 48
Cortot, Alfred, 88, 213, 216-217
Cotogni, Antonio, 98
Crooks, Richard, 131
Cummings, Joe, 28

dal Monte, Toti, 103, 113
Darby, W. Sinkler, 26
Darnley, Hubert, 39
Davidoff, 33
Davies, Sir Walford, "Hear My Prayer," 177
Dawson, Peter, 43, 176, 267
de Fabritiis, Carlo Oliviero, 174
De Gogorza, Emilio, 85
Delins, Frederick, 249
de Muro Lomanto, Enzo, 114
de Pachmann, Vladimir, 192-194
Destinn, Emmy, 85, 110-111
Discs, 5- and 7-inch, 17; 10- and 12-inch, 39
Didur, Adamo, 32
Dillnutt, George, 48
Donovan, Dan, 5
D'Ogly Carte, Sir Rupert, 175
Dulari, 57
Durinoid Company, 12

Eames, Emma, 16
Eddy, Nelson, 131
Edison, Thomas A., 5, 8, 9, 18
Ediss, Connie, 39, 40

Electric and Musical Industries, Ltd., English merger of Gramophone Company and Columbia Graphophone Company, 85; companies included, 259
Electrical recording in later 1920's, 79; "mobile van" a convenience, 176
Electrola Company (Berlin, 1926), 79
Elgar, Sir Edward, 242-255; association with Menuhin, 246
Elman, Mischa, 88, 151, 154, 211, 218
Erb, Karl, 263
Essex, Violet, 175

Farkoa, Maurice, 17, 40
Farrar, Geraldine, 16, 103, 204
Fawn, Jimmie, 40
Fay, Harry, 43
Fields, Gracie, 31, 267; with Tetrazzini, 110
Finkelstein Company, 28
Fischer, Edwin, 146, 194
Flagstad, Kirsten, 134-136
Flat disc talking machine, 9; first wax record, 11; plastic material, 12; clockwork motor, 15
Fleta, Miguel, 88
Foley, Charles, 204
Ford Motor Company and Menuhin, 221
Fuchs, Marta, 263
Furtwängler, Wilhelm, 125, 126, 141-142, 146-147

Gaisberg, William, 45, 48, 84, 90, 243
Galli-Gurci, Amelita, 16, 115, 216
Galvany, Maria, 169
Gaskins, George J., 7, 10
Gatti-Casazza, Giulio, 232
Gerhardt, Elena, 263
German, Edward, 241
German copyright law, hardship for Wagner and Brahms estates, 137
Giannini, Dusolina, 17, 166
Giannini, Ferruccio, 17
Gigli, Beniamino, 78, 98, 172, 207, 259
Gilbert and Sullivan operas, records of entire series, 175; popular throughout English-speaking world, 176
Gluck, Alma, 16, 85
Glyndebourne Mozart Festival theatre, 171. *See also* Christie, John
Glynne, Walter, 176
Godowsky, Leopold, 194, 206, 218
Golden, Billy, "Listen to the Mocking-Bird," 7, 9

270]

INDEX

Gorky, Maxim, 235, 236
Goura Jan, 55, 56
Graham, George, 10
Gramophone, first record, 9; in England, 24-25; in Leipzig, Vienna, Budapest, Milan, Madrid, 26; in Russia, 26-33; in India, 55-58; Japan, 58-62; China, 62; Burma, 64; widely used by soldiers in dug-outs during First World War, 79; human voice, military bands, orchestras, jazz and swing bands on, 83; recording of conversation unsuccessful, 261; educational uses, 261; collections of records by music lovers, 262; speeches recorded by English and American companies, 262; for the blind, Library of Talking Records, 263; records used as adjunct to stage and screen productions, 264; used to teach human speech to parrots, and nightingale song to canaries, 264
Gramophone, The, 265
Gramophone Company, 25
Gramophone disc, advantages, 19
Gramophone record business, early competition, 44; pooling of patents, 45. *See also* Electric and Musical Industries, Ltd.
Graphophone, 5
Gregory, Charles, 266
Gruschelnitska, 32
Guitry, Sacha, 261

Halland, Edward, 176
Hampe, Max, 37
Harty, Hamilton, 151
Heifetz, Jascha, 61, 88, 154, 216-218
Hempel, Frieda, 37, 103
Henry, Mrs. Leigh, 261
Hidalgo, Elvira de, 169, 235
Higgins, Harry, 117, 123, 157
"His Master's Voice," 25
Holt, Harold, 267
Horowitz, Vladimir, 191, 194
Hubermann, Bronislaw, 208, 209, 212
Huguet, Giuseppina, 103
Hunting, Russell, 8, 19, 42, 87, 267
Hurok, Solomon, 228, 231
Hüsch, Gerhard, 263

India, status of music thirty years ago, 57
Inghilleri, Giovanni, 166
Italy, second recording trip, 45; Caruso, 46; during First World War, 76; records of folksongs of peoples in Austrian armies played to induce desertion, 78; sales of opera records very large, 165; the claque, 169

Jackson, Sir Barry, 243, 251
Jacobs, Leopold, 24
Janki Bai, 57
Janssen, Herbert, 263
Japan, vogue of Western musicians and records, 61
Jeritza, Maria, 116
Johnson, Eldridge R., 15
Johnson, George W., 8, 41
Jones, Bessie, 176
Jones, J. W., 19, 45
Jones, Sarah, 176
Journet, Marcel, 85
Joyce, Peggy Hopkins, 230
Judson, Arthur, 154

Kajanus, 141
Karns, B. F., 13
Kavetskaya, 32
Kiepura, Jan, 88
Kirkby Lunn, Mme., 112
Kipnis, Alexander, 263
Klemperer, Otto, 141
Knowles, R. G., 39
Koussevitzky, Serge, 141, 152-154, 235, 253
Kreisler, Fritz, 16, 62, 154, 203-208, 209
Kubelik, Jan, 112, 151, 210
Kurz, Selma, 103
Kwartini, 32

Lambert, Frank, 17, 40
Lauder, Sir Harry, 43
Lawton, Frank, 40
Lebel, 26, 27, 32
Legge, Walter, 263
Lehmann, Lotta, 123, 126
Leider, Frida, 123, 129
Leno, Dan, 39, 40
Leoncavallo, Ruggiero, 165
Lloyd, Marie, 39
Lough, Ernest, 177

McCormack, John, 16, 85, 154, 158, 263
MacDonald, Charles, 10
Mackenzie, Compton, 265, 267
Mahler, Gustav, 156
Manners, Lady Diana (Lady Duff-Cooper), 227

[271]

INDEX

Mapleson, Col. James Henry, 96
Marconi, Francesco, 98
Mascagni, Pietro, 115, 165
Masini, Angelo, 166
May, Edna, 40
Melba, Nellie, 37, 42, 103, 111–113, 150
Melchior, Lauritz, 123, 126, 130–134, 141, 154, 207
Mengelberg, Josef Willem, 141
Menuhin, Hephzibah, 220
Menuhin, Yehudi, 218–221; association with Elgar, 246–249
Messal, 32
Meyers, Johnny, 7, 10
Michaelis, Alfred, 45, 46
Michailova, Maria, 72, 85
Moore, Gerald, 227, 263
Moore, Grace, 118
Mott, Charles, 244
Mozart, George, 39, 43
Mozart Festival theatre at Glyndebourne, 171. *See also* Christie, John
Muck, Karl, 141, 153

Nápravnik, Eduard Frantsovitch, 141, 148
National Gramophonic Society, 266
Neshdanova, 103
Nevsky, Peter, 29
Newton, Ivor, 227
Nikisch, Artur, 84, 125, 144–146, 152, 198

Ogilvie, F. W., 267
Olczewska, Maria, 123, 129
Oldham, Derek, 175
O'Terrell, John, 11
Owen, William Barry, 23

Paderewski, Ignace, 37, 181–184, 267
Pagliughi, Lina, 103, 166
Panina, 29
Pathé Brothers Studios, 9
Patti, Adelina, 37, 38, 150; experiences in recording her voice, 91–93
Pavlova, Anna, 229
Pearce, Ted, 267
Pennsylvania Railroad Company, 14
Pertile, 166
Phonographs, early slot-machines, 5, 7
Pianists, often active to advanced age, 192
Pike, Ernest, 43, 176
Pinza, Eric, 166
Pitt, Percy, 151, 250

Plançon, Pol, 39, 85, 151
Pons, Lily, 103
Ponselle, Rosa, 118
Powell, Lionel, 114, 115, 181
Power, Tyrone, 42
Prima donnas, favorites in various countries 1908-1914, 103; temperamental, but hard-working, 120
Printemps, Yvonne, 261

Quinn, Daniel, 7

Rabinovitch, Max, 234
Rachmaninoff, Serge, 88, 185–187
Radford, Robert, 175
Radio Corporation of America, 16
Rappaport, 26, 30
Raucheisen, Michael, 263
Record library at Hayes, England, 260. *See also* Clark, Alfred
Recording, on acoustic gramophone, apparatus, 37, 40, 48; shifting position of singer or speaker, 37; difficulties in, of actual performances "on the spot," 177
Records, early, 7, 18; early favorites among, in England, 40–43
Red Seal Catalogue, 16
Reeve, Ada, 39
Reich, Karl, and his canaries, 264
Reinhardt, Delia, 123
Renaud, Maurice Arnold, 39, 151
Repington, Col. Charles A'Court, 230
Rethberg, Elisabeth, 263
Richter, Hans, 84, 205
Robertson, Alec, 261
Robertson, Rae, 266
Rogan, Lieut. Col. Mackenzie, 83
Ronald, Sir Landon, 38, 39, 88, 92, 111, 150–151, 175, 243
Rosenthal, Moritz, 199
Rosoff, 72
Roswaenge, Helge, 263
Royal, B. G., 16, 24
Royalties of singers and musicians after First World War, 78; later, 88
Rubinsky, Max, 26, 27
Rubinstein, Arthur, 154, 188–191
Ruffo, Titta, 98
Russell, Scott, 40
Russia, introducing the gramophone, 26–33
Russian folk-songs, popularized in England after First World War, 71

272]

INDEX

Russian records, Moscow church bells, 72; the Lord's Prayer, by priest and church choir, 72; Cossack songs, 74; music from the Caucasus and other southeastern provinces, 74
Rutland, Violet, Duchess of, 227

Sabajno, Carlo, 149, 165, 167, 168
St. John, Florence, 150
St. John's Wood, London, many musicians who have lived there, 208
St. John's Wood Studios, 208
Sammarco, Giuseppi Mario, 112
Sammons, Albert, 246
Sanders, Joe, 24
Sargent, Malcolm, 151, 161, 209
Sauer, Emil, 199
Savage Club, London, Rachmaninoff at, 185
Schalk, Franz, 84, 126–128, 141, 158
Schnabel, Artur, 154, 160, 161, 196–200, 205, 207, 267
Scholes, Percy, book on *Learning to Listen*, 261
Schorr, Friedrich, 123, 129
Schumann, Elisabeth, 123–126, 129, 141, 230, 263, 267
Schwarz, F. A. O., 14
Scotti, Antonio, 16, 85, 98, 175
Segovia, Andrés, 209, 212
Shaw, George Bernard, 243, 244, 245, 246, 255
Sheppard, Bert, 39, 41
Sobinoff, 30, 33
Sousa, John Philip, 142
Spencer, Len, 7, 8
Sterling, Sir Louis, 9, 85, 86, 137, 207, 267
Stokowski, Leopold, 187
Stone, Christopher, National Gramophone Society, 266, 267
Stratton, Eugene, 39
Strauss, Richard, 124, 126, 127, 230, 242, 253
Stringed instruments affected by humidity and temperature, 212
Suess, Werner, 12
Szigeti, Joseph, 212

Tainter, Charles Sumner, 4, 5, 6
Tainter and Bell, patent for cutting sound on wax, 4, 17

Tamagno, Francesco, 90, 105, 135
Tamara, 29
Tartakoff, 33
Tauber, Richard, 267
Tetrazzini, Luisa, 48, 85, 98, 104–110; delighted with Gracie Fields' burlesque, 110
Thibaud, Jacques, 62, 189, 205, 213
Thornton, Edna, 175
Tibbett, Lawrence, 131, 175
Tilley, Vesta, 39
Toscanini, Arturo, 89, 126, 127, 141, 149, 151, 177, 206
Tree, Beerbohm, 252
Trianti, Alexandra, 263
Tsar, plan to record his voice, 29
Turner, Eva, 117
Tyler, Fred, 73

Van Rooy, Antonius, 84
Vialtseva, 31
Victor Talking Machine Co., 16, 19, 45
Victoria, Vesta, 39
Victrola, 16
Vienna Philharmonic Orchestra, 127
Volta Laboratory, 4, 10

Wagner, Siegfried, 136, 137
Wagnerian records, vast series made possible by electrical process, 132
Walker, ex-Mayor Jimmy, 207
Walpole, Sir Hugh, and Melchior, 131
Walter, Bruno, 123, 126, 127, 155–157, 267
Weber, Marek, 142
Weingartner, Felix, 62, 126, 128, 141, 267
Weiss, Anton, 128
Wells, H. G., 226, 230
Western Electric Company, research in electric recording, 85; new method made available to both Victor and Columbia on equal basis, 87
Wilde, Harold, 176
Williams, Trevor Osmond, and St. John's Wood Studios, 208
Williams, Vaughan, 241
Wolf, Hugo, albums of lieder, 263
Wood, Sir Henry, 131, 160

Yeomans, Walter, 261
Ysaye, Eugène, 84

Opera Biographies

An Arno Press Collection

Albani, Emma. **Forty Years of Song.** With a Discography by W. R. Moran. [1911]

Biancolli, Louis. **The Flagstad Manuscript.** 1952

Bispham, David. **A Quaker Singer's Recollections.** 1921

Callas, Evangelia and Lawrence Blochman. **My Daughter Maria Callas.** 1960

Calvé, Emma. **My Life.** With a Discography by W. R. Moran. 1922

Corsi, Mario. **Tamagno, Il Più Grande Fenomeno Canoro Dell'Ottocento.** With a Discography by W. R. Moran. 1937

Cushing, Mary Watkins. **The Rainbow Bridge.** With a Discography by W. R. Moran. 1954

Eames, Emma. **Some Memories and Reflections.** With a Discography by W. R. Moran. 1927

Gaisberg, F[rederick] W[illiam]. **The Music Goes Round.** 1942

Gigli, Beniamino. **The Memoirs of Beniamino Gigli.** 1957

Hauk, Minnie. **Memories of a Singer.** 1925

Henschel, Horst and Ehrhard Friedrich. **Elisabeth Rethberg:** Ihr Leben und Künstlertum. 1928

Hernandez Girbal, F. **Julian Gayarre:** El Tenor de la Voz de Angel. 1955

Heylbut, Rose and Aimé Gerber. **Backstage at the Metropolitan Opera** (Originally published as **Backstage at the Opera**). 1937

Jeritza, Maria. **Sunlight and Song:** A Singer's Life. 1929

Klein, Herman. **The Reign of Patti.** With a Discography by W. R. Moran. 1920

Lawton, Mary. **Schumann-Heink:** The Last of the Titans. With a Discography by W. R. Moran. 1928

Lehmann, Lilli. **My Path Through Life.** 1914

Litvinne, Félia. **Ma Vie et Mon Art:** Souvenirs. 1933

Marchesi, Blanche. **Singer's Pilgrimage.** With a Discography by W. R. Moran. 1923

Martens, Frederick H. **The Art of the Prima Donna and Concert Singer.** 1923

Maude, [Jenny Maria Catherine Goldschmidt]. **The Life of Jenny Lind.** 1926

Maurel, Victor. **Dix Ans de Carrière, 1887-1897.** 1897

Mingotti, Antonio. **Maria Cebotari,** Das Leben Einer Sangerin. [1950]

Moore, Edward C. **Forty Years of Opera in Chicago.** 1930

Moore, Grace. **You're Only Human Once.** 1944

Moses, Montrose J. **The Life of Heinrich Conried.** 1916

Palmegiani, Francesco. **Mattia Battistini:** Il Re Dei Baritoni. With a Discography by W. R. Moran. [1949]

Pearse, [Cecilia Maria de Candia] and Frank Hird. **The Romance of a Great Singer.** A Memoir of Mario. 1910

Pinza, Ezio and Robert Magidoff. **Ezio Pinza:** An Autobiography. 1946

Rogers, Francis. **Some Famous Singers of the 19th Century.** 1914

Rosenthal, Harold [D.] **Great Singers of Today.** 1966

Ruffo, Titta. **La Mia Parabola:** Memorie. With a Discography by W. R. Moran. 1937

Santley, Charles. **Reminiscences of My Life.** With a Discography by W. R. Moran. 1909

Slezak, Leo. **Song of Motley:** Being the Reminiscences of a Hungry Tenor. 1938

Stagno Bellincioni, Bianca. **Roberto Stagno e Gemma Bellincioni Intimi** *and* Bellincioni, Gemma, **Io e il Palcoscenico:** Trenta e un anno di vita artistica. With a Discography by W. R. Moran. 1943/1920. Two vols. in one.

Tetrazzini, [Luisa]. **My Life of Song.** 1921

Teyte, Maggie. **Star on the Door.** 1958

Tibbett, Lawrence. **The Glory Road.** With a Discography by W. R. Moran. 1933

Traubel, Helen and Richard G. Hubler. **St. Louis Woman.** 1959

Van Vechten, Carl. **Interpreters.** 1920

Wagner, Charles L. **Seeing Stars.** 1940